Enlightenment Unveiled

Expound into Empowerment

By Jen Ward LMT, RM

Jen Ward, LMT, RM

Copyright 2016 by Jen Ward
Jenuine Healing®
All rights reserved. No part of this publication may be reproduced in any form or by any means, including scanning, photocopying, or otherwise without prior written permission of the copyright holder.
ISBN-13: 978-1530232819
ISBN-10: 1530232813
Updated February, 2019

A Message from Jen

I have always been a sensitive person. As a child, I spent so much of the early years crying. It wasn't until well into my adulthood that I realized that I was feeling other people's pain. Every day was excruciating. Hearing music and interacting with people elicited such emotional pain that it was difficult for me to think of someone else having loss or feeling sad. Also, from an early age, I had this deep desire to be spiritual. I remember sorting out my personal stance on angels, God, and Purgatory when I was about four years old.

I was the youngest of ten children in an alcoholic home that was dysfunctional at best. Being introverted and invisible were my best survival tools. The only means of validation was in helping others. I kept all my thoughts and desires to myself and wasn't really aware of the keen insights I was collecting.

As I delved into my own spirituality, I would have dream memories that were so real that I knew them as my past lives. I remembered explicit scenarios of different ways I had died. People would ask me, "How do you know they are memories of you?" I would answer, "How do you know that memory of what you did yesterday was you?" It was a very vivid recollection.

I remember how I was murdered, what it felt like to die slowly, what happened when I died in war. I also remember being dead in one lifetime and not realizing it. I know the special hell of still thinking I am alive when the body is killed. Every scenario helps me now with clients who are having difficulties. Everything that ever happens now whether I am asleep or awake is research to help release people from similar issues.

The bulk of my social life was listening to people who called me with their problems. I have always listened with reverence. I was so grateful that someone wanted to talk to me that I would do anything I could in the moment to help them feel better. There was a special innate quality that I have that was revealed that I have always honored as sacred. It was always a subtle way I used to serve God.

Adulthood brought with it a relentless string of challenges that left me fighting for the simple amenities like food and shelter. Exhausted, broken and nearly defeated, a friend started taking me to sessions of an energy worker. The sessions seemed to lighten my burden like nothing else. I gained some self-esteem and enrolled in massage therapy school.

When I was in in school, we learned that tissues carry issues and it was quantified by how the students responded positively to massage. I could feel energy move around the body. I became proficient in massage and in demand during clinic hours. Not only could I feel energy in the body when I touched it, I could feel it even when I didn't touch it. I could also help it flow around the body just by intending it to do so. Each massage was reverent to me, and my intention to help someone feel better seemed to bring more results than the average massage.

Other modalities became easy for me to learn. Other people would spend thousands of dollars to learn special techniques; they would show them to me and I would just then know them. I started to figure out new ways to use modalities, and people started to have heightened experiences during my sessions. I brought my knowledge of how to move energy to people I talked to on the phone. I began using a technique known as being a medical intuitive. When I talked to someone, I could perceive their blockages and would gently will the energy to unblock. I could perceive sick organs and cloudy areas in the body. I would release the cloud with my intent and bring clarity back to the body.

My focus to help others was so intense that it seemed to collapse space in a way, and I could feel the dis-ease of their body like a stagnant cloud around me. I somehow learned how to "blow away" the cloud and dissipate someone's blockages. They would feel remarkably better. It also seemed to help me push stuck energy if I would emote sounds. Although uncomfortable to listen to, people tolerated them because of the incredible relief they felt when I made them. The sounds evolved into mimicking the sounds of the issues that were being released. Some were anger, sadness, frustration, etc. I could interpret the sounds I was making to access more information about the issues the person was holding.

People started calling me in emergency situations. One friend who had diverticulosis called me in the middle of the night because she didn't want to go to the emergency room. Since she refused to call an ambulance, I stayed present with her and tried to make her feel better with my "intention" and sounds. She relaxed after a while, and that particular issue never returned. She never had a recurrence of the bleeding that is a symptom of diverticulosis.

I did a similar type of session for my best friend's mother who was in and out of the hospital with diverticulosis. They were thinking she would not recover from it. Unaware of personal boundaries at the time, I thought about my friend's mother in the hospital and just started emoting and releasing like I would do if she were on the phone with me. My friend called me the next day and told me her mother was released from the hospital. The bleeding had stopped. Her mother lived another 20 years and never had another bout with diverticulosis.

My older brother called me in the middle of the night with a terrible headache. He was someone I very much wanted to help. I was never one he would usually reach out to, so it was very special. I started to feel his headache. It was like a vice. I started to feel all sweaty and unbearably uncomfortable. I can only explain that I felt like his issues were a river moving like a tube past me. During the most intense part of the experience, a voice within me, my inner guidance, told me NOT to remove the whole river.

I stopped myself before releasing everything that I was capable of. I told him to go to the hospital. Later, through the grapevine, I learned that he had a mini-stroke that night. It was so minor, but he had a slight lisp. Intuitively, I knew that that lisp was the part that I was told not to release for him. He needed that slight reminder for his own spiritual lessons. He never acknowledged my help that night, and I don't even think he realizes what transpired.

I learned the correlation between emotional pain and physical pain from a woman who came to me with excruciating fibromyalgia. She was so sore that she couldn't be touched. I was still inexperienced, so I blurted out during the assessment, "You were gang raped in a past life." She looked at me horrified. I realized what I had done. She hadn't been gang raped in a past life; it happened to her 30 years past in this life. She never told anyone.

With her secret exposed between us, I started sobbing uncontrollably. She hugged me and was consoling me, but she really was hugging and consoling herself. It was the first time she acknowledged the trauma that she had endured. It took her a few months to come back to me again, but when she did, she reported that the pain was much less. She seemed happier and lighter with each session with me touching parts of her body and sobbing spontaneously. Her physical issues seemed to come from being so saturated with emotional pain that it bled into the body as pain.

I have developed such deep devotion to helping others. It has created such an acute sensitivity to someone's energy system that I can perceive when they aren't aligned in their center. I can help them shift back into center or realign by using the same intent that I use to release blockages. People will ask if I have studied this or that. I really haven't been indoctrinated with what I do. I just take the techniques that I have acquired and extrapolate on them.

I am also able to see a pattern with past lives and present day injuries. I am able to access akashic records and see past experiences layered upon a present day injury. If someone has a sore neck, for example, I may see layers of lifetimes coming into play. While I am connecting with someone, I can be watching them go to the gallows, being decapitated, choked, etc. From my perceptions, I will create a set of SFT (Spiritual Freedom Technique) taps to fit their specific trauma. I will have this person release the specific trauma in all moments.

I can also tell people how the dynamics of the past life are affecting their present life. This is usually something very specific that I could not know arbitrarily. The information creates receptivity that helps people trust me enough to release their issues. This was the case for one woman whom I had seen decapitated in a past life. I saw her as a queen going through a chamber of a castle to be executed by decapitation. I also saw that in the present life, she collected crowns and was very sensitive to people coming up behind her. Hearing this, she was more receptive to the SFT given her to release the trauma she was holding in her neck.

Once there is an understanding of what is causing a specific pain, and it is validated, the body is free to let go of the pain. In this sense, pain is used as a cry for help to address very emotional issues.

One thing I never understood is why the LOA (law of attraction) didn't work for everyone. If one person could have abundance, why didn't everyone? I determined that if the LOA didn't work for someone, it wasn't because they were too depraved but because they made a different agreement with life that rendered the law of attraction inoperable.

It occurred to me that in past lives many of us were in monasteries. As part of our devotion, we took vows of poverty, silence, solitude, etc. We said them as sacred oaths to God, and we made them forever. I combined this knowledge with my abilities to assist energy flow and created a protocol of SFT taps for people to do on themselves as part of a session with me. The goal is to undo past life vows that are counterproductive to Joy, Love, Abundance and Freedom. This protocol has been very effective in assisting others.

I started making the SFT taps specific for individuals, and they seemed to get great results. My one girlfriend was a successful and attractive woman in her forties who never dated. There was no outer reason. I observed her wearing a ring on her wedding band finger. She said it was from her dear aunt and she always wore it. In that moment, I saw her as an old nun who wore a wedding band because she was married to God.

I created an SFT tap for her to recant her vow to be married only to God in all lifetimes. She obliged. The next day, she was asked out by someone she was interested in. It never amounted to anything, but it was a validation to her that the tap worked. A couple of months later, she started to date her old boyfriend and became engaged a couple months later.

I have found that it doesn't matter if I do a one-on-one session or a group of people at a time. In a group, there seems to be an energy shift in all. Many people don't realize the correlation between the sessions and what has transpired. They just seem to feel lighter in the moment and think their life has just spontaneously turned around. That is fine as long as they get what they need and are better people to those around them. This work seems to be my purpose, and I look forward to the process of helping as many people as possible. When one person shifts, the people around them seem to symbiotically shift as well. I believe that the more people that shift, the more humanity can be affected in a positive way. This seems to be my purpose.

Many years ago, I met a very intelligent man that silently suffered being in society. I didn't realize the depth of his depravity until it was too late. As I assisted him, he became very grateful. He would send me gifts and gave me attention that no man had given me. I felt special. He was compelled to connect with me only as a means of relieving his suffering from intangible sources.

In my attempts to help him, I delved deeper and deeper into his psyche. It was a dark place. Through his delusions, I have learned about alternative realities, UFO's, the paranormal, the Illuminati, etc. My help gave him such relief that he wanted to take care of me.

We moved to an isolated area where neither of us knew anyone. He changed drastically towards me almost at once. Instead of seeing me as a blessing, he saw me as a threat and thought my talents were something that I stole from him. He became obsessed with my dog and very resentful of me. Before we had moved together, I developed Stockholm Syndrome and cut off all contact with my friends and family. It became easy for him to control me.

In a short time, I went from being a gift to the world in his eyes to the opposite. In a paranoid state he made me drink vinegar water throughout the day and had me induce niacin flushes upon myself daily. He told me I was evil and created a heightened state of terror and confusion in me that was maintained until I entered an altered state of bliss and non-ego for three days. I had the most horrific experiences with darkness and despair in alternate realities. I also saw the dichotomy of hell and the beauty of creation and how easy it was to manifest worlds.

I came out of the three-day experience different. My perceptions were even more sensitive. I seemed to be at peace with whatever happened. I willingly worked outside from morning to night on a small bowl of rice a day. He thought the fat on my body represented the selfishness of the world, and he wanted me to lose all excess weight. I was mentally tortured and repeatedly indoctrinated into how disgusting I was. I had to explain to him in the third person how pathetic I was. It would delight him, and it became the way we interacted.

A number of years ago, April 1st, I was too weak to perform the morning ritual of abuse. As I prepared myself for the workday, something made me stuff my ID in my work pants. He locked me out of the house for not working, and I walked four miles in a weakened state to get help. Nearly starved to death, I escaped. It took many months to get my mental faculties back. I again relied on an energy worker to balance me out.

A couple of years before all of this, I was told that I was a sangoma. A sangoma is a traditional African healer that emotes sounds and heals through channeling their ancestors. One of the prerequisites of becoming a sangoma is reaching the brink of death and bringing one's self back to life. Ironically, my experience of nearly starving to death satisfied the requirements of being a sangoma.

When I got back to my hometown, most of my old friends and family wanted nothing to do with me. I had a very difficult time acclimating back into the world. All I wanted to do was find a nursing home that would accept me and find a place where the onslaught of stimuli didn't reach me. It was a lonely and painful time, more so than usual. I was afraid to use my talents because they brought in so much of the indoctrination that I was bad. I never wanted to inadvertently hurt anyone.

I started talking to a wonderful man who helped me when all the intangible fears came in. He would have me visualize taking him by the hand and diving into the fears. He helped me realize that all my fears are illusions and helped me dissipate them. He helped me overcome my fear of helping others. People's deep-seated issues are not intimidating to me because of what I have lived through. My experiences have created a depth of understanding that I could never have attained without the experiences that I have had.

I began working in a small suburb as an animal communicator. People would seek me out innately through their pets to get their own issues met. I also became aware of those who have crossed over seeking me out to give messages to their loved ones. They would tell me things that were very accurate as a means to prove that it was about them. It never seemed dark to me because I treated it as a matter-of-fact messaging system. I have an aversion to being considered a psychic or medium, so I have gone out of my way to not put those labels on myself. I never understood giving people information unless it benefits them in some way. It has been part of my goal to teach people how to assist themselves and not rely on a third party.

A year after being back, I ran into my nephew who is a genius in business. He was going through a transition, and I assisted him. In return, he introduced me to his business partners, and they created a website for me so I could help others. They helped me create a cyber-presence, and in return, I was able to assist them with business issues just like I would address energy shifts in the body. They made me feel safe in the world to share my talents. They even took the time to teach me social media like WordPress and Twitter.

I discovered a protocol for helping lost pets. Animals have a mechanism to help them find their way home. (We all have seen *The Incredible Journey*.) But I discovered that lost pets go into primal mode. So, if I tune into them and do an emotional release on them, they snap out of primal mode and just go home. It has a high rate of effectiveness. I started helping more people find their lost pets and working on creating more of a presence for myself in the world.

I do most of my work in remote phone sessions. It is easy for me to feel people's issues even before our session. It is hard to describe what happens in a phone session. I articulate people's issues to them better than they can articulate for themselves. I do an initial release on stagnant energy (blow it away) and then I get a better sense of what needs to be addressed. Clients are shocked into releasing their issues if they are open because their mind has no way to refute the shifts.

It seems that all I have experienced in this lifetime has been field study to assist others in becoming their own healer. People who are interested seem to pick up on what I do and help others. Many clients will say that they were praying or meditating for answers and were told to have a session with me. I feel that I have the stamina to assist large groups to shift back into alignment so that they can continue their own spiritual quest without giving up their power. The more individuals realize what they are capable of, the more they will empower themselves and those around them.

Now I am facilitating private remote sessions for people all over the world. I reach into the depth of the pain of those who come to me. I am able to pull out the core issues that have taken them off course and assist them into shifting back into alignment. People come to me saying they were at the end of their rope, praying to God, and they were led to me.

I am very humbled and surprised by the support that I have received. I am amazed and grateful for the response I have received from those I have helped. There is a love bond between myself and everyone I assist. My passion is to elevate the quality of existence for as many souls as possible using any gifts that I may have.

Jen Ward, LMT, RM

Table of Contents

A Message from Jen i
Your Gift 1
Section I: Spiritual Freedom Technique 5
    A Modern-Day Crusader 5
    The Start of the SFT Taps 5
    Release Being Married to God 7
    Recanting All Vows and Agreements 8
    Removing All Curses 10
    Removing Old Blessings 11
    Removing the Pain and Limitations of Karmic Ties 12
    Severing All Strings and Cords 14
    Removing the Pain and Limitations of a Karmic Connection 14
    Taking Back Your Joy 16
    Withdrawing Our Energy 19
    Bypassing the Mind 20
    Shifting One's Paradigms 22
    Transcending One's Issues 23
    Repairing the Skin on Your Energy Field 24
    Aligning All Our Bodies 26
    Being Centered in Divine Love 27
    How We Show Up in the World 28
    The Energetic Cleanse 30
    SFT Dictionary 34
Section II: SFT Taps 37
    1. A Shortcut 38
    2. A Client's Dramatic First Session 40
    3. Real Time Assistance 46

4. Taps to Transcend the Third Dimension 48
5. Mass Enlightenment 52
6. Disspating War..56
7. Releasing Fear Marathon 59
8. Eradicating War 64
9. Loyalties..68
10. Releasing the Trauma of Dying 70
11. Removing Violence from Society 77
12. Releasing Oppression..81
13. Breaking Up Thought Forms 85
14. Balancing the Yin and Yang Energies 90
15. Being an Individual...92
16. Releasing Insecurities..96
17. Releasing Everyone Else's Bullshit 99
18. Open the Inner Curtain to Love 102
19. The Reconnection Process 106
20. Balancing Yin and Yang 109
21. Releasing Old Work Paradigms 111
22. Undo Programming...114
23. Dissolving All Old Paradigms and Constructs...................................116
24. Empowerment: Issues Involved in Falling to One's Death 119
25. Frozen Shoulder 121
26. Your Own Energy Conversion..124
27. I AM!...126
28. Improving Self-Worth 128
29. The Correlation Between the Microcosm and the Macrocosm....132
30. Releasing Beliefs Around Poverty 136
31. Validation 139
32. The Takers...140

33. Buying Money 142
34. Maintaining Integrity 144
35. The Mule-Hearted Client 146
36. Unharnessing the Slimming Effects of Brown Fat 148
37. Removing Self-Limitations 151
38. Technique - Shatter the Glass House 156
39. Avoiding Suicide and Coming to Terms with Life 157
40. Regaining Fluid Energy 161
41. A Healer's Healing - Contempt for the Lords of Karma 164
42. Clearing the Karmic Slate 168
43. Alleviating Dis-ease on a Cellular Level 171
44. Releasing Dark Energies 176
45. Releasing the "Nice" Syndrome 179
46. Empowerment 182
47. Finish Those Projects! 184
48. Removing the Snowball Effect 186
49. Beings of Light 188
50. The Need to Be Liked 192
51. The Benefits of Being an Individual 194
52. Releasing Self-Loathing 197
53. Give a Gift to Humanity 201
54. Perfect the Dance 205
55. Understanding Food and Weight Issues 208
56. Concentrated Love 211
57. Reconnecting to One's Divinity 218
58. Uplifting Humanity 223
59. Releasing Torture 226
60. Repair Damage of Drug Use 229
61. Releasing Subtle Forms of Masochism 232

62. Primed for Enlightenment 237
63. Removing Fat Cells 241
64. Make Everything New Again 244
65. Healing in All Dimensions 246
66. Story of Saving a Spouse 249
67. Removing All Genetic Dis-eases 253
68. Uplifting Humanity by Releasing the Vanities 256
69. Embracing One's Higher Purpose 262
70. Releasing the Addiction to Television 265
71. Healing One's Own Fibonacci Sequence 267
72. Even More Taps on Food Issues 270
73. Release Being Conditioned 272
74. Embracing Your Ultimate Truth 274
75. Happy Birthday! 276
76. Father's Day Taps 278
77. The Underbelly of Mother's Day 281
78. Reclaiming Truth 284
79. Redefining Motherhood 287
80. Cleansing Ourselves of Energetic Parasites 290
81. Release Being Indoctrinated 292
82. Change Allegiance 295
83. Releasing Pain Marathon 297
84. Releasing the Drama from Friendship 301
85. Success Marathon 303
86. An Aversion to Eating 307
87. Autoimmune Disease 310
88. Attracting Money 314
89. The Need to Join 316
90. Being a Perpetual Success 319

91. An Energetic Vitamin 322
92. Vibrate with Love 324
93. Creating Better "Vision" 327
94. Be a Pipeline of Divine Light, Love and Song int This World 328
95. Manifesting Universal Joy 330
Testimonials About Jen's Work 333
About the Author 355
Other Books by Jen Ward 357

Your Gift

Life is not linear. You are not looming towards old age, disease, and death. We are all buoyed in a perpetual state of exponential Joy, Love, Abundance, Freedom and Wholeness. Our atoms our not conjoined in the sinewy mass of connective tissue. They are a colloidal collection of consciousness made up of individual frequencies of Light and Sound imprinted with the directive of individuality that is you.

Children innately understand this and exist in a perpetual state of bliss and acceptance. But then those that they respect or turn to as "all knowing" slap their hands, tell them that they are bad, and tell them they will have liberties when they "grow up." That programs these beautiful perfect expressions of wonderment to turn from perpetual Joy, Love, Abundance, Freedom, and Wholeness. They are conditioned to turn away from wonderment and fixate on getting older. They are told that they then can partake of the artificially induced freedom of being an adult. The payoff is a dangling carrot or a unicorn that never gives a resolve or a satisfactory return.

This has been our fate lifetime after lifetime, generation after generation. It has become such an ingrained pattern that it is hardly ever challenged except in the quotes of some great teachers that have come to earth hinting at the hypocrisy of our thought patterns. But instead of heeding their words, we galvanize their personalities and forget their message. They are such simple things to heed and yet are glazed over by those who use their message to further enslave the soul in an over-taxed mentality.

"Let he who is without sin cast the first stone," "Love thy neighbor as thyself," "Lest ye become like the little children, ye will not see the kingdom of heaven," "My father's house is a mansion and has many rooms." These are stating that there are so many ways of perceiving the world beyond this one, and they are all valid. "The things that I do, you are capable of doing, and greater." We are all great healers, teachers, inspirations, and devotees of the sanctity of spirit.

Each great teacher that comes to the earth encourages the individual to break through the conformity that is taught and reach into their depth to manifest greatness. There is such a short shelflife on their message though because it soon becomes bastardized after the messenger has been defiled, tortured, and killed.

The best thing to do is recognize truth when you are given it in a golden chalice and drink as much as you can. Gorge on truth when you are able. You know it. Truth easily assimilates in the body, like a nutritious meal to the starving. Be gluttonous about filling yourself with it and yet be as generous as possible in sharing it. You never know how long that stream of truth will be offered to you untainted and pure.

I am capable of tapping into truth. I did not realize that I had access. I did not expect to be able to inspire, teach, or heal others. The potential of such lay dormant underneath layers and layers of pain, self-derision and the contempt of those who know me. They resent the reminder that they are accessing a slight fraction of their potential. They resent the reminder that they have chosen mediocrity. They would argue that mediocrity was thrust upon them if they ever had the courage to be honest with themselves. But it was a choice. At some point, they chose the stroking of the ego and the embellishment of pettiness.

But here, in a sea of strangers, I have found my true calling and family of the heart. Those I pour effortlessly and willingly all that I have access to in hopes that they will find the key to access it themselves. Although it still seems like the same selfish world, it is not. This world is moving towards the manifestation of its true potential. The souls that know me here, recognize what we do here is no small fate. We have been seeding this world for lifetimes for what we realize in this present existence. The world, like each child, has the capability and capacity to be oh so much more. We all have an innate sense of it. What I share here is keys to understanding and techniques to access such greatness, not just for one but for all.

Every night I go to sleep I ask, "How can I convey truth for others? What will help them to grasp their own empowerment?" Every morning I ask the Universe, "What are others struggling with? What can I share to ease their self-doubt and break through the illusion of suffering?" Last night, I was told to convey to others this: A great technique is to approach life as if they are the infinite being that they are instead of a suffering human, which is the illusion.

The Universe showed me how humans utilize the techniques on my page, not to access their innate empowerment, but from the limited vantage point of relieving their suffering of the moment. In doing that, they are cowering to the ego. The ego will shove all this resistance at them, and they will shrug and say that there are too many taps to do or too many paragraphs in my post. So they skim it and go on to something that is less involved and placates their fickle attention for a moment.

What I share here is a rare opportunity for people to shift in consciousness. They are so pummeled, desecrated, and raped of their virtue that they have little left of trust or belief in something more. They are like the abused animal that runs into its cage rather than taste freedom because it is all it knows. I share repeatedly and consistently hoping that something will coax them out of the apathy of despair. But they can no longer trust that someone is not motive driven or that someone does not want to deplete them further.

But there are those loving, kind souls that do rescue animals for their own unselfish reasons. There are also souls that have such compassion and love for individual suffering that they pour their whole self into alleviating what they can. They are not polished and shiny or adorned in false media glitz. They are organic, simple, and pure, and serve out of a deep compulsion to ease suffering and fulfill a sense of purpose. They dissolve illusion and empower the individual, every individual.

For myself, serving others seems like the only way to make sense of all that I have endured to get to this point. Serving others is my personal lifeline to reason. It makes sense that forces that drive power and greed would meet the atoms of goodness and integrity with what feels like a perpetual menacing blow. But it is merely the spiritual law of balance being visited on me as an individual. It is nothing that goodness and kindness have always needed to transcend. I am not being punished. I am merely being met with the opposite energy to what I am. You are not being punished either. You are just being met with the opposite energy to your goodness. That is why understanding spiritual laws and transcending their effect on us is so beneficial. This is all possible and doable.

I did not plan to write this, but this is what pours out when I put my hands and heart to the keyboard. It is written with encouragement from intangible souls that assist you as guides lovingly serving to awaken a groggy planet. It is my honor to speak with them and for them and to walk with the truth that they have suffered in physical form to deliver. It is your gift if you are willing to accept. Your life is not beneath theirs. You do not have to earn their love and wait to catch a glimpse of them. All you have to do is challenge your own inner mechanism of the ego to pull down the curtain of unworthiness and then walk and converse with them freely. This is what is offered through the techniques I post.

May you bathe in the love and kindness that is lavished on you here. May you break through the facade of resistance and accept all that is offered. May you realize your worth instead of waiting to deem yourself worthy. May you perpetuate love and kindness to break through the facade of ignorance and despair and dissolve the walls of separation between yourself and all of life. You are worthy. You are dynamic. You are empowered. You are free.

Section I: Spiritual Freedom Technique

A Modern-Day Crusader

Everything is energy in different frequencies of movement. We are not separate like we believe. We are a stream of energy of one vibration within a stream of energy of a different vibration. Our words, feelings and thoughts are energy as well. They are all swirling around us. We are all entwined in this beautiful dance of our energy streams.

Since I perceive in energy, I see people's thoughts and feelings as well as their physical body. It is so acute that I perceive thoughts and feelings almost as well as physical action. In fact, since man lies to himself so easily, it is much easier to look at his finer energies to understand who he is. An example would be that if someone else saw a fit, well-dressed man, they may see him as confident. But I will be able to see his insecurities, evidence of times he was bullied or not nurtured, and I will see an overcompensation where others may not.

Everyone can see in energy, but they don't have the understanding to articulate it and formulate what they are perceiving. It isn't magic or occult. It is just articulating a subtle form of expression. In this way, I feel like a crusader. If everyone perceived in energy, they would believe their own instincts and live in truth. It could change the dynamics of the world in a positive way.

These taps are a means of shifting one's energy before they have a full understanding of it. The evidence shows up physically and one will feel better immediately, yet the vibrational shift is more profound than imaginable.

The Start of the SFT Taps

The protocol that I use in doing taps was given to me inwardly by my Spirit Guides. The first taps that were given to me were revealed to me by talking to an energy healer that was one of my instructors at massage therapy school. She explained that in past lives so many of us were in monasteries. She said that we had taken certain vows of devotion. But we didn't just take them for one lifetime. Many had taken vows that specifically stated forever.

I learned the effectiveness of tapping through a modality called BodyTalk. It was part of the procedure used to create energetic shifts in my BodyTalk sessions. It occurred to me that it would be helpful to recant past vows. When I went to my next BodyTalk session, I had my BodyTalk facilitator at the time help me recant vows I may have taken in a past life. It was very powerful. I told my friend about recanting the vow, and she did the same thing when she went to her BodyTalk session. She had such a great reaction to releasing her past that it was a breakthrough in her personal healing work. From her response, I felt that it was an effective way to help others. When people called me for help, I would walk them through the process of recanting ancient vows over the phone.

Here are the first taps:

Say each statement three times out loud while CONTINUOUSLY tapping on the top of your head at the crown chakra and say it a fourth time while tapping on your chest at the heart chakra. Say each word deliberately. They are not just words but a vibration that you are initiating to shift energy. Pause after each word. Say it in a commanding but even tone, not as a question. Forgo saying it in a singsong tone or with bravado. Say them all. Notice the semi-colon before "in all moments." This is to emphasize the pause before those three words.

> **"I recant my vow of poverty; in all moments."**
>
> **"I recant my vow of humility; in all moments."**
>
> **"I recant my vow of silence; in all moments."**
>
> **"I recant my vow of solitude; in all moments."**

"I recant my vow of chastity; in all moments."

"I recant my vow of celibacy; in all moments."

"I recant my vow of servitude; in all moments."

"I recant my vow of martyrdom; in all moments."

"I recant my vow of deprecation; in all moments."

"I recant my vow of deprivation; in all moments."

Little did I realize that leading people through releasing these vows would be the beginning of a powerful protocol.

I used to have some friends who were Buddhists. They worked in the healing profession. They were very good at it. They were amazing, loving people. The only thing was their personal lives were a mess. They had no lasting relationships and they weren't financially secure. They shared their Buddhist vow with me many times. Their vow was not to transcend until every sentient being had transcended. This stuck with me. I questioned within myself how someone would stay in this world if they had gained the wisdom to transcend but refused to do so. It occurred to me that the way that would happen was by collecting more karma to one's self.

It occurred to me that people who resonate with Buddhism may have taken this vow that my friends had taken. So sometimes, if I know someone has an affinity to Buddhism, I will give them this special tap to do:

"I recant my vow to NOT transcend; in all moments."

Release Being Married to God

I have a very pretty friend who was not attracting any potential mates. We were sitting together talking, and I looked down at her ring finger. She was wearing a ring on her wedding ring finger. Suddenly, as we were sitting there, she transformed in my eyes to a little old nun. I was seeing her in her past life.

It suddenly occurred to me that she had taken a vow to be married to God in a past life. That vow was interfering with her ability to meet potential husbands in this life. Meeting much resistance, I finally encouraged her to take the ring off. I also had her do this particular tap:

"I recant my vow to be married only to God; in all moments."

She felt different afterwards. Coincidentally, she had someone call her the next day and ask her out on a date. She was engaged a few months later.

Recanting All Vows and Agreements

It occurred to me that any two people who have any interaction at all have agreed to that dynamic on some level. It may not feel like someone would agree to being treated poorly, but it may be done out of habit. If someone was beaten down by someone in a past life, they may fall into that same role in this lifetime. If one could release having dynamics with unhealthy people out of habit, they could be more free.

The first thing to do when trying to free oneself is to stop agreeing to it. Since one doesn't remember that they have agreed to a certain dynamic, it is always good to just assume that they have. So the first tap in the protocol is to say:

"I recant all vows and agreements between myself and (person's name); in all moments."

There may be a great sense of relief in just doing this one tap. A strange phenomenon I have found is that when the tap is relevant to the person, they will have difficulty saying it. They will trip over their words or say it as if it were a question. They will say it really fast and not pause after the phrase. They will also sometimes say it in a singsong voice like they are telling a story.

The reason the taps include the phrase "in all moments." is because in metaphysical terms, all our past moments are happening at once. Since we have been trained to be linear thinkers, this explanation may seem confusing. So think of saying "in all moments." as going into those experiences and changing the agreement where they first occurred.

Imagine that all the times we have ever experienced something and think about it are out in the ethers somewhere. The "us" in the body wants to change, but all these other aspects of us that are still echoing through the universe make up most of our experience of what we do in our physical life. That is why it is not so easy to change a pattern of low exercise to healthy living when we choose to. Perhaps all these unconscious aspects of us are dictating what happens in this physical realm. Just suppose. So by tacking on the words "In all moments," we are addressing all those other expressions of our activity in the universe and commanding them to shift dynamics as well. We are pulling all expressions of "us" that ever existed totally into the moment. This is a powerful awareness to be able to do this. It may be a leap of faith in the physical realm. But it is having a dynamic command of self-empowerment in the subtle realms.

A mistake people make is saying "in all my moments." I correct them. We are not just changing the dynamics in our own experiences but also in the lives of others who are involved. Otherwise, it is not as efficient a tap as it could be. The whole purpose of these taps is to change ourselves at the core. It is like taking all our experiences, scooping them together, and collecting them and aligning them all into the one present moment of now.

I also found that it is helpful to recant our vows between more than just people. It is helpful if someone feels wronged by a certain organization to recant those vows and agreements. Many people have lived many lifetimes through the Crusades, so they may have contempt for the church or the king of the time. If they don't know who it is, they can use a description. They may say, the King of France or feudalism.

They may even release their vows and agreements with a concept. A professional soldier may have agreed to go to war in the past and be compelled to do so in this life. So a good tap to do would be recanting all vows and agreements with war in all moments. The list is endless since it is our agreements with these things that keep us anchored in this time and space.

By the way, recanting our dynamics with time and space can create a very profound, surreal shift.

Removing All Curses

The second tap in the protocol series that was given to me by my Guides was about removing curses. People think that a curse is ominous, as in black magic. But a curse is anything that was stated as a truth fueled by passion, and limits the individual that it was directed at. Here are some samples of curses that may sound familiar:

"You will never meet anyone who loves you as much as I do!"

"You will never amount to much!"

"You will never make money being a (profession)!"

These kinds of things can be hurtful in one lifetime. But if we heard something like this in a past life, it may put a glass ceiling on our future experiences. If we have enough of these glass ceilings on us, they can render us ineffective. So the more we remove these curses, the freer we become.

Also, it is important to remove the curses we have put on others as well. We can't really be free if we have someone else tied to us. Cursing others is a way to strap them to us.

The second tap of the protocol is:

"I remove all curses between myself and (person's name); in all moments."

Whomever or whatever you recanted your vows and agreements with in the first tap, you would follow up with removing all curses between yourself and that person or issue.

The mistake people make in doing this tap is they try to put the other person before themselves. Don't ever do that. You are the most important person in this procedure. This needs to be stated.

Removing Old Blessings

There is a new tap in the sequence of extracting all of an issue out of the energy field.

The new step in the protocol is, "I remove all blessings between myself and (the person or issue); in all moments." I discovered this step while doing a session on a dynamic healer. She noted that it was funny that when we released all curses between her and the issue, she saw all these positive aspects of the issue. But when we released all the blessings between herself and the issue, it was then that she saw all the scenarios release regarding the issue. They were things that never seemed relevant to her until we did the blessings tap.

The examples I was shown in my head that support the need to release the blessings between someone and the issue drove the point home. I saw someone who in the present day is without children but in the past came from a very large family that was overwhelming. She wished to never have to have children again. If people are childless in this life, that would have been their blessing in the past.

So a blessing is wishing for the opposite of what you wanted in the past and have in the present, but don't desire any more. A woman who was being sacrificed to a god in the past may wish she was plain or unattractive in the present so that she would never be targeted for her beauty. A man who watched people in power abuse others would be grateful to never be in that position himself. A person who lived on the farm and had to tend to animals his whole life would wish he would never have to care for an animal again. These lacks in this life would have been blessings in a past life. That is what the new tap removes from the energy field of those performing it.

Removing the Pain and Limitations of Karmic Ties

The third tap in the protocol for my work is about our connection with everything around us. Whenever we touch, think, feel, or remember something, there is a tiny string of energy between us that we are strengthening with our attention. If we looked at ourselves from a certain energetic perspective, we would look like a cocoon wrapped in all these karmic ties.

To be free is to cut all these karmic ties yet still be here having the experiences that we enjoy. This is what is meant by the statement "to be in this world but not of it." It is also the purpose of detachment. When we give something our attention, we are creating more ties to it in this world. That is why all the campaigns to raise awareness are misguided.

It doesn't look like any of the things that we raise awareness for are going away anytime soon. Because of the attention we give them, we actually tie them tighter to our world. We just become used to them and accept them as the norm. The people who bow out and refuse to give their attention to negative conditions are actually doing more to eradicate the cause than those who dedicate their energy to it. This is why you will never see me wearing a pink ribbon. A pink ribbon is literally tying the "c" word into people's lives.

This tap is the part of the protocol that dissolves all those ties between yourself and something else. After you have removed all vows and agreements with the person or issue, have removed all curses, it is time to dissolve all karmic ties with it. So the tap would be:

"I dissolve all karmic ties between myself and _____; in all moments."

It is important to put yourself first in the statement. We are so used to taking the backseat to others that we will habitually want to state them first in the sequence. That would be wrong. It is important to get in the habit of putting yourself first in all things, and this is the statement and practice to do so. We are taught that putting ourselves first is selfish, or it is wrong to be self-centered. But this is the only place that we can be empowered, in our own center.

Also, some other protocols may say to cut all ties. But some types of creative people will get distracted by the dangling strings that are created from saying it that way. Their mind may start getting distracted by concern of what the strings are doing. To dissolve them in the statement is the most efficient way to free one's self.

Once we hear about this technique, we may want to go around and dissolve all karmic ties with everyone and everything. And we can. But when we give these things our attention again, it will just reconnect them. We would then digress to a series of mind loops to try to keep these connections severed. It could lead to a small bout with obsessive compulsive disorder (OCD). The more effective approach is to learn the whole protocol and run through it with everyone and everything that pulls on us. In that way, we are actually freeing ourselves on a very deep level.

Think about it, to be free of the person who causes you the most angst. Or to be untethered to concepts of war and disease. That is what this protocol is all about. It sounds unfathomable because we have been tied up in them for so long that we have given up hope of being free of them. But once people get the undeniable sense of being lighter after using the protocol that I am sharing, they will want to use it over and over again to get themselves free.

The great thing is, the more we free ourselves, the more we free those around us. And if enough people learn the protocol and start using it, we can free a great part of the world from the karmic strings of many of the plights that have plagued the world. It is not done out of trying to control others. It is done by gently and methodically freeing ourselves and loosening the grip of these things so others can get on board and free themselves as well. It is the one way to empower ourselves and others, and it is the total antitheses of what we are conditioned to do in the present.

Severing All Strings and Cords

Whenever there is a physical connection between two people, a tiny string of energy is formed between them. If there is no attention put on that connection, the string will dissolve of its own accord. But with repeated connection and continuous attention, the energetic string that is formed becomes so strong that it can become a shackle between two people. It takes a conscious intention to sever such strings that have been allowed to strengthen through both repetitive interaction and a strong emotional reaction. Whether it is a positive dynamic or a negative one, the connections serve no purpose except to control.

> "I sever all strings and cords between myself and
> _____; in all moments."

Removing the Pain and Limitations of a Karmic Connection

After people have dissolved all karmic ties with someone or something, they may feel overburdened. It is that same feeling when someone has just dumped all their problems onto them. Without the warm and fuzzy feeling of the connection and the distraction that is generated from the connection, they are left feeling the heaviness of what they allowed the other party to store in them. Wouldn't it be great to just let go of that heaviness so as not to feel the need to throw it back at the other party by wielding anger at them?

We can release that heaviness through tapping it out. It is a clean way of disposing of issues that are being stored in our energy field. How freeing and empowering it is to just imagine releasing all that is holding us anchored in a lower vibration of pain and angst.

The next tap in the protocol that I have been given is:

"I remove ALL the pain, burden, limitations and engrams that _____ has put on me; in all moments."

The wording is important.

In my private sessions, I have found many ways that some clients try to sabotage themselves when saying this. Say the word "ALL" to make it most thorough. By not saying the word all, the mind leaves wiggle room to hold onto some stuff. Also, some clients want to put an "s" on the end of the word "burden." But leaving it singular makes it more expansive somehow. In addition, some clients will be stuck in saying the statement in the tone of a question. This renders it less effective. The way I have clients counter this is by asking them to pretend to be mad and say the statement in an angry tone. This seems to be the only way they are able to shift out of the ineffectiveness of the question tone.

Another point to pay attention to is saying the statements slowly and intentionally with much spacing between the words. The words are an intention to move and shift energy. Running through them is a subtle form of avoidance. It is not effective. As difficult as it is to stay present and focused, that is what empowerment entails. Doing the taps is an easy pass in working through dense karmic issues. But the issues are still being worked through. The clients are not going around the karmic issues but straight through them. That is why the taps may seem difficult to do, and that is exactly why they need to be done with focus and intention. It is a small price to pay for the overall energetic shift.

The word "engrams" refers to energetic ridges that we develop in our energy field that cause us to do things out of habit. They are similar to grooves on an old vinyl record. I see the energy field from the inside of the person sometimes as a waxy mound like a honeycomb nest. By gently melting the mold and smoothing out the ridges, we can actually remove habitual thoughts, beliefs and actions from our behavior. This may be a great visual for the reader to work with in contemplations. Look at your energy field from the inside and melt all lines and ridges so it is perfectly smooth.

When we use visualizations, we are giving our mind a job to help assist us in our desired goal. The mind works against us because it is not given enough direction and takes over the situation. It is like a teenager who thinks it is more empowered than the parent. As the parent, we have let the teenager gain control, and it is time to take back the reins and steer our own cart. Visualizations and taps are a great way to do that.

After we have removed all the pain, burden, limitations, and engrams that someone or something has put on us, we are going to want to remove all that we have put on that same someone or something. It is a matter of totally cleaning the slate and not having that other component coming after us for reciprocation. The tap would be:

"**I remove all the pain, burden, limitations and engrams that I have put on _____; in all moments.**"

The short version of this is: "**I remove all that I have put on _____; in all moments.**"

Usually when clients feel victimized by someone, if they go far enough back in their history together, they will realize that they were the perpetrator before. The one who seems like an older soul is especially more likely the one who abused power first and got tired of the game. Many of us are merely waiting for others to tire of the game we ourselves have already lost interest in, long ago. We are not victims; we are just merely tired of the game before everyone else is.

The short version is used when releasing the dynamics between someone that you are not feeling any love towards, like a rapist. The longer version is used to address the dynamics between yourself and a loved one.

Taking Back Your Joy

After we have dissolved all karmic ties with someone or something and have removed all that has been dumped on us, we may feel depleted. It is no different than breaking up with someone that you have poured your love into and realizing that they took way more than they reciprocated. So we are left feeling lost and empty when we have been used, cheated, abused, energetically raped, and left in pieces. Wouldn't it be great to go back and get back all that has been taken, not to be spiteful but merely to be whole?

Scientists know that energy has weight and mass. No matter how subtle, if we had the instruments to measure it, we would realize that it is intangible to some degree but it is still matter. If we had sensitive enough instruments, we could weigh and measure it. Because it does have some sort of mass and volume, it can be retrieved. The way we do this is with an intention and a tap.

An intention is an energetically charged thought. It is directed by the mind and fueled by the heart. The heart-mind combination is the winning combination behind every success. It can be our intention to retrieve what has been taken from us. Those who don't think it is possible may have never tried it.

The next tap in the protocol has three versions. There is a general one, a more thorough one, and a very thorough one. These are not just words. Positive words are like a vitamin to the body. This tap is an actual retrieval of the energy that has been taken from the person who invokes this tap.

Here are the three versions of the same tap to retrieve one's energy:

"I take back all that _____ has taken from me; in all moments."

"I take back all the Joy, Love, Abundance, Freedom, Life, and Wholeness that _____ has taken from me; in all moments."

"I take back all the Joy, Love, Abundance, Freedom, Health, Success, Security, Companionship, Creativity, Peace, Life, Wholeness, Beauty, Enthusiasm, Confidence, Spirituality, Enlightenment, Family, Intellect, and the Ability to Discern that _____ has taken from me; in all moments."

As this tap is being done, it may actually feel like you are being inflated. Some people may feel like their chest is opening up, or they are feeling taller. Some may feel extended all over. Some may start to feel tingling throughout their body.

To maintain a balance, it is important to give back all that you have taken from the same party. If it is someone that you don't have a history with, you may just say a generic tap:

"I give back all that I have taken from _____; in all moments."

If it is someone that you care about, like a relative, you may want to use this version:

"I give back all the Joy, Love, Abundance, Freedom, Life, and Wholeness that I have taken from _____; in all moments."

If you are going to do the taps with the subject being someone that you love like a spouse or child, you may want to do this version:

"I give back all the Joy, Love, Abundance, Freedom, Health, Success, Security, Companionship, Creativity, Peace, Life, Wholeness, Beauty, Enthusiasm, Confidence, Spirituality, Enlightenment, Family, Intellect and the Ability to Discern that I have taken from _____; in all moments."

If you are recanting all vows and agreements with an establishment instead of a person, and you are getting all that has been taken from you from an establishment, you will want to follow up by giving back all that you have taken from all others that the establishment caused you to take from them. You wouldn't give back to the establishment but to the people that the establishment caused you to hurt. For example, if you were a soldier in war, you may want to give back to all those that war has caused you to take from. Here is what it looks like:

"I give back all the Joy, Love, Abundance, Freedom, Life, and Wholeness that I have taken from all others due to _____; in all moments."

It is important to do all the taps in the protocol because it is a thorough combination of the dynamics that are causing a lack of some kind in your life. The mind will resist doing these. It will use many tricks to cause you to resist saying them. If you have trouble saying the words, that is a clear indicator that they are exactly what needs to be done to bring a shift. Another sabotage is the conscious mind deciding that a particular tap is not necessary to do. If you tell yourself one particular tap is not important, please break through that discerning concept and do it anyway. You may be surprised by the reaction.

Withdrawing Our Energy

Anything that is in our life is there because we have drawn it to us. In some way, we have given it energy to be a part of our existence. Use the analogy of giving a child who is having a temper tantrum attention and recognize how that feeds the condition. But if the child is ignored, the behavior dries up more quickly. We are fueling our world in the same way.

Anything that we don't want in our experience, we can simply withdraw our energy from to be free of it. It is human nature though to ruminate over the things we don't like. How many times do we find ourselves thinking about food when we are trying to lose weight, worrying about the bills when we are feeling a lack of money? Could we be feeding that lack with our attention?

When training a dog, it is understood that they don't know the word no. If they hear the command, "no couch," their mind will drop the word no and they will think that they are wanted on the couch. That is how it works. Maybe our minds work that way as well. Maybe when we think about what we don't want, our minds think we want more of that thing, even if it is lack.

It is the same with ruminating over the past. The mind does not register the past and the future. It only registers the present. So when someone talks about their issues from the past, the mind is creating our moment. By thinking of our past problems, we are programming ourselves to have problems in the moment. Our mind is a computer. It gives us what we ask for. In its simplistic black and white sense, if we are focusing on problems, we must want more of them. So it manifests more of the same for us. That is why focus and attention on our desired results are so effective. The taps are a great way to assist.

All the attempts to rectify manifesting what we don't want haven't worked for some. So the next tap in my protocol is to override the mind's belief that you want it to manifest more of what you really don't want.

Here is the tap:

"I withdraw all my energy from _____; in all moments."

We add the phrase "in all moments." to all the taps because there is a metaphysical belief that all we have ever felt, thought, believed or done is happening consecutively in the moment. The phrase "in all moments," brings all of these peripheral experiences into the intention, so they are not working against the present, conscious intention we are sending out.

This is a powerful tap to do in the protocol. Imagine how powerful it would be if everyone on the planet did the taps to withdraw all their energy from war, poverty and illness. The more individuals who do this protocol, the more we can make these experiences less of a reality for all.

Bypassing the Mind

The next steps in my personal protocol with the tapping are very effective in bypassing the mind. There are many people who fail at using affirmations because as soon as they say something positive, the mind pulls up all the times when that statement did not prove to be true. If someone said the affirmation, "I am healthy and fit," the mind would refute it with all the proof that the body is out of shape and remind the conscious self of all the diet attempts that failed. So the affirmations serve as arguments for the mind.

The taps themselves bypass the conscious mind. A way to make them even more effective is by wording them in such a way that the mind does not even know how to refute them. We are a frequency of sound or an emanation of light. By acknowledging the self in a way other than a solid physical form, the taps bypass the mind's ability to understand or scrutinize what is happening.

The mind does not have an overview of the self as a sound frequency or light emanation. So if we command a change in our sound frequency or light wave, the mind has no way to stop it. It is immobilized from its lack of ability in understanding how to override the command. It can be considered sneaking up on the mind to create a positive shift.

For example, we could try to talk ourselves into being happy until we are blue in the face. But the mind will work diligently to remind us of all the evidence that we are not. So with my protocol, we would do two different taps: one that addressed the individual as light emanation and one that addressed the individual as sound frequency. We would say, "I remove all sadness from my sound frequency," and "I remove all sadness from my light emanation." How is the mind going to refute these?

So whatever it is that one is dissolving all their karmic ties with, they will also want to remove it from their sound frequency and light emanation.

"I remove all _____ from my sound frequency; in all moments."

"I remove all _____ from my light body; in all moments."

Since everything is a movement of atoms, everything has a vibration, even us. Everything in our lives is synchronized to vibrate similarly with us. If we don't want something in our lives, we simply don't agree to it. If we don't want strife, we avoid it as much as possible. This is obviously an oversimplification, but the way to not agree with something on an energetic level is to refuse to resonate with it. The tap would be:

"I release resonating with _____; in all moments."

Using the same reasoning, we would use a similar tap to address the individual as a light emanation. The tap would be:

"I release emanating with _____; in all moments."

The mind is rendered helpless from stopping an incredible shift.

Shifting One's Paradigms

I was listening to a motivational speaker talk about our life patterns. He called them paradigms. He was explaining that if we change our behavior, it will change our paradigms. It made me think that it would make more sense to change the paradigms than the behavior. Since the patterns are directing the behavior, it seemed more logical to focus on changing the paradigms themselves and that would change the behavioral patterns. In doing this, we are changing our vantage point. Are we looking at a situation from the vantage point of a pathetic grunt? Or are we seeing ourselves from the vantage point of the empowered state of omniscience? It is a choice that we may never even have considered.

An analogy that comes to mind is, if you want the dog's tail to wag, do you try to manipulate the tail or do you motivate the dog to wag the tail?

I think of these paradigms that the speaker was talking about as an energetic base of who we are and how we show up. If we are showing up unhappy, then it would be important to move that whole base into happiness. I see it as an imaginary pyramid. When I do the taps about shifting my paradigm, I accompany it with the visual of actually moving a huge pyramid.

This part of the protocol is motivating the whole self to shift back into a natural state of wellbeing. Since it is our natural state to be in Joy, Love, Abundance, Freedom, Health, Success, and Wholeness, these are the words that are used in the tap. Sometimes when someone needs the extra oomph of other uplifting words, other positive words are added to the taps as well.

Here are two versions of the tap:

"I shift my paradigm from _____ to Joy, Love, Abundance, Freedom, Health, Success, and Wholeness; in all moments."

"I shift my paradigm from _____ to Joy, Love, Abundance, Freedom, Health, Success, Security, Companionship, Creativity, Peace, Life, Wholeness, Beauty, Enthusiasm, Confidence, Spirituality, Enlightenment, Family, Intellect and the Ability to Discern; in all moments."

Transcending One's Issues

People who help others are sometimes afraid of taking on karma for their efforts. It is a concern that some people try to put on me when I assist them. I have had insightful inner dialogues with my Spirit Guides on this topic.

One important thing to note is that fear is the opposite of love. If one is feeling fear, no matter how subtle, it means there is room for more love. All one has to do is make their love bigger. Fear of taking on karma is a fear.

A great visual is to imagine being plugged into an enormous source of expansive, emanating light that is a million times bigger than the sun. Imagine scrunching all this love down into a little ball, like scrunching down a soft sponge. Visualize stuffing this ball into you, and when you let go of it, it fills you up from the inside and emanates out of your every pore. It is so brilliant and massive, that it either burns or pushes out everything but the love and light.

Another distinction to make is our vantage point. A person's issues have weight and mass. They can possibly waft to someone else like a cloud can pass to another part of the sky if it is a lateral move. That is why anyone helping someone else must be so hyper aware to keep their vantage point higher than whomever they are helping. The helper must keep their feelings, experiences and thoughts out of it. They must transcend in that moment all that they are assisting someone to release.

This is also something that we individuals can do when we are separating ourselves from our own issues. Instead of seeing ourselves swimming in them, we can visualize ourselves hovering in the sky above all the fray.

The tap for this and the next tap in the protocol is:

"I transcend _____; in all moments."

It is a very quick way to shift vantage points and pull ourselves out of the emotional or mental muck that we may have been indulging in.

Repairing the Skin on Your Energy Field

You know how some people are dynamic, or they have a magnetic personality? Why don't we all have that? We are all made of the same stuff. Why is it that some people are courageous and dynamic and some have no presence and are overlooked?

When I work with clients, I perceive their energy fields as deflated balloon-like structures. As we work to release stagnant energy and regain the attributes of "wholeness," I feel the balloon fill up. But for so many, the skin of the balloon (their energy field) is compromised. It isn't able to hold itself together because there is a rip or tear in the balloon. Sometimes it is completely shredded. I see holes or rips in this aspect of some people. Sometimes the container of their separate energy is non-existent.

If someone does not perceive the energy that flows through them, it could be their energetic structure has been violated or even destroyed. Some people who have experienced war or extreme abuse seem to have no outer casing on their energy field to contain it. The next part of my protocol is to repair the skin on the energy field with a tap.

The name for the skin on the energy field is the Wei Chi. It is important that all the makeup of our energy field is contained within our Wei Chi. Otherwise, we are merely a floating cloud that dissipates our own effectiveness. Doing the next tap is an important step in the tapping protocol I have developed.

"I repair and fortify my Wei Chi; in all moments."

I see the visual as a strong bubble of protection around us that is the wall of our energy field. I sometimes imagine angels repairing the walls with light using the same tools that are used to repair drywall. A good way to think of this barrier is like a two-way mirror where all the love and light can pass both ways, but the negative energy is singed on contact.

Also, whenever someone throws a fear statement at you or you are put in fear by events or natural disasters, merely visualize a protective bubble around yourself, your loved ones, your home, your special tree or anything else that you hold dear. It is an effective form of protection and it dissipates the fear.

Another version of the tap which is more complete, is:

"I repair and fortify my Wei Chi of all my bodies; in all moments."

We are made up of different components. They are different vibratory rates within us. The coarsest is the physical component, but then we have our emotional component which is our emotional body, our past memories which is our causal body, and our mind which is our mental body. When we repair the Wei Chi of all these different components, we allow them to maintain their integrity and borders in relationship to each other, so we aren't a mishmash of thoughts, feelings, and experiences swirling around with no coherency or discernment between the different bodies.

There is also an essence of us beyond the lower bodies, but the deeper we go in developing the more subtle senses, the deeper we also go in establishing a greater integrity within ourselves. When delving deeper into ourselves, here is a tap to define ourselves as a spiritual being:

"I repair and fortify the Wei Chi of my Spiritual Beingness; in all moments."

Aligning All Our Bodies

We are much more than a physical body. That is one layer of vibratory rate in our makeup. We have an emotional body, which is another vibratory rate. In addition, we have a causal body where all the records of our past lives are stored. This is a different vibratory rate. We also have a mental body, which is a more refined vibratory rate. There are others, but these are the ones that are addressed in the next tap of my protocol.

There is a world that coincides with the vibratory rate of each body. When our physical body gives out, we simply slip out of it and continue our existence on the astral plane, which correlates with our astral or emotional body. Since we are then in our emotional body and on the astral plane, that world is as solid to us as earth is to our physical body.

All of these different vibratory rates of our different bodies should all be in unison with each other. They should all be a cohesive group and have an intricate interaction with the next. But due to pain and trauma, we start depending on one more than the other. Or, we start denying one body and overcompensate by relying on the others more.

How this may look energetically is similar to a bulging disc of a vertebra. At least, that is how I perceive it when working with someone. The way an unaligned body shows up to non-energy readers is in behavior.

A person who is not connecting well to his emotional or mental bodies could be overcompensating by being engrossed in physical activity. The term dumb jock comes to mind. Also, we have all met over-emotional people or people with intellects that seem removed from their emotions. These are all possible examples of people whose vibratory rates of their different aspects are not cohesive.

It may also show up in the chakra energy system of a person. Some of a person's chakras may have been processing more energy than others. This can cause a compensation in different ways. It can create emotional and mental denial, lethargy in the physical body or depression.

Here is the tap that is next:

"I align all my bodies; in all moments."

Being Centered in Divine Love

Once all the bodies are aligned, it is only a matter of igniting the intention for divine love to shoot through all of the bodies and to ignite the whole energy system. The mind may depict the physical, astral, causal, and mental bodies as a group of discs stacked in concentric circles with an opening in the middle. Or a bunch of inner tube-like structures lying on top of each other. This is fine for a rudimentary visualization of the different aspects of ourselves contained cohesively together.

There is a moment where creation is depicted as a spark bursting forth. This image is a good one to depict the visualization of the tap pouring energy into the whole system. A more thorough image for this tap is to visualize the emanating "spark of creation" accompanied by fluid energy running through the whole body from below the feet to above the head. Running energy combined with emanating energy and the spark of divinity are a thorough depiction of what this tap of being centered in divine love looks like.

The tap that one would say is:

"I am centered and empowered in Divine Love; in all moments."

The wording is very strong. Most people have been feeling less than empowered. So this tap, announcing to the whole system that one is indeed centered and balanced and empowered, is a confidence booster. All the different aspects of themselves that were working against each other are now finally working cohesively again.

The phrase "in all moments." is especially powerful because it goes into all the corners of the psyche. When and where the individual did not feel empowered, it reclaims its sovereignty. All aspects of the self are merged and working for the benefit of the whole being. Instead of giving allegiance to a spiteful king or some other power structure, the individuals are finally working under their own free will. It is very freeing to do this tap.

If someone was feeling especially ineffective before doing the protocol and needed an extra shot of empowerment, there is another tap that can be added. It's just an extra shot of reassurance, especially if someone was feeling negatively influenced.

"I burn out everything that is NOT Divine Love from my energy field; in all moments."

It is effective to sense things singeing and dissolving as one does this tap. We can actually feel a self-emanation experience and a burst in brightness.

How We Show Up in the World

The last tap in the protocol is about sharing our new state of empowerment in how we interact with the world. It is one thing to plug ourselves into Joy, Love, and Abundance. It is quite another step in empowerment to show up as these things in all of our interactions. The last tap in the protocol does just this.

"I resonate and emanate Divine Love; in all moments."

The long version of this is:

"I resonate and emanate Joy, Love, Abundance, Freedom, Health, Success, Security, Companionship, Creativity, Peace, Life, Wholeness, Beauty, Enthusiasm, Confidence, Spirituality, Enlightenment, Family, Intellect and the Ability to Discern; in all moments."

The Energetic Cleanse

Think of something that annoys you or you have been obsessing over. It can be a job, person, task, relationship, global issue or a habit. After you name the issue, say each statement out loud three times while tapping on the top of your head, and say it a fourth time while tapping on your chest.

"All engrams of _____ are removed; in all moments."

"All vivaxes with _____ are removed; in all moments."

"All tentacles of _____ are removed; in all moments.

"All my energy is withdrawn from _____; in all moments."

"All dependency on _____ is released; in all moments."

"Feeling beholden to _____ is eliminated; in all moments."

"All vows and agreements with _____ are recanted; in all moments."

"All contracts with _____ are nullified; in all moments."

"All curses with _____ are removed; in all moments."

"All blessings with _____ are removed; in all moments."

"All strings and cords with _____ are severed; in all moments."

"All karmic ties with _____ are dissolved; in all moments."

"All the pain, burden, limitations and engrams that _____ has inflicted are removed; in all moments."

"All the pain, burden, limitations and engrams that have been caused due to _____ are removed; in all moments."

"All that was taken from _____ is returned; in all moments."

"All the Joy, Love, Abundance, Freedom, Health, Success, Security, Companionship, Creativity, Peace, Life, Wholeness, Beauty, Enthusiasm, Contentment, Spirituality, Enlightenment and Confidence that _____ has taken is returned; in all moments."

"Resonating with _____ is released; in all moments."

"Emanating with _____ is released; in all moments."

"All of _____ is removed from my Sound Frequency; in all moments."

"All of _____ is removed from my Light Emanation; in all moments."

"My paradigm is shifted from _____ to Joy, Love, Abundance, Freedom, Health, Success, Security, Companionship, Creativity, Peace, Life, Wholeness, Beauty, Enthusiasm, Contentment, Spirituality, Enlightenment and Confidence; in all moments."

"All illusion is stripped from _____; in all moments."

"The first cause of enabling _____ is eliminated; in all moments."

"All masks, walls and armor are removed from _____; in all moments."

"All masks, walls and armor that were implemented due to _____ are removed; in all moments."

"All energy matrices of _____ are sent into the Light and Sound; in all moments."

"All complex energy matrices of _____ are escorted into the Light and Sound; in all moments."

"All portals to _____ are collapsed and dissolved; in all moments."

"All of _____ is transcended; in all moments."

"The Wei Chi of all bodies is repaired; in all moments."

"All bodies are aligned; in all moments."

"All are centered and empowered in Divine Love; in all moments."

Some people feel guilty saying the taps at first if they are going through them about someone they love. But it is not a betrayal. It actually releases issues between them that need not be issues. The relationship is based more clearly on love, and clarity and freedom are gained. I had to argue more than once with someone who did not want to say they were releasing hating someone they apparently loved. My argument is that they are not releasing loving the person; they are releasing hating them. If you have released hating them, then it's no longer an issue. The protest in doing the taps is evidence that they need to be done.

SFT Dictionary

There are some very complicated metaphysical concepts that do not need to be so difficult to understand. Anything that is fathomable in the Universe should be able to be simplified so a child can understand it. For instance, there are no words that explain the energy pull between two things. That would be the word *vivaxes*. As we become more enlightened, we will need more and more words to explain our ever-expanding relationship with energy.

Claws: Sometimes, and in some instances, a person will feel psychically gripped by an issue. The best way to depict the feeling of this is with the word claws.

Engrams: Engrams are the way past issues are stored in our energy field. Think of how a groove in a vinyl record plays a song repeatedly when a needle is inserted in the groove. An engram is a groove in a person's energy field that plays a behavior repeatedly.

Enlightenment: This is the formula process of a person meeting all of the negativity within themselves and stripping it away so they are no longer at the mercy of the ego and can see themselves more as a reflection of the higher realms than in reactionary mode.

Light Bodies: We seem like solid energy, but we are really made of layers of energy consisting of different vibrations. Our physical body is the coarsest. Then the emotions create a layer of vibration around that. People know that layer as the astral level of vibration. Then there is the level that contains the memory of every past experience. This layer is called the causal plane and the records are called the akashic records. After that layer of vibration is the mental realm. This is the same layer as the ego, and it is why it is difficult to see beyond the mental realm because the ego tries to prevent it. Above that level, the duality of the lower vibrations are dropped and the energy beyond that is of such a purity, it registers as a neutrality. That is why feeling good is not the highest expression of love but loving neutrality or detachment is a more spiritual state. The ego will convey this as bliss but in its true state, it is neither positive nor negative.

Light Emanation: We are not solid matter. In energy, we are a Light Emanation and a Sound Frequency woven together to give the illusion of matter.

Matrixes (also matrices): Stagnant energy can exist in cloud form. We walk through it all the time during the day. It can affect our moods. If a person walks through energy and it identifies with their vibration, it may collect in an individual and seem like an intrusion.

Complex Energy Matrix: When an energy matrix intrudes upon your energy system and identifies itself with a personality, it may convince you and it that it is an aspect of you or that it is a totally different individual that has taken you over in some way. It is merely stagnant energy that needs to be dissipated. No melodrama necessary. Just release it with the taps.

Portal: An energetic gateway.

Psychic Stream of Energy: A compilation of a similar vibration of thoughts and emotions that creates a cloud-like energy that can affect those who are subjected to it.

Sound Frequency: One of the two aspects of ourselves, the other one being Light Emanation. All energy is either Light or Sound. Knowing ourselves as Sound Frequencies and Light Emanations is breaking ourselves down to our true state devoid of ego and ego limitations. It is as a Sound Frequency or Light Emanation that we are capable of traveling in all realms and knowing ourselves as omniscient, omnipotent and omnipresent. It is also a means of communicating with Source or God in Its native tongue.

Strings: When two energy sources touch, a string of connecting energy is formed between them. If attention is kept on this string, it can become reinforced with obsessive or repetitive thoughts. These strings need to be broken if one is going to be free of the object of the taps.

Tentacles: Energy that reaches out and attaches to someone, perhaps to take from them or feed off their energy.

Vivaxes: An energy pull between two or more people, places or things.

Vortex: A vortex is an energy pull similar to a gravitational pull between two components. For example, there is a vortex between the sun and all the planets and there is a vortex between the earth and moon.

Wei Chi: The "skin" on the surface of a person's energy field that provides a natural barrier to energies interrupting one's natural function. It gets pierced and broken during trauma and then it is more difficult for an energy to hold its electromagnetic charge. Someone whose Wei chi is intact may have a natural magnetism.

Please see the website www.jenuinehealing.com/sft-dictionary/. Additional definitions are being added all time. You can also make requests for definitions here.

Section II: SFT Taps

1. A Shortcut

If you had an unbelievable gift of helping people, would you sit on it, or would you share it as much as possible? That is my dilemma daily. The ability to move energy and to remove stagnant energy was something that I have trained many lifetimes to do. Some people who do not understand it want to lecture me on not using it, or diminish me out of ego, or dismiss me out of disbelief. That is their choice.

The same training that gave me these abilities also taught me the ethics that go with it. There are spiritual parameters to follow. The world is changing from third dimension to fifth dimension. It is happening. People are being uplifted in consciousness as we speak. I am a part of that. I do my part. If I were to say that a few years ago, I would have been scoffed at or deemed insane. The fact that my point of view is accepted by some exceptional people is evidence of a shift.

The fact that I am a female and assisting the world in such a dynamic way is evidence that female energy is taking its place in balance with male energy. I could have incarnated as a male. But no. It is part of the advancement of consciousness that I am in a female body.

I facilitated a short and powerful tap for everyone last night before going to sleep. In the middle of the night, I was wide awake and had to go to the computer. A few minutes later, a dear friend was writing out her soul travel experience to me of being awake when asleep and believing she was dead and having her karmic sentence handed out. She survived that inner experience of dealing with all that entailed, was stripped of it, and arrived at a beautiful ocean. This person was different from the experience. She was enlightened.

It was my proof that the tap I did was beneficial to individuals who were asking for it. Some people had been praying and working towards what I put out there that night. Maybe you felt it too. Here is what I tapped: "I implement and process for humanity all the taps that I have formulated; in all moments." I then did the same tap for all individuals.

I did it with the encouragement of my Spirit Guides. The spiritual principle is that one can affect change from within. I am in physical form. I can facilitate a change within a group that I am a part of. That does not mean that it is overriding free will. It means that I am assisting all those all over the planet who are ready to shift and need a little help. Would you do less?

"I implement and process all the taps that Jen has formulated; in all moments."

"I implement and process for society, all the taps that Jen has formulated; in all moments."

"I implement and process for humanity, all the taps that Jen has formulated; in all moments."

"I implement and process for all of life, all the taps that Jen has formulated; in all moments."

These are exciting times. The sky is no longer a limit.

2. A Client's Dramatic First Session

I facilitated a private remote session with a new client. Her good friend had had sessions with me, and she has seen the profound shift in her friend, so she was receptive to my work. This helps because of how deep the sessions work. The more of a trust factor I have with the client, the more profound of a shift can happen. When setting up the session, she said that she had no real issues except for dealing with an ex-partner that she was going to be meeting with. Of course, I realized that that was not the case. It never is that simple.

As soon as we connected, I realized how receptive she was. I perceived a deep loneliness in her. She also facilitated energy work in the form of massage therapy, but when she was taught to allow the clients' issues to flow into the earth to release through her feet, she was merely jamming the issues into her own body. She was not energetically following through. So she was jam-packed with a lot of issues of her own and all of her clients. At the beginning of the session, she felt like iron.

The reason this happened came through later in the session. It touched on a current theme that ran through her lifetimes. It was a profound insight for her to realize, and it made a certain sense to her when it was revealed. She had lost both her legs during a past life, and the ingrained memory or habit of that (what I call an engram) was preventing the energy from flowing down her legs and into the ground. There was a disconnect between her and the earth.

"I release feeling disconnected from the earth; in all moments."

"I connect to the earth; in all moments."

"I recycle all energy back into love by perpetually pouring it into the earth; in all moments."

As I led her through instructions as to how to do the taps, she had a very difficult time doing them. The instructions are: Say each statement three times while tapping on your head and say it a fourth time while tapping on your chest. She said that she had a disability of some kind that prevented her from following simple instructions. I understand that because I experience a similar thing. So I challenged her which brought another emotional round of tears.

I explained to her that she thinks beyond linear thought just like I do. So every time she is given instructions, she has to take time to translate it back into the tedious method of linear thought, and it appears that she is slow. I reassured her that all of humanity is moving beyond linear thought, and she is just ahead of the curve. Explaining that she is disabled is the only way to explain what is happening to those who only know linear thought. I do that too. But I did not want her believing her own explanation when she is so advanced. In fact, one of the first taps I led her through had to do with her first lifetime on earth and how lonely it was.

"I release feeling abandoned on earth; in all moments."

"I release rejecting earth; in all moments."

For many people, their first lifetime on earth is a sore disappointment. Living on earth compared to other planets is like being immersed in a sarcophagus. It is that stifling. Plus, on other planets, we have had a beautiful, long, powerful tail. So many people, when they get on earth, have trouble balancing with just the two legs instead of the powerful tripod of legs and tail that having a tail affords. These people may have trouble with their lower back, tailbone, or hips. She confirmed that she had chronic issues with her hip, which surprised her when she felt a release with the next tap.

"I release the trauma of losing my tail; in all moments."

"I reattach my tail; in all moments."

These taps, as strange as they were to her consciously, brought great relief to the whole hip area. She felt space in her hip area that was not there before, and we both felt heat in her lower back that I worked at moving through her whole spine by releasing the issues that were jamming her up energetically.

"I remove all the anger that I have stored in my beingness; in all moments."

"I release cursing earth; in all moments."

"I release hating earth; in all moments."

I was told by my Guides a while ago that people who defile the earth so easily have little affinity for it. They were brought here begrudgingly and so treat the earth as if they are disgruntled children that resent their home situations. They need to awaken to gratitude for being here on earth and release old grudges of being brought to this planet unwittingly. They need to stop looking up at the stars to be saved and accept that all their old friends from their home planet have already incarnated here. In an indirect way, this will assist in relieving the pillaging of earth that is happening through the rape of all its fossil fuels.

"I release waiting to be rescued from earth; in all moments."

"I release looking to the stars for redemption; in all moments."

"I accept my earthly conditions; in all moments."

"I release the systemic rape of earth; in all moments."

Many people who pray to the heavens were initially waiting to be saved by their native planet from the fate of being on earth. But now, it merely dissipates earth, and people need to accept that they are here on earth and pour their love and energy back into the earth, or it will eventually be depleted as it is run to the ground and all its energy is dissipated.

"I release dissipating the earth of its energy; in all moments."

"I release diluting my energy by pouring it into space; in all moments."

"I release diluting the earth's empowerment; in all moments."

The next issues that were revealed in my new client, who was amazed that she was having such profound shifts of energy so quickly, had to do with the experiences that were creating trauma during lifetimes on earth.

"I release being turned into a eunuch; in all moments."

"I release the trauma of having my legs cut off; in all moments."

Underneath that trauma, another past life revealed itself where she was lobotomized. That thing that she called a disability in herself, even though she was perfectly healthy, was a past life engram of the trauma of being lobotomized.

"I release the trauma of being lobotomized; in all moments."

As I led her through this tap, the energy in her head opened up, and she felt light and expansive. I felt the issue in her right frontal lobe that was being addressed and repaired. She felt it too. She was not the same person that she was at the beginning of the session or who she had been for many lifetimes. She now seemed able to formulate the taps much easier.

I asked her if she felt lighter, and she did. I always describe this feeling as being like a Mylar balloon. She described it as being expansive as coral. This was an issue. Coral is not contained. This told me that the natural casing on her energy field was compromised. This casing is the Wei Chi. I led her through the taps to repair the Wei Chi, not only on her physical body, but on her astral, causal and mental bodies as well.

"I repair and fortify the Wei Chi of all my bodies; in all moments."

"I align all my bodies; in all moments."

"I am centered, empowered, and immersed in Divine Love; in all moments."

After this, I addressed the theme that was running through her lifetimes. She was always having appendages cut off. It was creating a systemic cringing in her energy field. When I told her this and about the lobotomy, it was very validating to her. She suddenly realized why she felt flawed and incapacitated at the core. The taps and the understanding together worked to create a drastic shift in her. She also recalled how difficult it was for her to watch anyone get cut on a show. She was excited to note the reaction it caused in her, and this validated what I was revealing about her.

Because it was a recurring theme, we addressed the first time that she ever got cut. This is called the initial cause or first cause. Since we work with all the lifetimes of a person at once, the way to remedy a reoccurring unwanted theme is to eliminate the first cause, or the first time it ever happened in all the lifetimes of that person. It is like the events are a line of dominoes, and we remove that first domino that knocks down all the other dominoes.

"I eliminate the first cause in regard to being cut into; in all moments."

"I eliminate the first cause in regard to having appendages cut off; in all moments."

This was the new client's first introduction to my work. She thought she was contacting me for a superficial reason. But she innately knew that what we would address would work more deeply. After working so deeply, I addressed the more superficial issues that motivated her to desire a session with me. But her life is ever changed by this investment of an hour with me.

There was much more that we released. We released all the vows that she had taken in lifetimes of monastery living and issues with relationships. But the taps that I shared above are the ones that brought the deepest, most profound and drastic shifts to her energy. May you feel a shift as well by reading this and doing the taps.

3. Real-Time Assistance

Here are a dialogue and taps that came through a spontaneous exchange. A client connected to me between sessions because she was feeling in her own words...

"A bit spiny and ego, fear-driven today after a deep God download yesterday, weird how that can happen. Looking forward to our next session and please share anything that feels like right guidance in this moment... xoxo."

[Say each statement slowly and consciously out loud. Articulate each word and make a point to pause after each phrase. Say each statement three times while tapping on your head. Then say it a fourth time while tapping on your chest. Take a deep breath after finishing the series.]

"I release recoiling out of habit; in all moments."

"I release the fear of my kundalini energy; in all moments."

"I release the fear of going insane; in all moments."

"I release dancing with power; in all moments."

My client shared here: "Chills. I've done the taps. My solar plexus relaxed a bit."

"I release being frozen in a submissive pose; in all moments."

"I release coagulating in pain; in all moments."

"I release heaving in anguish; in all moments."

"I release reverberating in apprehension; in all moments."

"I unfurl my energy to the depth and core of my being; in all moments."

"I overlay my greatness on the vestibule of humanity; in all moments."

"I ebb and flow with and between the heartbeat of divinity; in all moments."

"I surge and rejoice in the powerhouse of love, light, and celestial song; in all moments."

Her energy totally shifted.

4. Taps to Transcend the Third Dimension

I facilitated a session with someone whose job is to protect the natural wooded lands. She was feeling loopy and unfocused and did not know how to deal with it. She did not even understand it herself but felt a huge relief when I articulated it for her. She has been toggling between being a very effective forceful energy in her job and being the expansive energy where she feels more comfortable. Her energy field was wavering between the contrasting conditions. What she didn't realize was that this was reflective of her toggling between the third and fifth dimension.

When the Mayan calendar ended, and the world was supposed to come to an end, it was the means to register earth moving from the third dimension to being in the fifth dimension. Those of us who are sensitive are realizing the shift and getting a sense of more and more individuals holding a higher vibrational rate. The very fact that I can write openly about the spiritual and energetic things that I do is evidence of the shift. Many of us have been working diligently to assist in the raising of consciousness on earth for lifetimes. It is beyond validating to be at this precipice.

There are still those who are hanging on to the comfort of the vibrations of the third dimension. They are resisting moving into a higher understanding quickly. But they are moving. Have patience with them. They are easing their big toe in gently. To some reading this, it is a new and exciting concept that seems too good to be true. That is okay. It is all okay. The third dimension is like an old worn-out pair of sneakers that seems a better option than breaking in a new pair of shoes.

In the session with this client, I kept seeing a huge conifer tree. I mentioned that it was sending her incredible love and strength. She knew who it was immediately and had a name for him. "That is grandfather tree," she said. She admitted that she was afraid to change the vibration because if she did, she would be leaving the love behind. As we worked, we both felt the love move up her spine and open the energetic channels. It got stuck at her throat because of the many experiences of being decapitated, hanged, and choked. But then we both felt it pull off over her head as if taking off a tight turtleneck sweater. She was more open and free. She felt such incredible love, and the illusion was gone.

Taps to transcend the third dimension:

[Say each statement slowly and consciously out loud. Articulate each word and make a point to pause after each phrase. Say each statement three times while tapping on your head. Then say it a fourth time while tapping on your chest. Take a deep breath after finishing the series.]

"I release the fear of transcending the third dimension; in all moments."

"I release being enslaved in the third dimension; in all moments."

"I remove all the shackles of the third dimension; in all moments."

"I recant all vows and agreements between myself and the third dimension; in all moments."

"I remove all curses between myself and the third dimension; in all moments."

"I dissolve all karmic ties between myself and the third dimension; in all moments."

"I remove all energetic cords from the third dimension; in all moments."

"I remove all the pain, burden, limitations, and engrams that the third dimension has put on me; in all moments."

"I withdraw all my energy from the third dimension; in all moments."

"I leave all the ignorance in the third dimension; in all moments."

"I leave all the pain in the third dimension; in all moments."

"I leave all abandonment and isolation in the third dimension; in all moments."

"I leave all slavery in the third dimension; in all moments."

"I leave all genocide in the third dimension; in all moments."

"I take back all the Joy, Love, Abundance, Freedom, Health, Success, Security, Companionship, Peace, Life, Wholeness, Beauty, Enthusiasm, Contentment, Spirituality and Confidence that the 3rd dimension has taken from me; in all moments."

"I release resonating with the third dimension; in all moments."

"I release emanating with the third dimension; in all moments."

"I remove all of the third dimension from my sound frequency; in all moments."

"I remove all of the third dimension from my light body; in all moments."

"I transcend the third dimension; in all moments."

"I shift my paradigm from the third dimension to the fifth dimension and above; in all moments."

"I am centered and empowered in Joy, Love, Abundance, Freedom, Health, Success, Security, Companionship, Peace,

Life, Wholeness, Beauty, Enthusiasm, Contentment, Spirituality and Confidence; in all moments."

Don't be afraid that if you do these taps you will be leaving your loved ones behind. The effect will be that you will actually make the transition much easier for them. You will see evidence in it by a more open heartedness and a receptivity that was not as noticeable as before. Enjoy!

There was so much energy flowing through me after writing these taps that I felt like a teenager on a Friday night afterwards. I was compelled to drive to the water. It was surreal. I felt that I was going to meet a love. As I drove, all the stations seemed to play only uplifting classical music. As I drove down the road, I got this surreal experience that I was expanding the road. It felt like undoing a seam and expanding the girth of earth.

When I got to the water, there was such a beautiful soft murmur of breeze, trees and water communing. There was a hint of duck whisper as well. It was mesmerizing. Then out of the new night sky, a heron came to the shore to visit with me. She showed me how she fished, and I stayed a bit.

5. Mass Enlightenment

There was a talk show on the radio. The people were talking about what a waste state parks are, that the land could be utilized for industries. It is heart sickening that so many people still can't recognize the cause and effect between their environment and quality of life. They would much rather rally around a disease than invest any energy into organically supporting wellness. Our physical and mental health are dependent on nature. Nature and trees themselves provide much more sustenance than most people realize. For some, it is so obvious.

Ignorance cannot be stamped out. It is like the villain in any stalker movie. It looks like it is dead and lifeless, but then it rears up on its knees, crawls away, and comes back in another form with a vengeance. No, ignorance has to be disassembled piece by piece and have all the components melted down and destroyed individually.

We must all make certain that we are not carriers of ignorance, that we are not harboring it in the back recesses of our mind. We must snuff it out of ourselves as a means of weakening it and disemboweling its hold on humanity.

Taps to remove ignorance:

[Say each statement slowly and consciously out loud. Articulate each word and make a point to pause after each phrase. Say each statement three times while tapping on your head. Then say it a fourth time while tapping on your chest. Take a deep breath after finishing the series.]

"I declare myself a surrogate for humanity in drying up ignorance; in all moments."

"I release harboring ignorance; in all moments."

"I release confusing ignorance for truth; in all moments."

"I release hiding ignorance behind self-righteousness; in all moments."

"I release perpetuating and defending ignorance; in all moments."

"I release habitually being imbued in ignorance; in all moments."

"I remove all the blinders to ignorance; in all moments."

"I recant all vows, agreements, and commitments to ignorance; in all moments."

"I release hiding behind ignorance; in all moments."

"I remove all curses between myself and ignorance; in all moments."

"I dissolve all karmic ties between myself and ignorance; in all moments."

"I remove all the pain, burden, and limitations that ignorance has put on me; in all moments."

"I remove all the pain, burden, and limitations that I have put on all others because of ignorance; in all moments."

"I take back all the Joy, Love, Abundance, Freedom, Health, Peace, Life, and Wholeness that ignorance has taken from me; in all moments."

"I give back all the Joy, Love, Abundance, Freedom, Health, Peace, Life, and Wholeness that I have taken from all others because of ignorance; in all moments."

"I withdraw all my energy from ignorance; in all moments."

"I release resonating with ignorance; in all moments."

"I release emanating with ignorance; in all moments."

"I remove all ignorance from my sound frequency; in all moments."

"I remove all ignorance from my light body; in all moments."

"I release resisting enlightenment; in all moments."

"I shift my paradigm from ignorance to enlightenment; in all moments."

"I shift my paradigm from ignorance to Joy, Love, Abundance, Freedom, Health, Peace, Life, and Wholeness; in all moments."

"I make space in this world to be enlightened; in all moments."

"I make space in this world for mass enlightenment; in all moments."

"I remove all blockages to enlightenment; in all moments."

"I remove all blockages to mass enlightenment; in all moments."

"I stretch my capacity to be enlightened; in all moments."

"I stretch my capacity to accept and perpetuate mass enlightenment; in all moments."

Why is it easier to believe that great people roamed the earth thousands of years ago instead of claiming our own greatness? It may be a difficult concept with all the experiences we have witnessed. But we have the experiences under our belts to glean from their wisdom and accept a greater fate than we presently allow ourselves.

If people were totally happy, healthy, abundant, and unencumbered, I would scoff at my attempts to benefit humanity in this way. But if there is room for improvement, why not? Why not just try something totally out of the ballpark? It may just add dimensions or a quality of life that was overlooked before. Is it worth risking one's apathy to try?

6. Dissipating War

One session left me trembling after I finished facilitating it. It was a very powerful remote session with a client who lives in and is from Turkey. It was an amazing session. Turkey feels like a vortex of positive energy. I didn't realize that before the session.

My client's English was not proficient, so I did not lead her through many taps and just released a lot of issues without them. I did lead her through the protocol for all thought forms, and she agreed to be a surrogate to release war for the collective "we." I know my protocol is an effective way to release issues. My intention is to assist enough people so as to dissipate war altogether in my lifetime.

I hear people arguing with me in their minds that this is not possible. But think about it. If people argue against this intention, they are advocating war. Arguing for the gray areas is still advocating war. It is a subtle play of the mind and the emotions, but that is what it is.

For those who understand that point or want to support this intention, please do the taps that I led my client through. We did them using the collective "we." As we continued, she was gagging a lot. If she could see energy, she would have seen that she was throwing up black energetic tar. Also, besides telling me she was going through the process of throwing up, she was so energized that she could not sit still in the session. Her session surpassed her expectations.

I invite you to do these taps to assist in dissipating the negativity that is prevalent in the world.

Taps to dissipate war in the world:

[Say each statement slowly and consciously out loud. Articulate each word and make a point to pause after each phrase. Say each

statement three times while tapping on your head. Then say it a fourth time while tapping on your chest. Take a deep breath after finishing the series.]

"We release being encapsulated in war; in all moments."

"We release agreeing to war; in all moments."

"We release the belief that war is inevitable; in all moments."

"We recant all vows and agreements between ourselves and war; in all moments."

"We remove all curses between ourselves and war; in all moments."

"We dissolve all karmic ties between ourselves and war; in all moments."

"We remove all the pain, burden, limitations, and engrams that war has put on us; in all moments."

"We take back all the Joy, Love, Abundance, Freedom, Health, Life, and Wholeness that war has taken from us; in all moments."

"We remove all war from our sound frequency; in all moments."

"We remove all war from our light body; in all moments."

"We release resonating with war; in all moments."

"We release emanating with war; in all moments."

"We transcend all limiting concepts of war; in all moments."

"We transcend war; in all moments."

"We redefine Life as Peace; in all moments."

"We are centered and empowered in divine love; in all moments."

Many people believe that war is a part of the spiritual experience, and it will always be on earth. That is a limiting belief. If people want to hone their spiritual skills, they will challenge all beliefs and break through all limitations. There will still be many lessons to learn if earth forgoes war. There are so many rich inner conflicts that cannot be delved into because of the distraction of outer war.

Peace on earth is not going to kill the human spirit. It is going to enrich us all to what is possible as we all come together as individuals in the agreement of peace. If you have never tried doing the taps, I invite you to try these. Please get a sense of the empowerment they can bring. That empowerment is a trait of our true essence.

If you have never shared my taps before out of worry about what your friends may think, maybe that hint of insecurity is the same issue that helps war thrive. I encourage people to do and share these taps. If nothing else, it is a small intention to remove the fuel of the present flames of dis-ease in the world. Please feel free to share these taps elsewhere as well. Please hashtag them out to the world.

7. Releasing Fear Marathon

Love is the opposite of fear. Where there is Love, there is no fear. There are many primal experiences that many of us are afraid of. If we can release their grip on us, it will automatically make room for more Love. Love is our natural state. The fear moves in to squelch out the Love. Here is to releasing big chunks of fear so that one can return to the natural state of Love.

Taps to remove fear:

[Say each statement slowly and consciously out loud. Articulate each word and make a point to pause after each phrase. Say each statement three times while tapping on your head. Then say it a fourth time while tapping on your chest. Take a deep breath after finishing the series.]

"I release the fear of dying; in all moments."

"I release the fear of being separated from my consciousness; in all moments."

"I release the fear of plunging to my death; in all moments."

"I release the fear of being tortured; in all moments."

"I release the fear of being decapitated; in all moments."

"I release the fear of hanging; in all moments."

"I release the fear of drowning; in all moments."

"I release the fear of being held under the water; in all moments."

"I release the fear of being buried alive; in all moments."

"I release the fear of being humiliated; in all moments."

"I release the fear of being sacrificed; in all moments."

"I release the fear of spiders; in all moments."

"I release the fear of being raped; in all moments."

"I release the fear of losing my children; in all moments."

"I release the fear of being abandoned; in all moments."

"I release the fear of abandoning my loved ones; in all moments."

"I release the fear of being suffocated; in all moments."

"I release the fear of the Angel of Death; in all moments."

"I release the fear of going to hell; in all moments."

"I release the fear of being betrayed; in all moments."

"I release the fear of running for my life; in all moments."

"I release the fear of starving to death; in all moments."

"I release the fear of the world ending; in all moments."

"I release the fear of going to war; in all moments."

"I release the fear of being singled out in a crowd; in all moments."

"I release the fear of speaking my truth; in all moments."

"I release the fear of being crippled; in all moments."

"I release the fear of being different; in all moments."

"I release the fear of dying; in all moments."

"I release the fear of being alone; in all moments."

"I release the fear of snakes; in all moments."

"I release the fear of being eaten alive; in all moments."

"I release the fear of losing my home; in all moments."

"I release the fear of being a nothing; in all moments."

"I release the fear of being invisible; in all moments."

"I release the fear of being a ghost; in all moments."

"I release the fear of disappointing God; in all moments."

"I release the fear of being a failure; in all moments."

"I release the fear of being stupid; in all moments."

"I release the fear of being disfigured; in all moments."

"I release the fear of cats/dogs; in all moments."

"I release the fear of the government; in all moments."

"I release the fear of alien invasion; in all moments."

"I release the fear of foreigners; in all moments."

"I release the fear of being enslaved; in all moments."

"I release the fear of being murdered; in all moments."

"I release the fear of losing my mind; in all moments."

"I release the fear of growing old; in all moments."

"I release the fear of being helpless; in all moments."

"I release the fear of making a mistake; in all moments."

"I release the fear of costing others their lives; in all moments."

"I release the fear of responsibility; in all moments."

"I release the fear of marriage; in all moments."

"I release the fear of ceremonies; in all moments."

"I release the fear of being Shanghaied; in all moments."

"I release the fear of being passed around; in all moments."

"I release the fear of being lost; in all moments."

"I release the fear of the dark; in all moments."

"I release the fear of being possessed; in all moments."

"I release the fear of being mutilated; in all moments."

"I release the fear of losing a limb; in all moments."

"I release the fear of authority; in all moments."

"I release the fear of losing power; in all moments."

"I release the fear of being buried alive; in all moments."

"I release the fear of ghosts; in all moments."

"I release the fear of being born; in all moments."

"I release the fear of governing parties; in all moments."

"I release the fear of religious factions; in all moments."

"I release the fear of dying; in all moments."

This list is just scratching the surface. A good way to get a sense of what past traumas have been experienced is by noticing those taps that cause a greater reaction. In seeing the vastness of the list, one can understand why the love gets pushed out. May all who do these feel a shift in their own ability to embrace the love.

8. Eradicating War

So many are uncomfortable speaking about war because it makes them a target for criticism. I don't want to be a target, but since I feel so much of the conflict in the world within my own body, I feel compelled to try and resolve it.

It is a great opportunity for the world to see war from a distant vantage point. If people stay detached, they will see both sides are good people, and innocence everywhere is suffering. People who get mad at this statement are being drawn into war. It really is as simple as seeing the good in people. If individuals don't fuel the conflict, it will naturally dry up like a limited supply of arsenals. Opinions, passion, finger pointing, great intellectual debate, actually generate the interest and support that fuels the conflict. That is why representatives of both sides are on news channels now.

We could all study the issues, take sides, argue points, and use our wits and talents to make one side right and one side wrong. Some people reading this right now want to let me have it for my naive approach. But has it been tried? That is, withdraw all support for vindicating either side, and just pour love and healing peaceful intentions in the whole region.

I am fortunate enough to NOT know the details. I choose not to know. Yes, both sides want their position known and are rallying support for their side on the news shows. To me, this is similar to two fighting children wanting to tell mom what the other did. Mom, in her infinite wisdom, takes no side and loves both children equally. She knows there are issues but trusts that there is enough love to work things out. Why can't we do the same?

Please don't try to educate me on the merits of either side. I will just see that as a justification for killing. With all our evolution of knowledge, to still be destroying what others hold sacred, destroys an aspect of ourselves. We are all connected. When a child on the other side of the world loses his teddy bear, it matters to me. When terror is inflicted on others, it affects us all. When mass murder over ideas is still sanctioned as a solution, we all show up as barbarians. Nothing is worth taking life. No God worthy of being worshiped condones murder.

Taps to eradicate war:

[Say each statement slowly and consciously out loud. Articulate each word and make a point to pause after each phrase. Say each statement three times while tapping on your head. Then say it a fourth time while tapping on your chest. Take a deep breath after finishing the series.]

"I declare myself a surrogate for the macrocosm in doing these taps"

"We release condoning war; in all moments."

"We release supplying energy to war; in all moments."

"We withdraw all our energy from war; in all moments."

"We release killing innocence; in all moments."

"We release choosing power over love; in all moments."

"We release defining God in petty terms; in all moments."

"We release choosing ideals over people; in all moments."

"We release the arrogance of man; in all moments."

"We think for ourselves; in all moments."

"We release being victims of war; in all moments."

"We release being an advocate of war; in all moments."

"We release the belief that God is vindictive; in all moments."

"We release enjoying the excitement of war; in all moments."

"We release being bored with peace; in all moments."

"We release having a disregard for the reverence of life; in all moments."

"We recant all vows and agreements between ourselves and war; in all moments."

"We remove all curses between ourselves and war; in all moments."

"We dissolve all karmic ties between ourselves and war; in all moments."

"We remove all the pain, burden, limitations, and engrams that war has put on us; in all moments."

"We remove all the pain, burden, limitations, and engrams that we have put on everyone due to war; in all moments."

"We take back all the Joy, Love, Abundance, Freedom, Health, Success, Security, Companionship, Peace, Life, Wholeness, Beauty, Enthusiasm, Confidence, Spirituality, and Enlightenment that war has taken from us; in all moments."

"We give back all the Joy, Love, Abundance, Freedom, Health, Success, Security, Companionship, Peace, Life, Wholeness, Beauty, Enthusiasm, Confidence, Spirituality, and Enlightenment that war has taken from everyone; in all moments."

"We release resonating with war; in all moments."

"We release emanating with war; in all moments."

"We remove all war from our sound frequency; in all moments."

"We remove all war from our light body; in all moments."

"We shift our paradigm from war to Joy, Love, Abundance, Freedom, Health, Success, Security, Companionship, Peace, Life, Wholeness, Beauty, Enthusiasm, Confidence, Spirituality, and Enlightenment; in all moments."

"We eradicate war as an option and a concept; in all moments."

"We transcend war; in all moments."

"We are centered and empowered in Divine Love for everyone; in all moments."

We all feel so helpless. But what if it was the EXACT OPPOSITE? What if just one of us could harness an intention so loving that it could end world fighting? What if just one of us could draw in such a surging, vast amount of divine love that, like a tidal wave, could singe out all the embers of war? What if we have been enslaving ourselves to a complacency that is an illusion? What if we are all the proverbial elephant that has not realized yet that the chain that holds him tied to the post is a belief, and not an actual chain?

Some believe that peace will never happen on earth. They believe this is a warring world and have accepted that. I have been taught to challenge every belief no matter the source. Truth itself is always evolving. Challenging everything that we have been told is a way to continue to evolve ourselves.

9. Loyalties

Look at your loyalties. Who and what are the persons, situations, and things that are non-negotiable. See how they may be holding you back. For instance, some people stay in caustic situations because they absolve it from scrutiny by the blanket statement, "My _____ means everything to me."

Think of a teenager who is in a dysfunctional relationship. She may say her boyfriend means everything to her and uses blind loyalty to rationalize putting up with abuse. Think of someone who doesn't realize their own valuable contribution in a work setting. They stay in an unhappy situation out of loyalty. But is it really loyalty, or is it fear?

We have primal memories ingrained in our DNA of being trapped in scenarios where the lord of the land is king, and our loyalty to him is a matter of survival. We have been slaves, and as horrible as it is, we didn't want to be sold and taken to a worse scenario. There is the scenario of being thrown into a strange land, and the only comfort is the people we are with. There are so many times our loyalty was our only source of security.

Taps to recant ancient vows:

[Say each statement slowly and consciously out loud. Articulate each word and make a point to pause after each phrase. Say each statement three times while tapping on your head. Then say it a fourth time while tapping on your chest. Take a deep breath after finishing the series.]

> **"I release confusing loyalty for blind allegiance; in all moments."**
>
> **"I release looking the other way; in all moments."**
>
> **"I release losing myself in blind loyalty; in all moments."**

"I release blinding myself to loyalty; in all moments."

"I release being enslaved to loyalty; in all moments."

"I release giving my power over to loyalty; in all moments."

I release using loyalty to perpetuate denial; in all moments."

"I shift my paradigm from blind loyalty to awareness; in all moments."

By releasing blind loyalties, we make space in our world for a higher integrity. We remove the glass ceiling of other people and scenarios. We are more free and empowered.

10. Releasing the Trauma of Dying

More and more people are realizing that they aren't afraid of dying, but they are afraid of the process of dying. The process of dying is one of the things that I am privy to when people show me their past life issues. This is the dis-ease that many hold in the body as disease. I have seen the most horrific and unimaginable forms of death. By releasing the trauma of dying from clients, they feel much relief from the physical pain and generally gain more joy and freedom in their life.

We hold these issues in the places of the body that were compromised in a past death. Many people with neck issues were either hanged, decapitated, or choked to death. Many people with lung issues were either suffocated or drowned to death. People can get a sense of how they died by what they are afraid of, have an aversion to, or where they hold their pain.

We have all had so many experiences of death. Maybe the key to life is to keep doing it until it brings no fear or reaction in the body. This is what the great Athenian philosopher Socrates conveyed in his soliloquy after he drank the state-sanctioned hemlock and awaited his own death.

Here are some taps to do. I suggest you do them all and see which ones create a strong reaction. It may give you a greater clue in the totality of who you are as a spiritual being instead of someone just getting by through one lifetime. Doing these can actually change one's vantage point when looking at life. Another side benefit of these taps is that since we work "in all moments," it can assist in overcoming future traumas of dying.

Taps to release the trauma of dying:

[Say each statement slowly and consciously out loud. Articulate each word and make a point to pause after each phrase. Say each statement three times while tapping on your head. Then say it a

fourth time while tapping on your chest. Take a deep breath after finishing the series.]

"I release the pain and trauma of dying; in all moments."

"I release the pain and trauma of having my skull bashed in; in all moments."

"I release the pain and trauma of starving to death; in all moments."

"I release the pain and trauma of being eaten alive; in all moments."

"I release the pain and trauma of being hunted down and killed; in all moments."

"I release the pain and trauma of drowning; in all moments."

"I release the pain and trauma of freezing to death; in all moments."

"I release the pain and trauma of working to death; in all moments."

"I release the pain and trauma of dying of thirst; in all moments."

"I release the pain and trauma of dying in a firing squad; in all moments."

"I release the pain and trauma of being murdered in all lifetimes; in all moments."

"I release the pain and trauma of dying in childbirth; in all moments."

"I release the pain and trauma of suffocating to death; in all moments."

"I release the pain and trauma of being buried alive; in all moments."

"I release the pain and trauma of being left to die; in all moments."

"I release the pain and trauma of dying too soon; in all moments."

"I release the pain and trauma of dying in battle; in all moments."

"I release the pain and trauma of dying of a heart attack; in all moments."

"I release the pain and trauma of being gassed; in all moments."

"I release the pain and trauma of being burned at the stake; in all moments."

"I release the pain and trauma of dying of influenza; in all moments."

"I release the pain and trauma of dying in a mass grave; in all moments."

"I release the pain and trauma of having my baby ripped out of my body; in all moments."

"I release the pain and trauma of killing myself; in all moments."

"I release the pain and trauma of bleeding to death; in all moments."

"I release the pain and trauma of being gang raped; in all moments."

"I release the pain and trauma of dying in a dungeon; in all moments."

"I release the pain and trauma of dying for a cause I don't believe in; in all moments."

"I release the pain and trauma of dying on a foreign planet; in all moments."

"I release the pain and trauma of dying in utero; in all moments."

"I release the pain and trauma of the black death; in all moments."

"I release the pain and trauma of dying needlessly; in all moments."

"I release the pain and trauma of dying unexpectedly; in all moments."

"I release the guilt and trauma of dying before I fulfilled my purpose; in all moments."

"I release the pain and trauma of dying alone; in all moments."

"I release the pain and trauma of watching others die; in all moments."

"I release the guilt and trauma of killing others; in all moments."

"I release the guilt and trauma of leaving loved ones behind; in all moments."

"I release the pain and trauma of dying in a crash; in all moments."

"I release the pain and trauma of dying in an explosion; in all moments."

"I release the pain and trauma of falling to death; in all moments."

"I release the pain and trauma of dying as a leper; in all moments."

"I release the pain and trauma of being poisoned to death; in all moments."

"I release the pain and trauma of dying at the hands of the enemy; in all moments."

"I release the pain and trauma of dying at the hands of a friend; in all moments."

"I release the pain and trauma of being beaten to death; in all moments."

"I release the pain and trauma of dying of neglect; in all moments."

"I release the pain and trauma of being tortured to death; in all moments."

"I release the pain and trauma of going to the gallows; in all moments."

"I release the pain and trauma of dying at sunrise; in all moments."

"I release the pain and trauma of dying at sunset; in all moments."

"I release the pain and trauma of dying at sea; in all moments."

"I release the pain and trauma of dying in the desert; in all moments."

"I release the pain and trauma of dying in the wilderness; in all moments."

"I release the pain and trauma of dying from being murdered; in all moments."

"I release the pain and trauma of being choked to death; in all moments."

"I release the pain and trauma of being decapitated; in all moments."

"I release the pain and trauma of being hanged; in all moments."

"I release the pain and trauma of being martyred; in all moments."

"I release the pain and trauma of being sacrificed; in all moments."

"I release the pain and trauma of being stillborn; in all moments."

"I release the pain and trauma of dying of an overdose; in all moments."

"I release the pain and trauma of dying in a drunken stupor; in all moments."

"I release the guilt, pain and trauma of killing myself; in all moments."

"I release the pain and trauma of having my throat slit; in all moments."

"I release the pain and trauma of being sliced open; in all moments."

"I release the pain and trauma of dying in the arena; in all moments."

"I release the pain and trauma of being chosen to die; in all moments."

"I release the fear and trauma of the process of dying; in all moments."

"I release the pain and trauma of not crossing over; in all moments."

"I release the pain and trauma of being a ghost; in all moments."

"I release the pain and trauma of being harvested for parts; in all moments."

"I release the pain and trauma of being turned into a machine; in all moments."

"I release the pain and trauma of being brain dead; in all moments."

"I release the pain and trauma of a lingering death; in all moments."

This list should release a lot of the unconscious angst we carry within. It may give people a better understanding of their past lives. But it is totally fine to stay blissfully ignorant of the past and just do the taps to release the unconscious replay of old fears and trauma. The ultimate goal of doing these is merely to bring more Joy, Love, Abundance, Freedom, Health, Peace and Wholeness, to the present moment.

11. Removing Violence from Society

Do you know why there are so many people fascinated with violence and scary dramas? It is because they are trying to figure out what happened to them in the past. Since many people are denied the ability to look into their past and are told past lives don't exist, they have to look at it obliquely through TV shows and by perpetuating violence in the world.

It is a similar concept to an abuser who grows up to abuse others. They are trying to figure out the issue. Maybe this is why so many people are drawn to create violent films. It is a similar reason to why period pieces are created and enjoyed. It was a lifetime in which we lived, and we want to process it better within ourselves, or it was pleasant, and we long for those times again.

Did you know that people who have been abused enjoy horror flicks more than those who have not? It is like the fear elicited provides a comfort in them. It would be much more beneficial to society if we could all take responsibility for our past life traumas and work them out within ourselves instead of inflicting them on our families or society. Here are some taps to clear out the issues of violence. Maybe they will help to create a more peaceful way to release the issues instead of it needing to show up in our entertainment and our streets.

Taps to remove violence from society:

[Say each statement slowly and consciously out loud. Articulate each word and make a point to pause after each phrase. Say each statement three times while tapping on your head. Then say it a fourth time while tapping on your chest. Take a deep breath after finishing the series.]

"I declare myself a surrogate for humanity in doing these taps"
(optional)

"I release perpetuating violence; in all moments."

"I release the trauma of being violently killed; in all moments."

"I release confusing violence for love; in all moments."

"I release the trauma of losing my life to violence; in all moments."

"I release being in love with violence; in all moments."

"I release the guilt and trauma of being violent in all moments."

"I release hating myself; in all moments."

"I release fighting and dying in violence; in all moments."

"I release the trauma of being raised in violence; in all moments."

"I release infusing violence into my life; in all moments."

"I release being entertained by violence; in all moments."

"I release being fascinated by violence; in all moments."

"I release the trauma of violently hurting others; in all moments."

"I release the guilt and trauma of hurting my loved ones; in all moments."

"I release being indifferent to violence; in all moments."

"I release making excuses for violence; in all moments."

"I release the belief that I am unworthy; in all moments."

"I release being blind to violence; in all moments."

"I recant all vows and agreements between myself and violence; in all moments."

"I remove all curses between myself and violence; in all moments."

"I dissolve all karmic ties between myself and violence; in all moments."

"I remove all the pain, burden, and limitations that all violence has put on me; in all moments."

"I take back all the Joy, Love, Abundance, Freedom, Health, Peace, Life, and Wholeness that violence has taken from me; in all moments."

"I withdraw all my energy from violence; in all moments."

"I release resonating with violence; in all moments."

"I release emanating with violence; in all moments."

"I remove all violence from my sound frequency; in all moments."

"I remove all violence from my light body; in all moments."

"I shift my paradigm from violence to Joy, Love, Abundance, Freedom, Health, Life, and Wholeness; in all moments."

"I repair and fortify my Wei Chi; in all moments."

"I am centered am empowered in Divine Love; in all moments."

It is in working within ourselves and disconnecting our past trauma from the present that we can stop the need to bring violence into this world to "figure it out." We have all been the hero, victim, and villain in our past lives. These all blend within our present and make up the person that we are. The way to improve ourselves in every way is to come to terms with the parts that we don't like to see or deny in ourselves and remove them. It is a freeing and empowering thing to do so.

As freeing and empowering as it is to do this for ourselves, it is multiplied when doing it for all of society. By doing these taps for yourself and as a surrogate for humanity, you can stop being both the victim and the villain, and, in your own way, be a hero.

12. Releasing Oppression

I facilitated a private remote session with a woman who felt like a very clear soul. I get a sense of all the issues mingled into a person's energy field. But with her, it was much different. She felt very clear but also restricted. I described the feeling to her, and she said that it was how she felt. It felt like she was lying on her back, and someone had a gigantic thumb pressed into her chest.

The fact that I felt what she had trouble articulating was very validating to her. It felt it had been with her for so many of her incarnations that it was normal. It manifested in this lifetime as an obsession that society lacked control. To her, society seemed at the mercy of a malevolent force. Actually, it was her personal issue from many lifetimes ago.

I saw the core lifetime. She was some kind of bug or small creature that someone toyed with. She was their captured plaything. When we went through the taps that her energy told me would free her, she had a very strong reaction after being deeply validated. In that little life as a plaything, she did not have the mental capacity to process the trauma that she was experiencing. So when that issue was being stoked in the present lifetime, it was just as big and overwhelming as when she was a bug. To put a mental concept on what she was feeling now she had to make the issue as enormous as when she was a plaything. She made the feeling of powerlessness an assault on society itself.

After we did some taps, she allowed me to see many other lifetimes of suffocating oppression. I saw her with an energetic metal chain around her neck like the slaves had to wear in the movie Roots. She gasped at the realization that she hated watching that movie. Also, I felt that oppressed chest feeling manifest in a slave lifetime when she was in the bottom of a slave ship, and they stacked people on top of each other regardless of their discomfort.

As I shared with her the imagery I was perceiving, she was getting her own. It was both overwhelming and freeing to her. To me, two things became obvious. I realized that all the people who are still terrified at current events may have been subjected to suffering before their minds were able to compartmentalize it properly. So they manifest their pain as a larger-than-life enemy that is beyond reason. Also, it reminded me to be ever so gentle to every single soul that crosses my path so as to not inflict horrific experiences upon them. If bugs can register such pain then, of course, they can register kindness. So with every soul we meet, we help decide the course of their future incarnations by how we treat them.

Taps to release oppression:

[Say each statement slowly and consciously out loud. Articulate each word and make a point to pause after each phrase. Say each statement three times while tapping on your head. Then say it a fourth time while tapping on your chest. Take a deep breath after finishing the series.]

"I release being toyed with; in all moments."

"I release being someone's plaything; in all moments."

"I release being kept in a jar; in all moments."

"I release being squished; in all moments."

"I release being oppressed; in all moments."

"I recant all vows an agreements between myself and being oppressed; in all moments."

"I recant all vows and agreements between myself and all oppressors; in all moments."

"I remove all curses between myself and being oppressed; in all moments."

"I remove all curses between myself and all oppressors; in all moments."

"I dissolve all karmic ties between myself and being oppressed; in all moments."

"I dissolve all karmic ties between myself and all oppressors; in all moments."

"I remove all the pain, fear, burden, limitations and engrams that being oppressed has put on me; in all moments."

"I remove all the pain, fear, burden, limitations and engrams that all oppressors have put on me; in all moments."

"I take back all the Joy, Love, Abundance, Freedom, Health, Success, Security, Peace, Life, and Wholeness that being oppressed has taken from me; in all moments."

"I take back all the Joy, Love, Abundance, Freedom, Health, Success, Security, Peace, Life and Wholeness that all oppressors have taken from me; in all moments."

"I withdraw all my energy from being oppressed and all oppressors; in all moments."

"I release resonating with being oppressed and all oppressors; in all moments."

"I release emanating with being oppressed and all oppressors; in all moments."

"I remove being oppressed and all oppressors from my sound frequency; in all moments."

"I remove being oppressed and all oppressors from my light body; in all moments."

"I transcend being oppressed and all oppressors; in all moments."

"I shift my paradigm from being oppressed and all oppressors to Joy, Love, Abundance, Freedom, Health, Success, Security, Peace, Life and Wholeness in all moments."

If we can connect with these horrific things that happened to us and are stored on a primal level, we can be more in control of our thoughts, feelings, and actions in the present lifetime. We can also more clearly control ourselves from perpetuating harm onto others. We can be more consciously present in the moment.

The client checked in with me later that week. She said she was standing next to an African American and she felt this person release similar pain when she was near. It was a great validation of something that I have suspected. If it is not enough motivation to do these taps for yourself, do them to help the multitudes of others who hold a similar vibration of unrest.

13. Breaking Up Thought Forms

I facilitated a private remote session with a student of a spiritual path.

She was very in tune with her spiritual side and worked actively to see everyone as soul.

As we started the session, I was reminded of an inner experience I had recently where a Spirit guide reprimanded me. He looked pointedly in my face and told me, "YOU ARE NOT YOUR THOUGHT FORMS." I knew this was relevant to my client. Also, sometimes in a session, I will sing a song that is relevant to my client. I got a nudge to sing a particular song. As I started singing, my client convulsed in tears. The song that I sang was her favorite song that she listened to repeatedly when she first discovered her spiritual path. It was another confirmation to her that she was not betraying her teachings by having a session with me.

The following is all the taps from her session verbatim. A few of them made her convulse in tears.

Taps to break up thought forms:

[Say each statement slowly and consciously out loud. Articulate each word and make a point to pause after each phrase. Say each statement three times while tapping on your head. Then say it a fourth time while tapping on your chest. Take a deep breath after finishing the series.]

    "I release hiding behind thought forms; in all moments."

    "I release hiding within thought forms; in all moments."

    "I release using thought forms to diminish myself; in all moments."

"I release using thought forms to diminish others; in all moments."

"I break up all thought forms; in all moments."

"I release projecting thought forms on others; in all moments."

"I release wielding thought forms on others; in all moments."

"I release fueling thought forms with emotion; in all moments."

"I release using thought forms to feel superior; in all moments."

"I release using thought forms to diminish or destroy others; in all moments."

"I release using thought forms to diminish truth; in all moments."

"I release choosing thought forms over truth; in all moments."

"I release choosing thought forms over the Holy Spirit; in all moments."

"I release choosing thought forms over Joy; in all moments."

"I release choosing thought forms over Love; in all moments."

"I release choosing thought forms over Abundance; in all moments."

"I release choosing thought forms over Freedom; in all moments."

"I release choosing thought forms over Health; in all moments."

"I release choosing thought forms over Success; in all moments."

"I release choosing thought forms over Adventure; in all moments."

"I release choosing thought forms over Companionship; in all moments."

"I release choosing thought forms over Creativity; in all moments."

"I release choosing thought forms over Peace; in all moments."

"I release choosing thought forms over Life; in all moments."

"I release choosing thought forms over Wholeness; in all moments."

"I release choosing thought forms over Beauty; in all moments."

"I release choosing thought forms over Enthusiasm; in all moments."

"I release choosing thought forms over Contentment; in all moments."

"I release choosing thought forms over Spirituality; in all moments."

"I release choosing thought forms over Enlightenment; in all moments."

"I release diminishing God to a thought form; in all moments."

"I release diminishing my spiritual path to a thought form; in all moments."

"I release diminishing truth to a thought form; in all moments."

"I release diminishing Soul to a thought form; in all moments."

"I release diminishing the Light and Sound to a thought form; in all moments."

"I recant all vows and agreements between myself and all thought forms; in all moments."

"I remove all curses between myself and all thought forms; in all moments."

"I dissolve all karmic ties between myself and all thought forms; in all moments."

"I sever all strings and cords between myself and all thought forms; in all moments."

"I remove all the pain, burden, limitations, and engrams that all thought forms have put on me; in all moments."

"I take back all the Joy, Love, Abundance, Freedom, Health, Life, and Wholeness that all thought forms have taken from me; in all moments."

"I remove all thought forms from my sound frequency; in all moments."

"I remove all thought forms from my light body; in all moments."

"I transcend all thought forms; in all moments."

"I release denying the Spirit Guides; in all moments."

"I release the pain of being separated from the Spirit Guides; in all moments."

"I release the belief I am separated from the Spirit Guides; in all moments."

"I release denying the Spirit Guides request; in all moments."

"I release denying myself Mastership; in all moments."

"I am a powerhouse of Divine Love; in all moments."

Our Spirit Guides want us to be dynamic. They want us to take risks and live outside of convention. They don't want us to be complacent. I was initiated by a Spirit Guide in a past life. He is very direct and speaks very cleanly. He wastes no energy on the wrong word or the wrong thought. He doesn't tolerate wasted energy.

Also, my Spirit Guide told me in an inner experience that the tapping is a way of training individuals how empowered they are. In an inner experience, I was reading a sacred text and converting it into taps. The tapping is a preliminary step for people to get a sense of what is capable. But once everyone understands their potential, in a generation, the taps will become obsolete. It is a great teaching tool but to the awakened soul, really not necessary.

14. Balancing the Yin and Yang Energies

I have been receiving information about the balance of male and female energy. Male is associated with Yang energy and female is associated with Yin energy. But there is also a balance of the male and female energy within male energy and within female energy. It is important that those are balanced as well.

It is like the yin of Yin energy is an imbalance, and the yang of Yang energy is an imbalance. Say that someone is mostly Yin energy. The up qualities of yin energy are the expansiveness, the compassion, the intuitive components. But the negative components of Yin energy could be manipulative, sneaky, and influencing in an underhanded way. The negative components of the yang within the Yin are wanting attention, needing to be noticed, and making snide comments to discredit another. This would be an imbalance in the yin and yang within the Yin.

Taps to balance the male and female energy:

[Say each statement slowly and consciously out loud. Articulate each word and make a point to pause after each phrase. Say each statement three times while tapping on your head. Then say it a fourth time while tapping on your chest. Take a deep breath after finishing the series.]

"I balance my Yin and Yang energy; in all moments."

"I balance the yin and yang of my Yin; in all moments."

"I balance the yang and yin of my Yang; in all moments."

"I balance the yin and yang of the yin of my Yang; in all moments."

"I balance the yin and yang of the yang of my Yin; in all moments."

"I balance the yang and yin of the yin of my Yin; in all moments."

"I balance the yang and yin of the yang of my Yang; in all moments."

"I am centered and empowered in Divine Love; in all moments."

A balanced person has balanced yin/yang within their yin or within both their yin and yang regardless. It may seem like a very subtle distinction, but it can shift one's dynamics incredibly.

15. Being an Individual

The dynamics of the future are different from all past eras. In the past, there was a dependency on the group dynamic. It was necessary for survival. But in today's society and the society of the future, it is more important to be an individual. It is more important to have solace, be creative, think for one's self, and break out of the confines of conformity. It is a necessity in the new earth.

From afar, enlightened souls look like little grains of quinoa spiraling open and expanding when cooked. Love is the base in the pressure pot of life. Each individual is a grain being primed for its own expansion. Spiritual awakening is the new birthright. As in any simmer pot, some will unfurl sooner than the others. That is happening now.

My clients, the people who come to me, are perched on the verge of awakening. Some of them realize it. They know that I am assisting in the process. They feel ready and know they have worked towards this expansion for many lifetimes. The taps help to address the residual habits and fear that hold them back from what they have been working towards all their lifetimes.

One such beautiful soul admitted to me that she is afraid to be an individual. Ah...yes. The habit of survival has been to rely on the group. Thriving in the future is contingent on embracing one's individual splendor. It is a total shift in dynamics, a beautiful Zen irony.

Taps to overcome fears of being an individual:

[Say each statement slowly and consciously out loud. Articulate each word and make a point to pause after each phrase. Say each statement three times while tapping on your head. Then say it a fourth time while tapping on your chest. Take a deep breath after finishing the series.]

"I release defining individuality as being isolated; in all moments."

"I release defining individuality as being starved; in all moments."

"I release defining individuality as being abandoned; in all moments."

"I release defining individuality as being punished; in all moments."

"I release defining individuality as being in hell; in all moments."

"I release defining individuality as being dead; in all moments."

"I release defining individuality as being unloved; in all moments."

"I release defining individuality as being a failure; in all moments."

"I release defining individuality as being unsafe; in all moments."

"I release defining individuality as being overwhelmed; in all moments."

"I release defining individuality as being forsaken; in all moments."

"I release defining individuality as being rejected; in all moments."

"I release defining individuality as being unloved by God; in all moments."

"I release being afraid of being an individual; in all moments."

"I release the fear of being pulled out of the crowd and tortured; in all moments."

"I release being codependent; in all moments."

"I make space in this world to be an individual; in all moments."

"I remove all blockages to being an individual; in all moments."

"I stretch my capacity to embrace my individuality; in all moments."

"I redefine individuality as being Joyful; in all moments."

"I redefine individuality as being Loving; in all moments."

"I redefine individuality as being Abundant; in all moments."

"I redefine individuality as being Free; in all moments."

"I redefine individuality as being Healthy; in all moments."

"I redefine individuality as being Successful; in all moments."

"I redefine individuality as being Secure; in all moments."

"I redefine individuality as having Healthy Companionship; in all moments."

"I redefine individuality as being Creative; in all moments."

"I redefine individuality as being Peaceful; in all moments."

"I redefine individuality as being Alive; in all moments."

"I redefine individuality as being Whole; in all moments."

"I redefine individuality as being Beautiful; in all moments."

"I redefine individuality as being Enthusiastic; in all moments."

"I redefine individuality as being Content; in all moments."

"I redefine individuality as being Spiritual; in all moments."

"I redefine individuality as being Enlightened; in all moments."

"I am centered and empowered in my Individuality; in all moments."

"I am centered and empowered in Joy, Love, Abundance, Freedom, Health, Success, Security, Companionship, Creativity, Peace, Life, Wholeness; in all moments."

I write these taps to help people who want to change. I understand the resistance. If it were easy, everyone would be shifting. If you appreciate the taps, I am glad. If you don't want to do them, just don't do them.

16. Releasing Insecurities

When I was younger, I was one of those people who apologized to everyone around me. It was like I was apologizing for existing. I was saying, "I am sorry" all the time. It is humorous to me that I have become so direct due to the energy work and offend people through the process.

I used to want people to reassure me. Reassure me that I was good enough. I would fish for reassurance with anyone who was kind to me. It is the same way a love-starved dog will go to anyone to seek approval. I never felt comfortable in my skin. I could feel the actual shame that was layered between myself and everyone else. It felt similar to a blush and was permanent.

I never really complained or talked about my problems because I knew no one was interested. But I did obsess when someone was kind to me and relived that experience over and over as a way to feel happiness. It was an escape for me to fantasize about something nice happening to me or someone liking me. So I understand how much of life can be wasted in this state.

Imagine having no sense of self, desperately wanting to experience love, having acute sensitivities, and being immersed in dysfunction. Add to this the camouflage of people believing that you had it together because you were pretty and had some intelligence. This may be a lot of people's experience to varying degrees. That is the whole point.

My whole life has been a field study in gaining a deep understanding for those stuck in their private hells. It is part of the reason why I understand what a person truly needs. When I am not sympathetic, it is because I know in that moment that sympathy will not be effective. I have learned incredible techniques to help strip away that pain body that Eckhart Tolle writes about.

When people sympathize with someone, they are agreeing with a particular viewpoint that further meshes people into that unfavorable situation. It is like gluing the pain body or the experience more strongly into the true self. When I am harsh with people, I am getting the putty knife out and removing old wallpaper from them. Sometimes it has been up so long that it feels like part of the person. It will feel painful or unkind. But it is an effective tool to assist the person in being free.

Their ego will be so identified with the situation that it will feel like I am hurting it. The psyche will interpret that rawness that has been exposed as having their feelings hurt. Feelings should be hurt. The more fragile they are, the more they should be pulled from the person who wants to experience more freedom.

Taps to be a pipeline of divine love into this world:

[Say each statement slowly and consciously out loud. Articulate each word and make a point to pause after each phrase. Say each statement three times while tapping on your head. Then say it a fourth time while tapping on your chest. Take a deep breath after finishing the series.]

"I release apologizing for existing; in all moments."

"I release the need to make excuses; in all moments."

"I release perpetually defending myself; in all moments."

"I release needing reassurance; in all moments."

"I release seeking reassurance; in all moments."

"I release using reassurance to validate my existence; in all moments."

"I release confusing sympathy for love; in all moments."

"I release seeking sympathy; in all moments."

"I release being immersed in the quest for sympathy; in all moments."

"I release being surrounded by dysfunction; in all moments."

"I withdraw all my energy from all unworthy thoughts, feelings, and deeds; in all moments."

"I release being a bully; in all moments."

"I release bullying others; in all moments."

"I release protecting the pain body at all costs; in all moments."

"I make space in this world for a confident awareness of self; in all moments."

"I remove all blockages to having a confident awareness of self; in all moments."

"I stretch my capacity to having a confident awareness of self; in all moments."

"I am centered and empowered in a loving, confident, awareness of self; in all moments."

Feelings are so low on the survival scale. Avoiding feelings, to the emotional body, is like avoiding work and exercise to the physical body. Also, people will hide behind the facade of being nice. They will have this disconnect between their behavior and self-awareness. I have been fortunate to be able to observe the bully mentality in a few specimens. They really aren't aware that they are affecting people in such a way. They really believe that they are maligned and are victims in life.

17. Releasing Everyone Else's Bullshit

I facilitated a private remote session for a client who called me because she had no energy. The day before her session, her husband had a session with me. After her husband's session, she felt much better. From this information, these are the taps that came through for her to do in her session. They can be done for certain individuals, which we started out doing with her, but they brought so much relief that we worded them to include everyone.

Taps to release everyone else's bullshit:

[Say each statement slowly and consciously out loud. Articulate each word and make a point to pause after each phrase. Say each statement three times while tapping on your head. Then say it a fourth time while tapping on your chest. Take a deep breath after finishing the series.]

"I am impervious to everyone's bullshit; in all moments."

"I release agreeing to everyone's bullshit; in all lifetimes

"I release nurturing everyone's bullshit; in all moments."

"I release being a storage tank for everyone's bullshit; in all moments."

"I release being a crutch for everyone's bullshit; in all moments."

"I release being cordial to everyone's bullshit; in all moments."

"I release walking on eggshells around everyone's bullshit; in all moments."

"I release being a scapegoat for everyone's bullshit; in all moments."

"I release enabling everyone's bullshit; in all moments."

"I release empowering everyone's bullshit; in all moments."

"I release having my truth snuffed out by everyone's bullshit; in all moments."

"I remove everyone's bullshit form my beingness; in all moments."

"I release filling up my sacred space with everyone's bullshit; in all moments."

"I starve out everyone's bullshit; in all moments."

"I release complying to survive; in all moments."

"I recant all vows and agreements between myself and everyone's bullshit; in all moments."

"I remove all curses between myself and everyone's bullshit; in all moments."

"I sever all ties and cords between myself and everyone's bullshit; in all moments."

"I dissolve all karmic ties between myself and everyone's bullshit; in all moments."

"I remove all the pain, burden, limitations, and engrams that everyone's bullshit has put on me; in all moments."

"I take back all the joy, love, abundance, freedom, health, life, and wholeness that everyone's bullshit has taken from me; in all moments."

"I release resonating with everyone's bullshit; in all moments."

"I release emanating with everyone's bullshit; in all moments."

"I remove everyone's bullshit from my sound frequency; in all moments."

"I remove everyone's bullshit from my light body; in all moments."

"I shift my paradigm from everyone's bullshit to joy, love, abundance, freedom, health, life, and wholeness; in all moments."

"I transcend everyone's bullshit; in all moments."

"I repair and fortify the Wei Chi of all my bodies; in all moments

"I am centered and empowered in divine love; in all moments."

18. Open the Inner Curtain to Love

A client had requested a private remote session to address panic attacks. In her session, many disturbing visuals came through. The first one was being in the ground and having the shovels of dirt pound on her chest. She thought she was alive, but the body had died, and she refused to cross over because she thought the body WAS her consciousness. The feeling of the dirt being piled on her chest was similar to the sensation she experiences when she was having a panic attack.

She was so afraid to be separated from her consciousness that she stayed in the body after death because she believed that her consciousness resided in the body. Her whole session was about letting go of the old consciousness. Just like holding onto the physical body in that lifetime, she is holding onto old consciousness in this life. The consciousness of the world is changing. Unwillingness to change with it leaves people clinging to the old consciousness. The old consciousness is being removed. If people identify with it too strongly, they will have a fear of dying because they believe they ARE this old consciousness.

The next image was a sensation that she was in love with fear. There was a man that was absolutely cruel to her. He was the personification of fear. But she still had an intense passion for him. In her psyche, this manifested as a deep attachment and even love for fear. When I explained this to her, she said that there was someone who treated her like that in the present life. We had to release her attachments to fear.

The third image was a dark impression. It was of being born to fear. The details were of a group of cult members who lived in a dark coven. She was born into it. It was a horrific dark imagery. She had a sense of it once I told her about it. So I led her through a visualization that is a good one for anyone to use:

Enlightenment Unveiled

See the dark room within that has pain, terror and dysfunction. Imagine your chest cavity as having dark curtains on it. Visualize ripping open the curtains and allow the cleansing light of divine love to burn out everything in that room. Feel the lightness as the pain and terror is burned out. Anywhere there is pain or discomfort in the body, open up a set of curtains and let the cleansing light of divine love pour through. Also, here are some of the taps I led her through.

Taps to open an inner curtain to love:

[Say each statement slowly and consciously out loud. Articulate each word and make a point to pause after each phrase. Say each statement three times while tapping on your head. Then say it a fourth time while tapping on your chest. Take a deep breath after finishing the series.]

"**I release the fear of being separated from my consciousness; in all moments.**"

"I release identifying with the old consciousness; in all moments."

"I strip off the old consciousness; in all moments."

"I release the belief that consciousness resides in the body; in all moments."

"I release the fear of crossing over; in all moments."

"I release the fear of leaving my body; in all moments."

"I release the belief that I am going to hell; in all moments."

"I release choosing the body over crossing over; in all moments."

"I release being born to fear; in all moments."

"I release being in love with fear; in all moments."

"I recant all vows and agreements between myself and old consciousness; in all moments."

"I remove all curses between myself and old consciousness; in all moments."

"I release pulling back old consciousness; in all moments."

"I dissolve all karmic ties between myself and old consciousness; in all moments."

"I remove all the pain, burden, limitations, and engrams that old consciousness has put on me; in all moments."

"I take back all the Joy, Love, Abundance, Freedom, Health, Life, and Wholeness that old consciousness has taken from me; in all moments."

"I release resonating with old consciousness; in all moments."

"I release emanating with old consciousness; in all moments."

"I remove all of old consciousness from my sound frequency; in all moments."

"I remove all of old consciousness from my light body; in all moments."

"I shift my paradigm from old consciousness to Joy, Love, Abundance, Freedom, Health, Life, and Wholeness; in all moments."

"I repair and fortify the Wei Chi on all my individual bodies; in all moments."

"I align all my bodies; in all moments."

"I transcend old consciousness; in all moments."

"I am centered and empowered in Divine Love; in all moments."

If you really want to be thorough, go back after you have done all these taps and switch out the word "old consciousness" and put in the word "fear" and do all the taps again.

19. The Reconnection Process

There is a truth explaining that the human DNA is supposed to be 12 strands instead of two. There are different theories why it got stripped down to two strands. It was a means to keep humans grounded on earth, so they wouldn't visit their warring ways onto other planets. Unfortunately, it has kept humans infighting and self-serving for way too long.

The reason why some people are still so focused on war is that their DNA is stunted. It may even be a little less than two strands. Some of us have been preparing to have our DNA upgraded to 12 strands. Those of us who have received an upgrade are more sensitive to perceiving in energy, can accept our intangible gifts, get more of an overview on the cause and effect of every action, are more prone towards love than power, see the potential in all others, stay healthier and more robust, see a positive more uplifting future, and are free of the subliminal forms of manipulation, just to name a few changes.

I have been working to uplift the consciousness by assisting others in reknitting their DNA to 12 strands. I am not certain I can explain how to do this, but it starts as a loving intention. Many cannot see that it is possible to change the course of this earth, but I see it as inevitable. In fact, I sense that many greats of different eras may have chosen to incarnate now simply to assist in the upgrade.

If any of this resonates with you, you may want to try these taps to speed the process along in yourself and those you love.

Those of us who have upgraded will assist those around us in spontaneously upgrading to 12 strands. If this sounds like insanity to anyone, all they need to do is turn on the news and witness true insanity. Spontaneously upgrading, and the potential for all to be so much better than they have been, are the most sane things I can think of.

Taps to upgrade one's DNA:

[Say each statement slowly and consciously out loud. Articulate each word and make a point to pause after each phrase. Say each statement three times while tapping on your head. Then say it a fourth time while tapping on your chest. Take a deep breath after finishing the series.]

"I make space in this world for a 12-stranded upgrade of myself; in all moments."

"I remove all blockage to a 12-stranded upgrade of myself in this world; in all moments."

"I stretch my capacity to upgrade to a 12-strand expression of myself; in all moments."

"I remove all genetic propensity for dis-ease; in all moments."

"I release storing issues in my genetic code; in all moments."

"I sweep out all issues and debris from my genetic code; in all moments."

"I remove all rifts and schisms in my DNA; in all moments."

"I erase all old genetic programming; in all moments."

"I clean the genetic slate; in all moments."

"I recalibrate my entire energy system to accept healthy 12-strand DNA; in all moments."

"I replace the old two-strand genetic code with healthy 12-strand genetic code; in all moments."

"I upgrade my whole energy system to healthy 12-strand DNA; in all moments."

"I integrate healthy 12-strand DNA into my whole energy system; in all moments."

"I embrace my upgraded self; in all moments."

"I accept all my gifts; in all moments."

There are many uplifting side effects of doing these taps. May you enjoy embracing your subtle gifts.

20. Balancing Yin and Yang

In a male dominated world, it is easy for people to get their Yin and Yang out of balance. Many of my clients have revealed past lives where their male experiences were dominated with an abuse of power, and their female lifetimes were of being devastated by suppression. It comes to a point in their spiritual evolution where they are ready to transcend such patterns.

Since Yang energy is focused and direct, and Yin energy is expansive and all encompassing, it is beneficial to embrace both equally. In doing so, we can widen our effectiveness in any endeavor. Some try to marry their Yin and Yang, and though this may be a vital experience, the enlightened individual may get to the point of balancing the two and transcending the Yin-Yang dynamics completely.

Taps to balance the yin and yang:

[Say each statement slowly and consciously out loud. Articulate each word and make a point to pause after each phrase. Say each statement three times while tapping on your head. Then say it a fourth time while tapping on your chest. Take a deep breath after finishing the series.]

"I release preferring to be Yin; in all moments."

"I release preferring to be Yang; in all moments."

"I release associating Yang with an abuse of power; in all moments."

"I release the belief that Yin is weak; in all moments."

"I release my Yang dominating and suppressing my Yin; in all moments."

"I release hiding my Yin in my Yang; in all moments."

"I release the fear of being Yin; in all moments."

"I release the fear of being Yang; in all moments."

"I shift my paradigm from Yang to balance; in all moments."

"I shift my paradigm from Yin to balance; in all moments."

"I balance my Yin equally with my Yang; in all moments."

"I transcend the dynamics between the Yin and Yang; in all moments."

"I shift my paradigm from the Yin-Yang dynamics, to Joy, Love, Abundance, Freedom and Wholeness; in all moments."

The benefit of working on male/female issues from this vantage point is that it is more difficult for the mind to interfere and refute shifting to Joy, Love, Abundance, Freedom and Wholeness. It frees up so much of our energy to be comfortable in our own skin, whichever sex that may be.

21. Releasing Old Work Paradigms

People wonder why they are struggling to find work. It is because work is an outmoded concept that is not supported by the new paradigm. If people are struggling, it is because they refuse to let go of the old paradigm of work.

The new paradigm is doing what you love and being in abundance as a result. It is about serving in joy and having that joy be part of payment. In the new paradigm, there is more contentment in having enough. It is less about accumulating a number in a bank account and stockpiling things and more about experiencing wealth in all the intangible ways.

People want that security of a job, but many are not getting it. They struggle to find enjoyable work. They are really just feeling the conflict of wanting to follow the call of living in joy, but are afraid to let go of the old paradigm. Trying to tell them is like trying to get a thrashing person who thinks they are drowning to float.

So many people are on disability not because they have nothing to offer, but because they don't fit into the old crumbling paradigm of work. It is not so ingrained as it was just a few years ago when everyone worked 9-5. But it could be dismantled a lot sooner.

Taps to release old work paradigms:

[Say each statement slowly and consciously out loud. Articulate each word and make a point to pause after each phrase. Say each statement three times while tapping on your head. Then say it a fourth time while tapping on your chest. Take a deep breath after finishing the series.]

> **"I release being enslaved to the concept of work; in all moments."**

> **"I release the fear of being out of work; in all moments."**

"I release drowning in mind loops; in all moments."

"I release fighting the natural progression of life; in all moments."

"I release living in outmoded concepts; in all moments."

"I release trying to bring the past to the present; in all moments."

"I release the fear of my own freedom; in all moments."

"I recant all vows and agreements between myself and the concept of work; in all moments."

"I remove all curses between myself and the concept of work; in all moments."

"I dissolve all karmic ties between myself and the concept of work; in all moments."

"I sever all strings and cords between myself and the concept of work; in all moments."

"I remove all the pain, burden, limitations and engrams that the concept of work has put on me; in all moments."

"I withdraw all my energy from the concept of work; in all moments."

"I take back all the Joy, Love, Abundance, Freedom, Health, Life and Wholeness that the concept of work has taken from me; in all moments."

"I remove all of the concept of work from my sound frequency; in all moments."

"I remove all of the concept of work from my light body; in all moments."

"I transcend the concept of work; in all moments."

"I shift my paradigm from work to living my life's purpose; in all moments."

"I make space in this world to live my purpose; in all moments."

"I remove all blockages to living my purpose; in all moments."

"I stretch my capacity and confidence to live my purpose; in all moments."

"I am centered and empowered in living my purpose; in all moments."

The sooner people release the old paradigm of a fear-based life, the sooner they can embrace the inevitable joy, abundance, and freedom that is the new paradigm. They can start doing what they love.

There are so many stories about people quitting their day job because their hobby became so lucrative. They turned their hobby into a steady flow of income. People who are attached to the concept of work are afraid to do that. If they let go of all the angst of finding work, they could use that energy in the pursuit of their passion and being in abundance.

22. Undo Programming

You know all those commercials that we sit through? Their whole purpose is to connect a positive experience with their product so that you buy their product. All those cravings, all those extra snacks, all those new favorite "must haves" are programmed into you. Here is the cure. These taps will help to undo the programming.

Taps to undo programming:

[Say each statement slowly and consciously out loud. Articulate each word and make a point to pause after each phrase. Say each statement three times while tapping on your head. Then say it a fourth time while tapping on your chest. Take a deep breath after finishing the series.]

"I release confusing food for love; in all moments."

"I release confusing food for friendship; in all moments."

"I release confusing food for fun; in all moments."

"I release confusing food for security; in all moments."

"I release confusing food for sex; in all moments."

"I release confusing food for intimacy; in all moments."

"I release confusing food for adventure; in all moments."

"I release confusing food for family; in all moments."

"I release confusing food for confidence; in all moments."

"I release confusing food for a relationship; in all moments."

"I release confusing food for power; in all moments."

"I release confusing food for success; in all moments."

"I release confusing food for love; in all moments."

"I release confusing food for companionship; in all moments."

"I release confusing food for peace; in all moments."

"I release confusing food for likability; in all moments."

"I release confusing food for beauty; in all moments."

After doing these, you can trade out the word food and replace it with alcohol, beer, shopping, shoes, or what whatever your craving is.

23. Dissolving All Old Paradigms and Constructs

I facilitated a private remote session with someone who was experiencing being light-headed and hearing an inner buzzing in her ears. When I tuned into my client, I understood what the issue was. She was someone who wanted a traditional life that entailed family, home, marriage, and career. But she also wanted to empower her spiritual side and to uncover her healing gifts. The two polar opposite experiences were creating conflict in her.

She also didn't realize that being light-headed was a way to perceive energy. She also didn't realize that inner sounds were a way that some people commune with God, or more accurately, God speaks to us through the inner sounds. For many people, they can use the sounds that they inwardly hear to decipher the caliber of the inner connection they are experiencing.

Her draw to a traditional life was in direct conflict with her desire to be more expansive in awareness. She romanticized family, marriage, aspects of society, work, etc. But the consciousness of the world is moving towards an inner connectedness. That is why those of us who are becoming more expansive, are inwardly sharing that with others who are newly awakening to it. Her being attached to the old ways was working as a form of an anchor to the group collective. In a certain perspective, being attached to the old ways was holding the collective back.

These wonderful freeing taps came from that session.

Taps to dissolve old paradigms and constructs:

[Say each statement slowly and consciously out loud. Articulate each word and make a point to pause after each phrase. Say each statement three times while tapping on your head. Then say it a fourth time while tapping on your chest. Take a deep breath after finishing the series.]

"I release being dependent on old paradigms and constructs; in all moments."

"I release being anchored in old paradigms and constructs; in all moments."

"I recant all vows and agreements between myself and all old paradigms and constructs; in all moments."

"I remove all curses between myself and all old paradigms and constructs; in all moments."

"I sever all ties and cords between myself and all old paradigms and constructs; in all moments."

"I dissolve all karmic ties between myself and all old paradigms and constructs; in all moments."

"I remove all the pain, burden, limitations, and engrams that all old paradigms and constructs have put on me; in all moments."

"I take back all the Joy, Love, Abundance, Freedom, Health, Success, Confidence, Companionship, Creativity, Peace, Life, Wholeness, Spirituality, and Enlightenment that all old paradigms and constructs have taken from me; in all moments."

"I release resonating with all old paradigms and constructs; in all moments."

"I release emanating with all old paradigms and constructs; in all moments."

"I remove all old paradigms and constructs from my sound frequency; in all moments."

"I remove all old paradigms and constructs from my light body; in all moments."

"I shift my paradigm from all old paradigms and constructs to Joy, Love, Abundance, Freedom, Health, Success, Confidence, Companionship, Creativity, Peace, Life, Wholeness, Spirituality, and Enlightenment; in all moments."

"I transcend old paradigms and constructs; in all moments."

"I repair and fortify the Wei Chi of all my bodies; in all moments."

"I am centered and empowered in Joy, Love, Abundance, Freedom, Health, Success, Confidence, Companionship, Creativity, Peace, Life, Wholeness, Spirituality, and Enlightenment; in all moments."

24. Empowerment: Issues Involved in Falling to One's Death

We forget that hospitals, wheelchairs and painkillers are a relatively modern invention. In the past, when we fell or broke a limb, we lay there mangled and twisting, writhing in pain until someone put us out of our misery or death came to us. These memories still surface when we are confronted with health issues. They are the hiccups of past torments making their way to the surface for validation. They need not be permanent.

If past issues are acknowledged, and the body is validated, we can move through them quite quickly. See? It is not always something settling into us. Most times, it is something devastating trying to leave. That is the purpose of the taps: to acknowledge the pain quickly and to help it pass through.

One of my first clients was terrified of birds. It sounds silly to some. But the image that I saw was her as a young Native American man. He was climbing on the rocks of a cliff to access eggs in the nests. He lost his footing and fell to his demise. But death wasn't swift. He lay there watching the vultures circle him as he got weaker. They did not wait for him to die before they moved in and started picking at his flesh. They made their first strikes at the moist areas where the blood drained out, the intestines, and the eyeballs. This was how she left that life.

Taps with issues in falling to one's death:

[Say each statement slowly and consciously out loud. Articulate each word and make a point to pause after each phrase. Say each statement three times while tapping on your head. Then say it a fourth time while tapping on your chest. Take a deep breath after finishing the series.]

"I release the pain and trauma of falling to my death; in all moments."

"I release the fear of heights; in all moments."

"I release the horror of being eaten alive; in all moments."

"I release the fear of being eaten by birds/dogs/cats/natives (whatever it is); in all moments."

"I untangle the limbs of my body; in all moments."

"I untangle the energy of my body; in all moments."

"I release mingling my sense of adventure with fear; in all moments."

"I release allowing fear to override my sense of adventure; in all moments."

"I release feeling helpless and abandoned; in all moments."

"I release the belief that I am helpless and abandoned; in all moments."

"I shift my paradigm from helpless and abandoned to empowered and free; in all moments."

"I am centered in Joy, Love, Abundance, Freedom, Health, Success, Adventure and Wholeness; in all moments."

We are only as brave as the strongest memory of our deepest fear. When we understand that we are empowered by taking a non-reactive stance to unconscious triggers, we can just address them without being blindsided by emotional reactions. We don't even have to fully understand the emotional reaction to just address them head on. Our own resistance to addressing them then becomes sabotage because the taps work easily and effectively.

25. Frozen Shoulder

I facilitated a private remote session with someone who came to me for help with a frozen shoulder. Immediately, I got an impression of the issue. I saw her in a past life with a huge shield in the left hand, clenched to the body and in a very defensive stance. When we connected by phone for her session, she validated that it was indeed her left shoulder. She also validated that people in this lifetime seemed to attack her for no reason, and it did make her defensive. I explained to her that the attacks were reminders or hints to the conscious mind of what she had suffered in the past without having to remember details. Her inner energy was not fluid but stuck in the position of the warrior.

I can tell that I am accurate in accessing an issue because the client will have difficulty in hearing the taps I give them and retaining them enough to repeat them to me. It was very difficult for this client to get through any of the taps. The energy was so stagnant and locked in her body that it was difficult to connect with her enough to help her release by saying the taps.

The imagery of different lifetimes in war was layered within her. Besides the initial image, I saw her rotting in a dank dungeon chained to a wall, in many different battle scenarios, and definitely spending many lifetimes living, fighting, and dying in the Crusades. When someone has been in the Crusades, the song "Hallelujah" comes to me as a way to release the issues. She was so congested with these lifetimes that I sang "Hallelujah" to her. She cried profusely during it. This released the issues in her a bit. I then was able to lead her through some taps to free up her energy more.

Taps to remove the trauma of being in battle:

[Say each statement slowly and consciously out loud. Articulate each word and make a point to pause after each phrase. Say each statement three times while tapping on your head. Then say it a fourth time while tapping on your chest.]

"I declare myself a surrogate for humanity; in all moments." (optional)

"I release fighting for my life; in all moments."

"I release the trauma of being attacked; in all moments."

"I release being in attack mode; in all moments."

"I release defending my life; in all moments."

"I release being defensive; in all moments."

"I release the guilt and trauma of killing others; in all moments."

"I release hating the Church; in all moments."

"I release fighting and dying for a cause I don't believe in; in all moments."

"I release the trauma of being at war; in all moments."

"I release infusing apathy into life; in all moments."

"I release the trauma of being tortured; in all moments."

"I release the trauma of being imprisoned; in all moments."

"I recant all vows and agreements between myself and all battles; in all moments."

"I remove all curses between myself and all battles; in all moments."

"I dissolve all karmic ties between myself and all battles; in all moments."

"I remove all the pain, burden, and limitations that all battles have put on me; in all moments."

"I take back all the Joy, Love, Abundance, Freedom, Health, Peace, Life, and Wholeness that all battles have taken from me; in all moments."

"I withdraw all my energy from all battles; in all moments."

"I release resonating with all battles; in all moments."

"I release emanating with all battles; in all moments."

"I remove all battles from my sound frequency; in all moments."

"I remove all battles from my light body; in all moments."

"I shift my paradigm from all battles to Joy, Love, Abundance, Freedom, Health, Life, and Wholeness; in all moments."

"I repair and fortify my Wei Chi; in all moments."

"I am centered am empowered in Divine Love; in all moments."

At the end of the session, the client could feel the energy in her body as more fluid. She was happy and enthused with her session. She had been to many alternative and conventional healers. None were able to assist. I understood why. I had to really pin her down energetically to help her strip these issues off. It is similar to sitting on someone and stripping layers of tight clothing off of them. I went deep and was more relentless than they were able to be. Maybe by doing the taps above, we all can shift the tide of current events. Maybe we can work as inside agents to free and uplift humanity. Maybe we can unhinge the unconscious allure for war, and move humanity to peace! Who is willing to do this?

26. Your Own Energy Conversion

When I assist someone in private sessions, I feel their stagnant energy like a cloud and dissipate it by emoting sounds. In doing this, I am converting the energy from latent (dormant) to dynamic (flowing), and it's very effective. The client usually feels the heaviness move out and is surprised at the shift that they are witnessing within themselves.

Energy conversion is something that we all do to stay well and balanced. We convert food into calories for energy, and there are many conversions of energy that we can do for ourselves consciously. One of the reasons singing is so effective in lifting a bad mood is that it is converting energy that may have not been useful into something useful. It may be dissipating denser energy and moving it out of the body, and this is why singing is literally uplifting. When slaves sang, it may have been a way to convert their incredible pain from misery to resolve.

In the same way, exercise converts latent energy into dynamic energy, and there are more subtle forms of conversion as well. When we choose to be kind or positive, when we decide to support others, we are making conscious decisions to convert denser energy of feeling bad into something useful. But when we talk about problems, wallow in pain, try to get attention in negative ways, not only are we weighing ourselves down, but we are also attempting to pull others into our stagnant cloud for companionship.

[Say each statement slowly and consciously out loud. Articulate each word and make a point to pause after each phrase. Say each statement three times while tapping on your head. Then say it a fourth time while tapping on your chest. Take a deep breath after finishing the series.]

"I convert all problems into solutions; in all moments."

"I convert all self-pity into enthusiastic resolve; in all moments."

"I convert all limitations into opportunities; in all moments "

"I convert all complaints into compliments; in all moments."

"I convert all obstacles into bridges; in all moments."

"I convert all indecision into motivation; in all moments."

"I convert all limitations into possibilities; in all moments."

"I release storing energy as nostalgia; in all moments."

"I release giving all my energy to another; in all moments."

"I release using storage systems for my issues; in all moments."

Many have very heavy issues they are dealing with. But if there were a better understanding of the dynamics involved in all our interactions, with others and ourselves, maybe more people would take control of their inner conversion system. They could master the subtleties of life.

27. I AM!

Taps to feel great every day.

[Say each statement slowly and consciously out loud. Articulate each word and make a point to pause after each phrase. Say each statement three times while tapping on your head. Then say it a fourth time while tapping on your chest. Take a deep breath after finishing the series.]

"I Am Joy Personified; in all moments."

"I Am Love Personified; in all moments."

"I Am Abundance Personified; in all moments."

"I Am Freedom Personified; in all moments."

"I Am Health Personified; in all moments."

"I Am Success Personified; in all moments."

"I Am Creativity Personified; in all moments."

"I Am Peace Personified; in all moments."

"I Am Kindness Personified; in all moments."

"I Am Confidence Personified; in all moments."

"I Am Beauty Personified; in all moments."

"I Am Contentment Personified; in all moments."

"I Am Enthusiasm Personified; in all moments."

"I Am Wholeness Personified; in all moments."

"I Am Light Personified; in all moments."

"I Am Music Personified; in all moments."

"I Am Spontaneity Personified; in all moments."

"I Am Compassion Personified; in all moments."

"I Am Omniscience Personified; in all moments."

"I Am Omnipresence Personified; in all moments."

"I Am Omnipotence Personified; in all moments."

28. Improving Self-Worth

When I was born, my father was 52. He was already worn out, and as I was the tenth child and the seventh girl, he had hardly anything to give. I had a dream that seemed like an allegory for male/female dynamics. I don't usually share my dreams. But this may help someone with a similar recognition.

I was in an old warehouse apartment where I lived when I was at one of my lowest ebbs. I was letting a teenage girl stay with me for a bit. It was painful having her in my living quarters. She was just into having a good time and not very thoughtful of others. We and her friend went over to her aunt's house to see if she could stay there. It was chaotic.

At the aunt's home, there were me, the aunt, the girl that stayed with me, her friend, and the aunt's friend. There were also Richard Gere, my brother (who never showed himself but was in another room), and my father. I was interacting with the aunt trying to get this girl out of my home. The girl started inviting someone else to stay at my house. I was ruthless and shut her down telling her how it was not hers to offer. That felt good!

Richard Gere was walking around and talking to everyone at the party one on one. I was waiting for my turn. He came close, but he sat next to one of the cousins and ignored me. I was totally being ignored except the one time the aunt offered donuts, and I took the largest one just to fill myself up. It felt like the big one was enormous enough to plug up the discomfort of being invisible.

My father was in a suit that he owned when we were kids. He was walking around to everyone and apologizing for his actions. He was really sad and pathetic as he went around asking for forgiveness and trying to illicit sympathy. Part of me wanted his attention. But then he went to the woman who was staying with me BEFORE me and asked her forgiveness. I was livid. He came to me last. I was ruthlessly angry with him for coming to me last. I cut into him with my anger and then walked out of the house leaving him pressed up against the door looking at me. Then I woke up.

Upon awaking, I knew immediately why I was so angry. Richard Gere didn't come over to talk to me because my dad hadn't come over to talk to me. I realized in that moment that our relationship with men is directly related to our relationship with our father. However our father treats us is how we will experience men treating us.

I believe this awareness is me taking one for the team of womankind. It was good that I was angry. Anger is higher on the survival scale than apathy. It is the step before peace. Here is to helping everyone get to a more peaceful relationship with themselves.

Taps to improve self-worth:

[Say each statement slowly and consciously out loud. Articulate each word and make a point to pause after each phrase. Say each statement three times while tapping on your head. Then say it a fourth time while tapping on your chest. Take a deep breath after finishing the series.]

"I release doing things I don't want, so others will like me; in all moments."

"I release being taken advantage of; in all moments."

"I release having my kindness being misconstrued as weakness; in all moments."

"I release the habit of being used; in all moments."

"I release the need to be considered good; in all moments."

"I release giving away my innate essence; in all moments."

"I release compensating for being abandoned; in all moments."

"I release trying to earn love; in all moments."

"I release the belief that my only value is in giving of myself; in all moments."

"I release the belief that physical beauty is the highest asset; in all moments."

"I release coming out of my center for others; in all moments."

"I release being passive; in all moments."

"I release being overlooked by male energy; in all moments."

"I release being invisible; in all moments."

"I release the belief that I am unworthy of love; in all moments."

"I release buying love with sacrificial acts; in all moments."

"I release being abandoned by male energy; in all moments."

"I release gauging my worth by how men respond to me; in all moments."

"I release being subservient to men; in all moments."

"I recant all vows and agreements between myself and a male dominated existence; in all moments."

"I remove all curses between myself and a male dominated existence; in all moments."

"I dissolve all karmic ties between myself and a male dominated existence; in all moments."

"I remove all the pain, burden, limitations, and engrams that a male dominated existence has put on me; in all moments."

"I take back all the Joy, Love, Abundance, Freedom, Health, Success, Security, Companionship, Peace, Life, Wholeness, Beauty, Enthusiasm, Contentment, Confidence, Spirituality, and Enlightenment that a male dominated existence has taken from me; in all moments."

"I withdraw all my energy and support from a male dominated existence; in all moments."

"I transcend a male dominated existence; in all moments."

"I shift my paradigm from a male dominated existence to Joy, Love, Abundance, Freedom, Health, Success, Security, Companionship, Peace, Life, Wholeness, Beauty, Enthusiasm, Contentment, Confidence, Spirituality, and Enlightenment; in all moments."

"I am centered and empowered in Joy, Love, Abundance, Freedom, Health, Success, Security, Companionship, Peace, Life, Wholeness, Beauty, Enthusiasm, Contentment, Confidence, Spirituality, and Enlightenment; in all moments."

These taps are good for men to do as well. There was another part of the dream. Heidi Klum was there, and she was very beautiful. But when I started talking to her, an insecurity revealed itself. She is the epitome of beauty and success. Her insecurity in the dream was symbolic of a glass ceiling on the value of female energy as long as we are in a male dominated existence. The glass ceiling is being lifted. These taps will hurry it along for the individual. God Speed!

29. The Correlation Between the Microcosm and the Macrocosm

Everything that happens in our life is a reflection of what is happening in the world. Our life is the microcosm and the world at large is the macrocosm. What we see happening in the world is what is happening within ourselves. Sometimes we look around us, and we don't see how it relates to our own personal plight. But it does. The more we can let go of the issues within ourselves, the greater impact we can make on the world. Every power struggle, lack of communication, form of toxin or pollution that is happening "out there" is happening within. To change the world, we must deal with the issues within ourselves that we avoid. The more we do this, the more we empower others around us to do this and cause a chain reaction

But for many, the task of looking within is difficult. It may be easier for many to put all the blame outward and feel like helpless watchers in the world. It also is easier to love and help everyone else in the world rather than to love and honor ourselves. Here is a technique to pour all your intention out into the world and within at the same time. Think of the little man operating the big mechanism with gadgets. But instead of gadgets, it is intentions that operate the world.

See yourself encased in a circle of your own energy, protected and surrounded in Light and Love. See the world as a larger circle with your orb centered in the middle.

Taps to uplift the macrocosm and microcosm:

[Say each statement slowly and consciously out loud. Articulate each word and make a point to pause after each phrase. Say each statement three times while tapping on your head. Then say it a fourth time while tapping on your chest. Take a deep breath after finishing the series.]

"I align my microcosm with the macrocosm; in all moments."

"I remove all sadness from my microcosm and macrocosm; in all moments."

"I remove all fear from my microcosm and macrocosm; in all moments."

"I remove all lack from my microcosm and macrocosm; in all moments."

"I remove all dis-ease from my microcosm and macrocosm; in all moments."

"I remove all slavery from my microcosm and macrocosm; in all moments."

"I remove all failure from my microcosm and macrocosm; in all moments."

"I remove all uncertainty from my microcosm and macrocosm; in all moments."

"I remove all abandonment from my microcosm and macrocosm; in all moments."

"I remove all war from my microcosm and macrocosm; in all moments."

"I remove all death and decay from my microcosm and macrocosm; in all moments."

"I remove all need from my microcosm and macrocosm; in all moments."

"I remove all fragmentation from my microcosm and macrocosm; in all moments."

"I remove all ugliness from my microcosm and macrocosm; in all moments."

"I remove all apathy from my microcosm and macrocosm; in all moments."

"I infuse Joy into my microcosm and macrocosm; in all moments."

"I infuse Love into my microcosm and macrocosm; in all moments."

"I infuse Abundance into my microcosm and macrocosm; in all moments."

"I infuse Health into my microcosm and macrocosm; in all moments."

"I infuse Freedom into my microcosm and macrocosm; in all moments."

"I infuse Success into my microcosm and macrocosm; in all moments."

"I infuse Security into my microcosm and macrocosm; in all moments."

"I infuse Companionship into my microcosm and macrocosm; in all moments."

"I infuse Peace into my microcosm and macrocosm; in all moments."

"I infuse Life into my microcosm and macrocosm; in all moments."

"I infuse Contentment into my microcosm and macrocosm; in all moments."

> "I infuse Wholeness into my microcosm and macrocosm; in all moments."

> "I infuse Enthusiasm into my microcosm and macrocosm; in all moments."

> "I infuse Beauty into my microcosm and macrocosm; in all moments."

If one is discouraged with the state of affairs in the world, these taps may be a way to feel effective in holding a loving intention for all. Each small shift in each of us creates a shift in the whole. It may seem silly to some, but what may be more ridiculous is having the power the whole time and not utilizing it.

30. Releasing Beliefs Around Poverty

It is surprising how many good, spiritual people are not living in abundance. It seems that those who lead a good life and are kind and loving to others would naturally attract wealth. To me, spirituality is Joy, Love, Abundance, Freedom, and Wholeness.

People are empowered to manifest more than they realize. Ask Anthony Robbins what he thinks of people not living a fulfilling life. If they are not having a life filled with Joy, Love, Abundance, Freedom and Wholeness, it may be their misconception of what God expects of them. In past times, a life of self-denial may have been expected. Maybe that old belief system is still ingrained somewhere in the psyche. If so, here is assistance in releasing it and other outdated ideas.

Taps to release beliefs around poverty:

[Say each statement slowly and consciously out loud. Articulate each word and make a point to pause after each phrase. Say each statement three times while tapping on your head. Then say it a fourth time while tapping on your chest. Take a deep breath after finishing the series.]

> "I release the belief that God wants me to be poor; in all moments."

> "I release the belief that God wants me to suffer; in all moments."

> "I release the belief that God wants me to martyr myself; in all moments."

> "I release the belief that God wants me to abase myself; in all moments."

"I release the belief that God wants me to be contrite; in all moments."

"I release the belief that God wants me to be passive; in all moments."

"I release the belief that God wants me to be meek; in all moments."

"I recant my vow of martyrdom; in all moments."

"I recant my vow of poverty; in all moments."

"I recant my vow of humility; in all moments."

"I recant my vow of self-deprecation; in all moments."

"I recant my vow of self-deprivation; in all moments."

"I release confusing deficiency with loving God; in all moments."

"I release defining spirituality as having poverty; in all moments."

"I release the belief that money is evil; in all moments."

"I release the belief that happiness is a sin; in all moments."

"I release carrying the weight of the world on my shoulders; in all moments."

I shift my paradigm to Joy, Love, Abundance, Freedom, and Wholeness; in all moments."

"I make space in this world for my personal Joy, Love, Abundance, Freedom, and Wholeness; in all moments."

"I remove all blockages to being centered in Joy, Love, Abundance, Freedom, and Wholeness; in all moments."

"I stretch my capacity to accept Joy, Love, Abundance, Freedom, and Wholeness; in all moments."

In many past times, life was cruel and harsh. The only comfort may have come from believing that enduring suffering endeared one to God. It was a great survival tool of the time. But it may be time to have another experience. I challenge everyone to question their core beliefs and realize that they are still worthy of God's Love even if they are rich beyond their wildest dreams.

31. Validation

Validation is when we desire outwardly what we already know intuitively. We have been taught to distrust ourselves so much that we don't value something unless we receive it from an outside source. Please know that the universe validates you. Whatever you perceive as your truth is valid. You are an amazing part of the whole and connected to the All.

Taps to boost confidence:

[Say each statement slowly and consciously out loud. Articulate each word and make a point to pause after each phrase. Say each statement three times while tapping on your head. Then say it a fourth time while tapping on your chest. Take a deep breath after finishing the series.]

"I release the shame and embarrassment of being invalidated; in all moments."

"I release the need to be validated; in all moments."

"I strengthen my inner conviction; in all moments."

"I empower my own intuition; in all moments."

"I tap into direct knowing; in all moments."

"I am centered and empowered in direct knowing; in all moments."

32. The Takers

I facilitated a session where the client just couldn't get motivated. It wasn't difficult to get a sense of the core issue. Wherever we go and whatever we do, we run into two types of interactions: those that give to us and those that take from us.

Those interactions with people who take from us are not bad, and people may not even realize that they are taking. We all would like to think of ourselves as givers all the time, but that would be naive. In my sessions, we work on a client's interactions in all lifetimes. This client was one who had been taken from. Through his spiritual disciplines, he had practiced being neutral in all his interactions, but that didn't preclude others from engaging with him as they will.

Some of us attract a certain type of exchange. We are all trying, at the core, to experience ourselves as divine love, but in our everyday experiences that can be interpreted as receiving attention, being better than another, or accruing what another person has. But it is pointless to be frustrated with others that are merely holding their particular place on the survival scale. These taps will help release a universal issue without being directed at another.

Taps to avoid takers and taking:

[Say each statement slowly and consciously out loud. Articulate each word and make a point to pause after each phrase. Say each statement three times while tapping on your head. Then say it a fourth time while tapping on your chest. Take a deep breath after finishing the series.]

"I release being a taker; in all moments."

"I release taking; in all moments."

"I release being susceptible to taking and takers; in all moments."

"I release being manipulated by taking and takers; in all moments."

"I recant all vows and agreements between myself and all taking and takers; in all moments."

"I remove all curses between myself and all taking and takers; in all moments."

"I dissolve all karmic ties between myself and all taking and takers; in all moments."

"I remove all the pain, burden and limitations that all taking and takers have put on me; in all moments."

"I take back all the Joy, Love, Abundance, Freedom, Life and Wholeness that taking and takers have taken from me; in all moments."

"I release resonating with taking and takers; in all moments."

"I release emanating with taking and takers; in all moments."

"I remove all taking and takers from my sound frequency; in all moments."

"I remove all taking and takers from my light body; in all moments."

"I shift my paradigm from taking and takers to Joy, Love, Abundance, Freedom, Life and Wholeness; in all moments."

We all have been givers, and we all have been takers. It isn't black and white. Some take from us by giving, and it is also possible to give to someone by accepting what they wish to give. It is only when we can get an overview of all our lifetimes that we can realize incredible compassion for ourselves and all others.

33. Buying Money

In a session, it came to me why so many people are in lack. Instead of using money to buy happiness, they are using happiness to buy money. They are using all their abundance of Joy, Love, Freedom and Wholeness as currency to buy money.

People who spend all their time at a job they don't like just for the pay are buying money. If people hate their job, they are using their love to buy money. If they are unhappy, they are using their joy to buy money. If they are feeling trapped in a job, they are using their freedom to buy money. If they are feeling pulled between their home life and their job, they are buying money with their wholeness. Here are taps to stop selling one's happiness.

Taps to Attract Money:

[Say each statement slowly and consciously out loud. Articulate each word and make a point to pause after each phrase. Say each statement three times while tapping on your head. Then say it a fourth time while tapping on your chest. Take a deep breath after finishing the series.]

"I release selling my Joy to buy money; in all moments."

"I release selling my Love to buy money; in all moments."

"I release selling my Abundance to buy money; in all moments."

"I release selling my Freedom to buy money; in all moments."

"I release selling my Health to buy money; in all moments."

"I release selling my Success to buy money; in all moments."

"I release selling my Security to buy money; in all moments."

"I release selling my Companionship to buy money; in all moments."

"I release selling my Talent to buy money; in all moments."

"I release selling my Peace of Mind to buy money; in all moments."

"I release selling my Wholeness to buy money; in all moments."

"I release selling my Life to buy money; in all moments."

"I release chasing money; in all moments."

"I shift my paradigm from chasing money to having Abundance; in all moments."

"I am centered in Joy, Love, Abundance, Freedom, Health, Success, Security, Companionship, Peace, Life, and Wholeness; in all moments."

It may seem like we have to do what we have to do to make money. But for so many, it doesn't seem worth it. Maybe these taps will free us from a habitual belief system that is selling ourselves short.

34. Maintaining Integrity

My clients are some of the most dynamic people on the planet. They are dedicated to using their talents to assist others and living their purpose. It is sometimes difficult to know when one is veering off center when they are so empowered. If I see it, I will address it, and it may not be pleasant.

It is difficult when the ego starts feeling empowered when one is living their dynamic purpose. When someone comes to me, it is my job to hold him or her accountable.

There are streams of energy that people can project to accomplish goals. But they can also get caught up in them. We have all seen good people start in a career of politics or entertainment and have watched their inner light be snuffed out on the way to fame. I keep my clients honest.

One dynamic client is a life coach. She was on the top of her game. She was getting great acknowledgment and validation but was starting to get swept up in it. It was nothing that someone else would see. But being privy to akashic records, I could see a possible future where she would be slightly less attuned to listening to the needs of those who come to her and more interested in her role.

When dealing with ego, it is important to strip it away. The technique is sometimes brutal. It is the kindest thing to do for someone who wishes to truly serve, but it does not feel good. It is vulnerable to lose a layer of the ego. If I did not help this client now, she would still be successful, considered beautiful and dynamic, but she wouldn't be quite on the mark as far as giving from a pure place.

Taps to maintain integrity:

[Say each statement slowly and consciously out loud. Articulate each word and make a point to pause after each phrase. Say each statement three times while tapping on your head. Then say it a fourth time while tapping on your chest. Take a deep breath after finishing the series.]

"I release selling out; in all moments."

"I release choosing power over love; in all moments."

"I release choosing ego over living my purpose; in all moments."

"I release being coerced by fame or fortune; in all moments."

"I make space in this world for organic love; in all moments."

"I remove all blockages to manifesting organic love; in all moments."

"I stretch my capacity to manifest organic love; in all moments."

"I serve from a pure place; in all moments."

There are so many dynamic, polished people striving for the top of the heap. The public has become savvy to sincerity or lack of it. What sets a person apart from the others is forgoing the competition realm and giving to truly serve and empower others.

35. The Mule-Hearted Client

I facilitated a session with a client who was very frustrated and confused at her own ambivalence. She was aware that she had many talents and gifts but seemed to not be able to share them. She seemed to have a very subtle contempt for the incompetency of others and yet seemed to seek their approval. Even though she felt manipulated by their compliments, she seemed to allow them to appease her. The dynamics of it seemed to leave her feeling helpless and not in control. She also felt overburdened.

In her session, a past life image of a donkey came through. She was really stubborn and made to carry such a heavy load. Beating her did not get a response. The only thing that would motivate her in that life was sweet talk. To her, in that life, sweet talk was the closest thing to love that she received. On a subtle level, she was still registering sweet talk as a viable form of love. It was so ingrained in that past life from the loneliness and pain of the beatings that it had imprinted on her and was affecting the present life.

After I led her through a bunch of taps, she felt the heaviness of this invisible burden lift from her. She was much lighter. Hopefully, she will be less vulnerable to shallow praise.

Taps to release being manipulated:

[Say each statement slowly and consciously out loud. Articulate each word and make a point to pause after each phrase. Say each statement three times while tapping on your head. Then say it a fourth time while tapping on your chest. Take a deep breath after finishing the series.]

"**I release being manipulated by praise; in all moments.**"

"**I release craving validation; in all moments.**"

"I release seeking approval; in all moments."

"I release the need to be appeased; in all moments."

36. Unharnessing the Slimming Effects of Brown Fat

There are two types of fat. There is the white fat and the brown fat. People who can eat anything they want have more of the brown fat. Many of us would be happy if we had brown fat instead of white fat. The brown fat burns up the white fat for fuel.

My friend said something genius today. She said that the taps that I recently posted about our dynamics with the fat cells were going to empower the brown fat to seemingly amp her metabolism. Of course. Why not? Why not create taps for that?

Taps to unharness the slimming effects of brown fat:

[Say each statement slowly and consciously out loud. Articulate each word and make a point to pause after each phrase. Say each statement three times while tapping on your head. Then say it a fourth time while tapping on your chest. Take a deep breath after finishing the series.]

"I amp up my metabolism; in all moments."

"I encourage my stem cells to create more brown fat; in all moments."

"I regenerate the production of brown fat in my body; in all moments."

"I commend the PRDM16 molecules to produce brown fat; in all moments."

"I empower the BMP-7 protein to produce brown fat; in all moments."

"I uptake my body's levels of melatonin; in all moments."

"I make space in this world for the mitochondria of my fat cells to have express levels of UCP1 protein; in all moments."

"I remove all blockages to the mitochondria of my fat cells to have express levels of UCP1 protein; in all moments."

"I stretch the capacity of the mitochondria of my fat cells to have express levels of UCP1 protein; in all moments."

"I make space in my body for more brown fat; in all moments."

"I remove all blockages and limiting beliefs to having more brown fat in my body; in all moments."

"I stretch my body's capacity to manufacture brown fat; in all moments."

"I recalibrate my body to empower the brown fat; in all moments."

"I awaken and empower my body's brown fat to use up all the white fat; in all moments."

"I command my body to use up all the white fat; in all moments."

"I shift my body's paradigm from white fat to brown fat; in all moments."

"I am centered and empowered in brown fat; in all moments."

Science hasn't found a way to make brown fat more prevalent in the body with a pill, but they have come up with a trick. The trick is to turn the water from hot to cold repeatedly while showering. Since the brown fat is used in mammals to prevent them from freezing during hibernation, the chills hold a key to creating it. So maybe while doing the taps, visualize being outside in the winter with almost nothing on. The visual of shivering may create a better conduit to manifest results. Also since the brown fat is more prevalent in babies, it may be helpful to visualize yourself as an infant as well.

So when this tap series works for people, they will realize that the other series of taps must work as well. Maybe these particular taps are a key to creating a healthier and more empowered world. By doing these, we are uplifting humanity one tap at a time.

37. Removing Self-Limitations

We may all be compartmentalized by how we show up in the world. There is a subtle judgment that goes on, both externally and internally with all the little labels that define us. We are grouped with those with similar characteristics. We are all on the conveyor belt of life getting sorted and counted and scrutinized for imperfections. Why? Why are we allowing ourselves to be counted and boxed in on all sides? Does it add to our happiness? Does it make us more valuable? No, quite the opposite. It makes it easier for us to be grouped, minimized and discounted.

It's up to each one of us to individualize ourselves. Some try to do it in a negative way. It is not necessary. Some are screaming out to be noticed. Maybe it's not really the need for validation as much as a need to stop invalidating themselves. They can help their plight by not ignoring all the things that interest them merely to fit in. They can stop going along with the consensus of the groups they are affiliated with and speak their own heart.

Taps to remove limitations:

[Say each statement slowly and consciously out loud. Articulate each word and make a point to pause after each phrase. Say each statement three times while tapping on your head. Then say it a fourth time while tapping on your chest. Take a deep breath after finishing the series.]

"I release being limited by my current ethnicity; in all moments."

"I shatter the glass ceiling of my current ethnicity; in all moments."

"I transcend all limitations of ethnicity; in all moments."

"I release being limited by my current gender; in all moments."

"I shatter the glass ceiling of my current gender; in all moments."

"I transcend all limitations of gender; in all moments."

"I release being limited by my current age; in all moments."

"I shatter the glass ceiling of my current age; in all moments."

"I transcend all limitations of age; in all moments."

"I release being limited by my current sexual orientation; in all moments."

"I shatter the glass ceiling of my current sexual orientation; in all moments."

"I transcend all limitations of sexual orientation; in all moments."

"I release being limited by my current size; in all moments."

"I shatter the glass ceiling of my current size; in all moments."

"I transcend all limitations of size; in all moments."

"I release being limited by my current occupation; in all moments."

"I shatter the glass ceiling of my current occupation; in all moments."

"I transcend all limitations of occupation; in all moments."

"I release being limited by my current marital status; in all moments."

"I shatter the glass ceiling of my current marital status; in all moments."

"I transcend all limitations of marital status; in all moments."

"I release being limited by my current family; in all moments."

"I shatter the glass ceiling of my current family; in all moments."

"I transcend all limitations of family; in all moments."

"I release being limited by my current education; in all moments."

"I shatter the glass ceiling of my current education; in all moments."

"I transcend all limitations of education; in all moments."

"I release being limited by my current conditions; in all moments."

"I shatter the glass ceiling of my current conditions; in all moments."

"I transcend all limitations of conditions; in all moments."

"I release being limited by my current beliefs; in all moments."

"I shatter the glass ceiling of my current beliefs; in all moments."

"I transcend all limitations of beliefs; in all moments."

"I release being limited by my current religion; in all moments."

"I shatter the glass ceiling of my current religion; in all moments."

"I transcend all limitations of religion; in all moments."

"I release being limited by my politics; in all moments."

"I shatter the glass ceiling of my politics; in all moments."

"I transcend all limitations of politics; in all moments."

"I release being limited by my current geographical location; in all moments."

"I shatter the glass ceiling of my current geographical location; in all moments."

"I transcend all limitations of geographical location; in all moments."

"I release being limited by my current opinions; in all moments."

"I shatter the glass ceiling of my current opinions; in all moments."

"I transcend all limitations of opinions; in all moments."

"I release being limited by my current habits; in all moments."

"I shatter the glass ceiling of my current habits; in all moments."

"I transcend all limitations of habits; in all moments."

"I release being limited by my current fears; in all moments."

"I shatter the glass ceiling of my current fears; in all moments."

"I transcend all limitations of fears; in all moments."

"I release being limited by my currently being human; in all moments."

"I shatter the glass ceiling of my currently being human; in all moments."

"I transcend all limitations of being human; in all moments."

"I release being limited by all my current limitations; in all moments."

"I shatter the glass ceiling of all my current limitations; in all moments."

"I transcend all limitations of being limited; in all moments."

The more people do these taps, the more we can unwind the unconscious hold of unacceptable conditions. It is a way of doing something productive without sticking our neck out there. It can be very validating to be passively proactive.

38. Technique - Shatter the Glass House

Visualize yourself as just an expansiveness. Nothing defines you except qualities of Joy, Love, Abundance and Wholeness. See this expansive you on a shoreline next to a beautiful ocean.

Wait. Look again. You notice that you are in a glass house that you didn't notice at first. Each wall is constructed of a certain label that is used to define you. On the outer walls are the bigger things that you identify with: your country, ethnicity, religious affiliations. The ceiling could be the label of being a human. There are many interior walls of physical characteristics, likes and dislikes, associations, and talents. There are uncomfortable parts of the house, rooms you don't like that are constructed of insults, self-depreciating descriptions and things you aren't happy with.

See the whole house from afar. See it as dusty and awkward and limiting. See every angle of every label that was ever put on you creating a component of this house. Get prepared to shatter the whole creation!

Taps to shatter glass ceilings:

[Say each statement slowly and consciously out loud. Articulate each word and make a point to pause after each phrase. Say each statement three times while tapping on your head. Then say it a fourth time while tapping on your chest. Take a deep breath after finishing the series.]

"I shatter the glass house; in all moments."

"I crush all the shards of glass to fine powder; in all moments."

See the powder as fine as sand at the fringe of the beautiful ocean. You are now free to be anywhere and everywhere. You can be in the ocean or in the sunshine. You are free!

39. Avoiding Suicide and Coming to Terms with Life

So many of us have been devastated by the life's journey to get to this point. Merely maintaining our own sense of boundaries may be a huge accomplishment. For someone who has been battered and beaten down by the purifying nature of living, having a peaceful existence is the life lesson to absorb. An existence where no one is beating down the door, no one is being pulled out of their home and dragged off to prison, no one is being forced to kill and defend his life is the respite that a weary soul needs to go on.

If people are used to this kind of upheaval in their past life records, having a peaceful existence may be maddening to them. It may be like post-traumatic stress of all their other lifetimes. The psyche of a person may be trying to sort it all out.

I have assisted families where a person has committed suicide. The guilt and shame of believing that it could have been prevented is devastating. Usually, some close friend or family members may want to kill themselves afterwards as well. They think this is of their own doing. What they don't realize is that after someone severs their own lifeline, they immediately regret it. They are instantly pulled into a hellish experience of their own making that they cannot return from. Anything that they were experiencing moments ago, when they were still breathing physical air, has been magnified to such a degree that it feels like child's play in comparison.

Those who have pushed themselves over to the other side immediately regret it and start pulling on those still in the physical realm. The persons still here will process that pulling as physical guilt and will want to end their life, too. That is the emotional anguish that they need to separate themselves from. The person who has crossed over made a choice. They needed that experience to appreciate the value of their life. They will get there. There is no need to join them.

Taps to avoid suicide:

[Say each statement slowly and consciously out loud. Articulate each word and make a point to pause after each phrase. Say each statement three times while tapping on your head. Then say it a fourth time while tapping on your chest. Take a deep breath after finishing the series.]

"I release being beaten down by life; in all moments."

"I release wanting to end my life; in all moments."

"I release the belief that I don't matter; in all moments."

"I remove all the hatred and pain I have collected in life; in all moments."

"I release absorbing the anguish of others; in all moments."

"I release being in sympathy with someone who has taken their own life; in all moments."

"I release the guilt and trauma of taking my own life; in all moments."

"I release being on the outside looking in; in all moments."

"I release wanting to punish those I love; in all moments."

"I release wanting to take my life to exact revenge; in all moments."

"I release devaluing and dismissing life; in all moments."

"I release feeling like an outsider in my own existence; in all moments."

"I release being influenced by someone who has taken their own life; in all moments."

"I release recreating the trauma of living and dying; in all moments."

"I release defining life as death; in all moments."

"I release using pain to feel superior and self-righteous; in all moments."

"I release hating my own life; in all moments."

"I release the belief that my life is a waste; in all moments."

"I release wanting to die; in all moments."

"I recant all vows and agreements between both life and death; in all moments."

"I release befriending the Angel of Death; in all moments."

"I release summoning the Angel of Death; in all moments."

"I release over-analyzing life; in all moments."

"I release being fascinated with death; in all moments."

"I release wanting to kill myself to have an adventure; in all moments."

"I remove all curses between myself and both life and death; in all moments."

"I dissolve all karmic ties between myself and both life and death; in all moments."

"I remove all the pain, burden, limitations, and engrams that both life and death have put on me; in all moments."

"I withdraw all my worry from both living and dying; in all moments."

"I take back all the Joy, Love, Abundance, Freedom, Health, Success, Security, Companionship, Peace, Life, Wholeness, Beauty, Enthusiasm, Contentment, Spirituality and Enlightenment that both life and death have taken from me; in all moments."

"I transcend both life and death; in all moments."

Those who are being seduced to kill themselves must hear from someone who can toggle both sides of existence to learn what it is really about. It is a form of manipulation from psychic energies or a form of self-hypnotism to want to kill oneself. The nightmare never ends for someone who takes his or her own promising life.

If you know someone who is struggling with this issue, please share this exercise. Many great souls struggle with this issue.

People feel unimportant or that they are insignificant. That is the lie. That is caused from lifetimes and lifetimes of having their truth desecrated. They become apathetic and just give up their power. But, if they are really so insignificant, why not speak their truth because who will notice if they are indeed so insignificant? Why not speak one's truth boldly and courageously? It is a way to challenge a core belief that one is ineffective. If nothing else, it gets one out of apathy and immerses them in entertaining themselves with their courage to hold to their convictions. Either they will be more effective than they realize, or they will make their life more interesting by amusing themselves with their choices.

40. Regaining Fluid Energy

I facilitated a remote session for a client who was having trouble with her hip. As soon as I tuned into her, it felt that I could only feel the energy in the top torso of her body. There was no sensation in the bottom half of her. Her energy was not flowing through her body but was cutting off at her waist. No wonder she was in pain.

I saw her past life as a slave in the making of the Pyramids. She had a rope tied around her waist, and the end was attached to a huge slab of stone. A HUGE slab of stone. It got away from them, and with the rope twisted around her, the rope sliced her right in half. It was a grueling demise. She said she felt like she never made any progress in life and never had any fun. She also said that she was bracing to have a horrific death. It seems that she had many of those, and now she was in the habit of expecting them, maybe even manifesting them.

As I led her through the taps, she stopped and was distracted by observing herself. Suddenly, her legs felt very heavy. The energy that was not flowing suddenly filled up her lower torso and she experienced it as heaviness. As we continued to have her do the taps, her whole body felt very heavy. It was the first time in at least this lifetime when her energy was so complete. Here are the taps I led her through.

Taps to regain fluid energy:

[Say each statement slowly and consciously out loud. Articulate each word and make a point to pause after each phrase. Say each statement three times while tapping on your head. Then say it a fourth time while tapping on your chest. Take a deep breath after finishing the series.]

"I release expecting to have a horrific death; in all moments."

"I release the belief that dying is a horrific experience; in all moments."

"I release defining dying as horrific; in all moments."

"I release the fear of dying; in all moments."

"I release being enslaved to a horrific death; in all moments."

"I release habitually having a horrific death; in all moments."

"I sever all strings and cords between myself and a horrific death; in all moments."

"I withdraw all energy from having a horrific death; in all moments."

"I shift my definition of dying to an effortless transition; in all moments."

"I define dying as awakening; in all moments."

"I accept the natural transition from being alive to awakening; in all moments."

"I release the trauma of being a slave; in all moments."

"I recant all vows and agreements with being a slave; in all moments."

"I dissolve all karmic ties between myself and being a slave; in all moments."

"I remove all the pain, burden, limitations and engrams that being a slave has put on me; in all moments."

"I release enslaving others; in all moments."

"I remove all the pain, burden, limitations and engrams that I have put on all others due to slavery; in all moments."

"I take back all the Joy, Love, Abundance, Freedom, Life, and Wholeness that slavery has taken from me; in all moments."

"I give back all the Joy, Love, Abundance, Freedom, Life, and Wholeness that I have taken from all others due to slavery; in all moments."

"I withdraw all my energy from slavery; in all moments."

"I release resonating with slavery; in all moments."

"I release emanating with slavery; in all moments."

"I remove all slavery from my sound frequency; in all moments."

"I remove all slavery from my light body; in all moments."

"I shift my paradigm from slavery to Joy, Love, Abundance, Freedom, Life, and Wholeness; in all moments."

"I transcend slavery; in all moments."

"I am centered and empowered in Joy, Love, Abundance, Freedom, Life, and Wholeness; in all moments."

41. A Healer's Healing - Contempt for the Lords of Karma

I facilitated a session with a very accomplished healer. I have incredible respect for her. She has helped so many at such a deep level, and yet she still has personal issues to deal with. When we started speaking, she got frustrated because I don't listen to issues. When I stopped her from explaining something to me, she said that she felt like she was on the witness stand and being prevented from defending herself.

Immediately, I saw an image of her between lifetimes. She was standing before the Lords of Karma. The Lords of Karma are energetic beings that serve by deciding if souls need to go back to earth, and if so, what the conditions of that lifetime will be. In this image, they were deciding to send her back. She was very frustrated and angry. There was one small issue that she was not understanding, so she had to incarnate because of it. When they questioned her, her energy stirred, and they encountered that it was a deeper issue than it first appeared. She thought she had been cleared to transcend, but upon closer scrutiny, there was an issue that needed to be cleared in another incarnation.

She was furious at the Lords of Karma, and it was playing out on earth. I led her through some taps that had to do with defying authority. Suddenly the great truth came through. It was the one lesson that she was missing. The point that made incarnating again necessary.

Earth is a schoolyard for people to learn about power and how not to abuse it. The way to learn this lesson is by being in positions of power. She harbored so much resentment at people who were abusing their authority, but they were doing the best they could. They were learning their lessons. And by being in the place that they needed to learn their lessons, they were living their sacred purpose. She was so respectful of people living their sacred purpose except if they were in a position of authority. There was a piece missing in her awareness. So by her interfering with those who abused power, she was interfering with their sacred purpose. She was carrying the burden in her body of all those that she interfered with as they served their sacred purpose in positions of authority.

What she finally got to realize was that all the times she was infuriated with people in authority, she was actually angry at the Lords of Karma for sending her back. Her session was an epiphany! This was the life's lesson. All the understanding that she learned from helping others understand their issues was simply to help her figure out the one lesson she had left to learn. Others were serving as they were capable, and her real anger with those in authority was really anger at the Lords of Karma.

She also had an issue with swearing in this lifetime. She never wielded energy through swearing, but it was something she did quite often. What she didn't realize was that whenever she swore, she was cursing the Lords of Karma. Her energy was braced in that moment of learning that she had to re-enter earth. She was stuck in the trauma of having to go back.

Taps to release feeling punished in life:

[Say each statement slowly and consciously out loud. Articulate each word and make a point to pause after each phrase. Say each statement three times while tapping on your head. Then say it a fourth time while tapping on your chest. Take a deep breath after finishing the series.]

"I release the frustration of being sent back; in all moments."

"I release defining life as a prison sentence; in all moments."

"I release hating the Lords of Karma; in all moments."

"I release arguing with the Lords of Karma; in all moments."

"I release feeling superior to the Lords of Karma; in all moments."

"I release being stuck in a perpetual state of being killed; in all moments."

"I recant all vows and agreements between myself and the Lords of Karma; in all moments."

"I remove all curses between myself and the Lords of Karma; in all moments."

"I sever all strings and cords between myself and the Lords and Karma; in all moments."

"I dissolve all karmic ties between myself and the Lords of Karma; in all moments."

"I remove all the pain, burden, limitations, and engrams that the Lords of Karma have put on me; in all moments."

"I take back all the Joy, Love, Abundance, Freedom, Health, Success, Security, Companionship, Creativity, Peace, Life, Wholeness, Beauty, Enthusiasm, Contentment, Spirituality, Enlightenment, and Dance that the Lords of Karma have taken from me; in all moments."

"I transcend the Lords of Karma; in all moments."

"I release being stuck in that moment of being sent back; in all moments."

"I recant all vows and agreements between myself and being sent back; in all moments."

"I remove all curses between myself and being sent back; in and between all moments"

"I sever all strings and cords between myself and being sent back; in all moments."

"I dissolve all karmic ties between myself and being sent back; in all moments."

"I remove all the pain, burden, limitations, and engrams that being sent back has put on me; in all moments."

"I take back all the Joy, Love, Abundance, Freedom, Health, Success, Security, Companionship, Creativity, Peace, Life, Wholeness, Beauty, Enthusiasm, Contentment, Spirituality, Enlightenment, and Dance that being sent back has taken from me; in all moments."

"I release resonating with being sent back; in all moments."

"I release emanating with being sent back; in all moments."

"I remove all of "being sent back" from my sound frequency; in all moments."

"I remove all of "being sent back" from my light body; in all moments."

"I shift my paradigm from being sent back to Joy, Love, Abundance, Freedom, Health, Success, Security, Companionship, Creativity, Peace, Life, Wholeness, Beauty, Enthusiasm, Contentment, Spirituality, Enlightenment; in all moments."

"I transcend being sent back; in all moments."

"I infuse Namaste into my sound frequency in all moments."

"I imbue Namaste into my light body; in all moments."

"I am centered and empowered in Namaste; in all moments."

"I am the personification of Namaste; all moments."

42. Clearing the Karmic Slate

What is worse: Killing someone with little remorse or being in a position to stop someone who is killing others and doing nothing about it? How about being forced to kill someone and feeling bad, or choosing to kill someone with absolute indifference? Is it less of a moral issue to kill someone who is inferior, or is that just a form of not taking responsibility? Are humans a more important life form than animals? Are humans more important than nature? Is it okay to kill as long as there is a reason, like food or safety? What if one does not understand the vantage point of those they have killed or are indifferent?

This is the dilemma that has been played out in all eras throughout history. The moral issue of taking life is so subjective that one wonders if the karmic consequences are subjective as well. Sometimes, someone who was not directly responsible for the death of others carries more of a guilty burden than those who carried out the kill. How does that register in guilt and heaviness? How does each get rectified?

Here are some taps that I led a client through in a private session. She wasn't privy to the images that I had to endure in releasing the following imbalances from her energy field. She knew it was a devastating shift from my horrific wailing after she performed taps. I was crying her anguish. In doing this technique, it is like energetically going back to the incidents that caused so much anguish and guilt, and releasing the imbalance. It is also an energetic way to give back what was taken from others unjustly. We cannot fully heal until we rectify our actions, and these taps are the way to do just that. If there is a lot of sadness released in doing these, there is also a lot of relief in releasing the sadness that we have caused. Knowing that we are giving back what we have taken from the innocent helps in pushing past the resistance. The client had a hard time doing these taps, but when I explained that it would free those she has wronged, she got through them.

Taps to clear the karmic slate:

[Say each statement slowly and consciously out loud. Articulate each word and make a point to pause after each phrase. Say each statement three times while tapping on your head. Then say it a fourth time while tapping on your chest. Take a deep breath after finishing the series.]

"I recant all vows and agreements between myself and all those I have caused to be killed; in all moments."

"I remove all curses between myself and all those I have caused to be killed; in all moments."

"I remove all the guilt and anguish that I have been carrying for all those I have caused to be killed; in all moments."

"I dissolve all karmic ties between myself and all those I have caused to be killed; in all moments."

"I remove all the pain, burden, limitations, and engrams that I have put on all those I have caused to be killed; in all moments."

"I remove all the pain, burden, limitations, and engrams from myself due to all those I have caused to be killed; in all moments."

"I give back all that I have taken or caused to be taken from all those I have caused to be killed; in all moments."

"I take back all the Joy, Love, Abundance, Freedom, Health, Success, Security, Companionship, Creativity, Peace, Life, Wholeness, Beauty, Enthusiasm and Contentment that was taken from me due to all those I have caused to be killed; in all moments."

"I remove all those I have caused to be killed from my sound frequency; in all moments."

"I remove all those I have caused to be killed from my light body; in all moments."

"I release resonating with the guilt of all those I have caused to be killed; in all moments."

"I release emanating with the guilt of all those I have caused to be killed; in all moments."

"I transcend all transgressions between myself and all those I have caused to be killed; in all moments."

"I shift my paradigm from all those I have caused to be killed to Joy, Love, Abundance, Freedom, Health, Success, Security, Companionship, Creativity, Peace, Life, Wholeness, Beauty, Enthusiasm and Contentment; in all moments."

"I am centered, imbued, and empowered in Divine Love; in all moments."

43. Alleviating Dis-ease on a Cellular Level

I facilitated a private remote session with an incredible BodyTalk practitioner. The energy between us was so intense that the phone signals were knocked out. So we continued through instant messaging. Since she is all about service, the taps that I was given to walk her through were all about service as well. She has graciously agreed to allow me to share them. They may be very helpful to empaths and sensitive people who feel the intensity of the world in their various bodies. Carrying issues in the body may be a universal issue. We may be helping all of humanity by freeing ourselves.

After we got through the taps, the phone connection cleared up and we could freely speak to each other again.

Taps to bring ease on a cellular level:

[Say each statement slowly and consciously out loud. Articulate each word and make a point to pause after each phrase. Say each statement three times while tapping on your head. Then say it a fourth time while tapping on your chest. Take a deep breath after finishing the series.]

"I release playing out the story in all my cells in the microcosm and macrocosm; in all moments."

"I release the fear of being without the story in the microcosm and macrocosm; in all moments."

"I untangle all lines of communication in the microcosm and macrocosm; in all moments."

"I release being rerouted; in the microcosm and macrocosm; in all moments."

"I release the primal anger and resentment in the microcosm and macrocosm; in all moments."

"I release all resistance to transcendence in the microcosm and macrocosm; in all moments."

"I release holding humanity back on a cellular level in the microcosm and macrocosm; in all moments."

"I dissolve all duality and hidden agendas on a cellular level in the microcosm and macrocosm; in all moments."

"I converge all paths to one that leads directly to higher purpose even on a cellular level in the microcosm and macrocosm; in all moments."

"I make space in this world and this reality for enlightenment on a cellular level in the microcosm and macrocosm; in all moments."

"I remove all blockages to enlightenment on a cellular level in the microcosm and macrocosm; in all moments."

"I stretch my capacity and propensity to induce enlightenment in this reality and all dual realities in the microcosm and macrocosm; in all moments."

"I dissipate all illusion with the brilliance of Divine Love on the cellular level in the microcosm and macrocosm; in all moments."

"I converge all realities to the brilliant path of purity and higher intention on a cellular level in the micro and macro in the microcosm and macrocosm; in all moments."

"I accept and embrace the brilliance and purity of higher purpose on a cellular level in micro and macro in the microcosm and macrocosm; in all moments."

"I am centered and empowered in the brilliancy of a higher purpose in the microcosm and macrocosm; in all moments."

"I emanate waves of higher purpose through my beingness even on a cellular level in the microcosm and macrocosm; in all moments."

"I connect to the infinite Ocean of Love, Light, Music, and Healing on a cellular level in the microcosm and macrocosm; in all moments."

"I release all silt on a cellular level in the microcosm and macrocosm; in all moments."

"I move fluidly and effortlessly through the infinite Ocean of Love, Light, Music, and Healing on a cellular level in the microcosm and macrocosm; in all moments."

"I AM the whole of the infinite Ocean of Love, Light, Music, and Healing on a cellular level in the microcosm and macrocosm; in all moments."

"I move out the pain of humanity like an incredible fluid wave on a cellular level in the microcosm and macrocosm; in all moments."

"I AM the wind, wave, shore, and sea on a cellular level in the microcosm and macrocosm; in all moments."

"I AM omniscient, omnipresent, and omnipotent on a cellular level in the microcosm and macrocosm; in all moments."

"I grace all of humanity with the intention of knowing them as omniscient, omnipresent, and omnipotent on a cellular level in the microcosm and macrocosm; in all moments."

"I encourage all humanity to stretch their capacity to know themselves as omniscient, omnipresent, and omnipotent on a cellular level in the microcosm and macrocosm; in all moments."

"I remove all blockages to all humanity knowing themselves as omniscient, omnipresent, and omnipotent on a cellular level in the microcosm and macrocosm; in all moments."

"I remove all blockages to all humanity knowing themselves as Universal Joy, Love Abundance, Freedom, Health, Success, Security, Companionship, Creativity, Peace, Life, Wholeness, Beauty, Enthusiasm, Confidence, Spirituality, and Enlightenment on a cellular level in the microcosm and macrocosm; in all moments."

"I encourage all humanity to stretch their capacity to know themselves as Universal Joy, Love Abundance, Freedom, Health, Success, Security, Companionship, Creativity, Peace, Life, Wholeness, Beauty, Enthusiasm, Confidence, Spirituality, and Enlightenment on a cellular level in the microcosm and macrocosm; in all moments."

"I embrace all life on a cellular level in the microcosm and macrocosm as Universal Joy, Love Abundance, Freedom, Health, Success, Security, Companionship, Creativity, Peace, Life, Wholeness, Beauty, Enthusiasm, Confidence, Spirituality, and Enlightenment on a cellular level in the microcosm and macrocosm; in all moments."

"I flush out the back wash in the gray matter in the spinal cord with Universal Joy, Love Abundance, Freedom, Health, Success, Security, Companionship, Creativity, Peace, Life, Wholeness, Beauty, Enthusiasm, Confidence, Spirituality, and Enlightenment on a cellular level in the microcosm and macrocosm; in all moments."

"I flush out all residual pocket of resistance that are holed up in the fossa on a cellular level in the microcosm and macrocosm; in all moments."

"I am centered and empowered in my free will on a cellular level in the microcosm and macrocosm; in all moments."

"I shift my paradigm from the third dimension to the fifth dimension; in the microcosm and macrocosm; in all moments."

44. Releasing Dark Energies

I never know what I am going to run into when I take on a client. I don't allow them to tell me anything, and I read their energy. I just finished a session with a client who was wonderfully pleased with it. She was referred to me by someone else who felt that I could help her.

Immediately, I picked up core issues of dark energy that were inhibiting her. From her perspective, she called it demonic possession. I immediately deflated the drama of it. Such energies feed on hate and fear. So I calmly told her that we would address the issues. Immediately, she was relieved and surprised at herself for not being more afraid. Since my work is all done in absolute love, there is no space for fear or anything else. I just told her that we would call whatever she was dealing with dark energies and give it no more identity than that.

She was from South America. People from other countries take influences more seriously than many in America. When we do the taps to remove curses and karmic ties, they know these things as literal releases. Some who work with me think they are figurative. She was assured that they are NOT. When I was working with her, it occurred to me that the taps would be more effective if she did them in Spanish. She did indeed feel a deeper shift as she translated them into Spanish.

She felt free and light as she did these taps. She was surprised at lightness, warmth, and tingling in her body. Energetically she was repeating two things to me: how surprised she was about how easy it was, and she just kept saying energetically repeating, "It's over, it's over."

The taps we did were done from a place of incredible love. We did not send hate or fear to anything. Love and respect for all life is the vantage point to take in doing these taps. There is no need for fear when one is so incredibly filled with Divine Love and reverence and compassion for all.

Taps to release dark energies:

[Say each statement slowly and consciously out loud. Articulate each word and make a point to pause after each phrase. Say each statement three times while tapping on your head. Then say it a fourth time while tapping on your chest. Take a deep breath after finishing the series.]

"I release being afraid; in all moments."

"I am loved, protected, and supported; in all moments."

"I rescind all invitations to all dark energies; in all moments."

"I shut all doors to all dark energies; in all moments."

"I recant all vows and agreements between myself and all dark energies; in all moments."

"I remove all curses between myself and all dark energies; in all moments."

"I dissolve all karmic ties between myself and all dark energies; in all moments."

"I remove all the fear, pain, burden, limitations, and engrams that all dark energies have put on me; in all moments."

"I take back all the Joy, Love, Abundance, Freedom, Health, Success, Security, Companionship, Creativity, Peace, Life, Wholeness, Beauty, Enthusiasm, Contentment, Music, Light, Confidence, Spirituality, and Enlightenment that all dark forces have taken from me; in all moments."

"I release resonating with all dark energies; in all moments."

"I release emanating with all dark energies; in all moments."

"I remove all dark energies from my sound frequency; in all moments."

"I remove all dark energies from my light body; in all moments."

"I shift my paradigm from all dark energies to Joy, Love, Abundance, Freedom, Health, Success, Security, Companionship, Creativity, Peace, Life, Wholeness, Beauty, Enthusiasm, Contentment, Music, Light, Confidence, Spirituality, and Enlightenment; in all moments."

"I transcend all dark energies; in all moments."

"I am centered and empowered in Divine Love; in all moments."

"I transform all dark to Light; in all moments."

Know that if you have found yourself to these taps that you are protected in love and light in doing them, and you are able to free yourself and others. You are loved and supported.

45. Releasing the "Nice" Syndrome

A new client came to me for her first session. Nothing came through for me in regard to helping her except one thing that was getting in the way. She was nice. It was coating all of her sound frequency to the point that it was irritating to hear her speak. Her energy was just nice.

When I asked her about it, she said that she hates it. It was such a part of her. It was so ingrained that I spoke directly to her energy and explained that it was not fooling me. I saw through the facade. I had her do a few ruthless taps to try and crack though and crumble the coating of nice that was keeping her stuck. She enjoyed them. I am not certain how I succeeded because usually I can tell by people's reactions that there is a shift. But with her, she just gave me more "nice."

I did get a glimpse of a recent past life where she was kept by three men and was repeatedly beaten, raped and made to serve them. She got pregnant and didn't know which one was the father and ended up drowning the baby in a mental fog. The memories were so devastating that she was using the nice as a tool for survival. I also saw a quick glimpse of many lifetimes at war. She was using nice for denial. She would just deny everything by being nice. But it had become a prison.

Taps to release the need to be nice:

[Say each statement slowly and consciously out loud. Articulate each word and make a point to pause after each phrase. Say each statement three times while tapping on your head. Then say it a fourth time while tapping on your chest. Take a deep breath after finishing the series.]

"I release being galvanized in nice; in all moments."

"I release using being nice as a form of denial; in all moments."

"I release the trauma that I am forgetting by being nice; in all moments."

"I release wasting all my energy being nice; in all moments."

"I release manipulating others by being nice; in all moments."

"I release the belief that nice is the highest action; in all moments."

"I release being programmed to be nice; in all moments."

"I release all nice programming and engrams; in all moments."

"I release being trapped in being nice; in all moments."

"I release defining nice as being holy; in all moments."

"I release using nice to be superior; in all moments."

"I release being enslaved to being nice; in all moments."

"I transcend being nice; in all moments."

"I shift my paradigm from nice to authentic; in all moments."

"I remove all nice from my sound frequency; in all moments."

"I remove all nice from my light body; in all moments."

"I release resonating with being nice; in all moments."

"I release emanating with being nice; in all moments."

"I shatter the glass ceiling of being nice; in all moments."

"I am centered and empowered in divine love; in all moments."

We think of being nice as the highest good. But it can be a prison of its own. A lot of damage can be done to ourselves and to others by the compulsion to be nice. Anything that is done in excess is a deviation from personal freedom.

46. Empowerment

Don't allow people to shove their reality onto you. Powerless people will try to tell you that this will happen if you don't do that. They are so ineffective in their own life that they want to feel empowered by helping you feel ineffective, too. Don't allow it!

Disengage them in whatever means you have to. Their prophecies are like curses on your life. Give yourself permission to disengage.

A curse is merely an unfavorable outcome directed at you with passion or conviction. Stop allowing them. Be an advocate for yourself.

Taps to remove curses:

[Say each statement slowly and consciously out loud. Articulate each word and make a point to pause after each phrase. Say each statement three times while tapping on your head. Then say it a fourth time while tapping on your chest. Take a deep breath after finishing the series.]

> "I remove all curses that have been put on me; in all moments."

> "I remove all curses that have been put on my family; in all moments."

> "I remove all curses that have been put on my community; in all moments."

> "I remove all curses that have been put on my country; in all moments."

> "I remove all curses that have been put on my people; in all moments."

"I remove all curses that have been put on the world; in all moments."

"I remove all curses that I have put on all others; in all moments."

47. Finish Those Projects!

People who don't finish what they start are people who might have died too soon in a past life. They were having a perfectly wonderful life, but then they died or were killed before they were ready. It created a schism in their energy that may surface when they are in the midst of a perfectly good project. They may sabotage the project because its completion, in some twisted way, may be associated with their death.

The more that someone does not finish a project, the more they reinforce the schism. If this resonates, try these taps.

Taps to help finish those projects:

[Say each statement slowly and consciously out loud. Articulate each word and make a point to pause after each phrase. Say each statement three times while tapping on your head. Then say it a fourth time while tapping on your chest. Take a deep breath after finishing the series.]

"I release associating the completion of a project with death; in all moments."

"I release the pain and trauma of dying too soon; in all moments."

"I release the fear of dying too soon; in all moments."

"I release all resistance to completing projects; in all moments."

"I make space in this world to complete all projects; in all moments."

"I remove all blockages to completing all projects; in all moments."

"I stretch my capacity to complete all projects; in all moments."

"I shift my paradigm from dying too soon to completing all projects; in all moments."

"I am centered and empowered in finishing all projects and living a long healthy life; in all moments."

48. Removing the Snowball Effect

In all your lifetimes on earth, there was a first time that you experienced something unpleasant that made it snowball into the present conditions that you now deal with. This is called the initial cause or first cause. Since we work with all our lifetimes at once, the way to remedy a reoccurring unwanted theme is to eliminate the first cause, or the first time it ever happened in all the lifetimes of that person.

It is like the events are a line of dominoes, and we remove that first domino that knocks down all the other dominoes in regard to a particular issue. These taps are profound. They are a gift to whomever is receptive enough to do them.

Taps to remove the snowball effect:

[Say each statement slowly and consciously out loud. Articulate each word and make a point to pause after each phrase. Say each statement three times while tapping on your head. Then say it a fourth time while tapping on your chest. Take a deep breath after finishing the series.]

"I eliminate the first cause in regard to sadness; in all moments."

"I eliminate the first cause in regard to fear; in all moments."

"I eliminate the first cause in regard to lack; in all moments."

"I eliminate the first cause in regard to enslavement; in all moments."

"I eliminate the first cause in regard to dis-ease; in all moments."

"I eliminate the first cause in regard to failure; in all moments."

"I eliminate the first cause in regard to insecurity; in all moments."

"I eliminate the first cause in regard to loneliness; in all moments."

"I eliminate the first cause in regard to war; in all moments."

"I eliminate the first cause in regard to death; in all moments."

"I eliminate the first cause in regard to fragmentation; in all moments."

"I eliminate the first cause in regard to ugliness; in all moments."

"I eliminate the first cause in regard to apathy; in all moments."

"I eliminate the first cause in regard to discontent; in all moments."

"I eliminate the first cause in regard to ignorance; in all moments."

"I eliminate the first cause in regard to vulnerability; in all moments."

"I eliminate the first cause in regard to weakness; in all moments."

"I eliminate the first cause in regard to being conditioned or programmed; in all moments."

49. Beings of Light

We are all beings of light. Then why do we not all emanate goodness and inspiration? In the physical form, we have all gone through experiences that create filters in our light body. They can make some people feel really heavy to be around and make most of us forget our natural state.

It is difficult to change this using the coarse workings of the mind because the mind is the mechanism that installed the filters in the first place. That is why it is so difficult to figure out our own spiritual needs. Using the mind to free ourselves is like trying to clean a streaked window using a dirty rag.

Here are some taps to remove the limiting filters and let in the pure rays of our ultimate light body emanate through even to the physical realms.

Taps to remove imperfections from one's light:

[Say each statement slowly and consciously out loud. Articulate each word and make a point to pause after each phrase. Say each statement three times while tapping on your head. Then say it a fourth time while tapping on your chest. Take a deep breath after finishing the series.]

"I remove all sadness from my Light Body; in all moments."

"I release emanating with sadness; in all moments."

"I infuse Joy into my Light Body; in all moments."

"I emanate with Joy; in all moments."

"I remove all hate and fear from my Light Body; in all moments."

Enlightenment Unveiled

"I release emanating with hate and fear; in all moments."

"I infuse Divine Love into my Light Body; in all moments."

"I emanate with Divine Love; in all moments."

"I remove all poverty from my Light Body; in all moments."

"I release emanating with poverty; in all moments."

"I infuse Abundance into my Light Body; in all moments."

"I emanate with Abundance; in all moments."

"I remove all slavery and imprisonment from my Light Body; in all moments."

"I release emanating with slavery and imprisonment; in all moments."

"I infuse Freedom into my Light body; in all moments."

"I emanate with Freedom; in all moments."

"I remove all sickness and dis-ease from my Light Body; in all moments."

"I release emanating with sickness and dis-ease; in all moments."

"I infuse Health into my Light Body; in all moments."

"I emanate with Health; in all moments."

"I remove all failure from my Light Body; in all moments."

"I release emanating with failure; in all moments."

"I infuse Success into my Light Body; in all moments."

"I emanate with Success; in all moments."

"I remove all insecurity from my Light Body; in all moments."

"I release emanating with insecurity; in all moments."

"I infuse Confidence and Security into my Light Body; in all moments."

"I emanate with Confidence and Security; in all moments."

"I remove all loneliness and abandonment from my Light Body; in all moments."

"I release emanating with loneliness and abandonment; in all moments."

"I infuse Companionship into my Light Body; in all moments."

"I emanate with Companionship; in all moments."

"I remove all war and chaos from my Light Body; in all moments."

"I release emanating with war and chaos; in all moments."

"I infuse Peace into my Light Body; in all moments."

"I emanate with Peace; in all moments."

"I remove all death and decay from my Light Body; in all moments."

"I release emanating with death and decay; in all moments."

"I infuse Life into my Light Body; in all moments."

"I emanate with Life; in all moments."

"I remove all fragmentation from my Light Body; in all moments."

"I release emanating with fragmentation; in all moments."

"I infuse Wholeness into my Light Body; in all moments."

"I emanate with Wholeness; in all moments."

"I remove all guilt and intentional programming from my Light Body; in all moments."

"I release emanating with guilt; in all moments."

"I am centered and empowered in Joy, Love, Abundance, Freedom, Health, Success, Security, Companionship, Peace, Life and Wholeness; in all moments."

"I am a pure beacon of Joy, Love, Abundance, Freedom, Health, Success, Security, Companionship, Peace, Life and Wholeness; in all moments."

The more shifts are made without the discernment of the mind, the more drastic and absolute the changes can become.

50. The Need to Be Liked

Did you ever notice that we are happy when people like us? Or that we like people better if they agree with us? It is all about that sense of belonging. In the past, we felt safe if we were with those who were of the same mindset. These days, there are so many more variables involved. Does it really matter if people agree with us? Can't we like them anyway?

In general, we think we can like everybody. But how many times have we heard something about someone that didn't resonate with our moral belief system, and we changed our opinion of them slightly? How many times have we held back from sharing our beliefs because we knew the listening audience felt differently?

Taps to release the need to be liked:

[Say each statement slowly and consciously out loud. Articulate each word and make a point to pause after each phrase. Say each statement three times while tapping on your head. Then say it a fourth time while tapping on your chest. Take a deep breath after finishing the series.]

> **"I release being wishy-washy; in all moments."**
>
> **"I release the need to be liked; in all moments."**
>
> **"I release the fear of being disliked; in all moments."**
>
> **"I release compromising my truth to be liked; in all moments."**
>
> **"I release abandoning my truth; in all moments."**
>
> **"I release living a lie; in all moments."**
>
> **"I release caring what people think about me; in all moments."**

"I release judging others; in all moments."

"I release trading my integrity for popularity; in all moments."

"I release giving my power to the opinions of others; in all moments."

"I draw upon and am empowered by my own truth; in all moments."

"I am centered and secure in my own truth; in all moments."

Once people get over the habit of needing to be liked, they can truly experience what it feels like to be appreciated for who they really are.

51. The Benefits of Being an Individual

The issue isn't that we aren't powerful. The issue is that we don't understand the incredible potential energy that we have when we connect the wires between our heart and mind. When enough of us figure out the blueprint, we will all be as effective as Gandhi, as insightful as Einstein, as loving as Mother Theresa and as motivating as Mandela.

We as individuals are all world changers. We are made to be that. But when we throw our energy into a group and allow that group to manage our sails, we lose the breeze. We are only as great as the greatest member of our group, and we are hindered by the least of them. Why do you think so many of us have gotten beaten down to such an extent? Why not decide that humanity itself is the only thing we give our lifeblood to. We can support all the groups we want, but from the vantage point of our own individuality. It is not about dropping out; it is about plugging more in.

This means thinking for ourselves, seeing the hidden agenda in every statement, feeling the energy pull of every intention, and giving only to those whose intentions truly benefit humanity. Once one pulls oneself free of the fibers of others' agendas, it is clearer to see the subtle form of control to which they have given their power. One can break the spell. That is the importance of claiming one's individuality.

Taps to be an individual:

[Say each statement slowly and consciously out loud. Articulate each word and make a point to pause after each phrase. Say each statement three times while tapping on your head. Then say it a fourth time while tapping on your chest. Take a deep breath after finishing the series.]

"I release the primal fear of being separated from the herd; in all moments."

"I release hiding in groups for security; in all moments."

"I release being enslaved to group dynamics; in all moments."

"I release being dependent on groups; in all moments."

"I release losing my identity in groups; in all moments."

"I shatter the glass ceiling of all groups; in all moments."

"I recant all vows and agreements between myself and all groups; in all moments."

"I remove all curses between myself and all groups; in all moments."

"I dissolve all karmic ties between myself and all groups; in all moments."

"I sever all strings and cords between myself and all groups; in all moments."

"I remove all the pain, burden, limitations, and engrams that all groups have put on me; in all moments."

"I remove all the pain, burden, limitations, and engrams that I have put on all others for the sake of a group; in all moments."

"I take back all the Joy, Love, Abundance, Freedom, Health, Success, Security, Companionship, Peace, Life, Wholeness, Beauty, Enthusiasm, Confidence and Enlightenment that all groups have taken from me; in all moments."

"I withdraw all my energy from all groups; in all moments."

"I release resonating with all groups; in all moments."

"I release emanating with all groups; in all moments."

"I remove all groups from my sound frequency; in all moments."

"I remove all groups from my light body; in all moments."

I shift my paradigm from all groups to Joy, Love, Abundance, Freedom, Health, Success, Security, Companionship, Peace, Life, Wholeness, Beauty, Enthusiasm, Confidence and Enlightenment; in all moments."

"I transcend all groups; in all moments."

"I am centered and empowered in the divinity of my own individuality; in all moments."

"I make space in this world for the realization of the empowerment of my own individuality; in all moments."

"I remove all blockages to the realization of the empowerment of my own individuality; in all moments."

"I stretch my capacity to manifest and accept the empowerment of my own individuality; in all moments."

"I am centered and empowered in Divine Love; in all moments."

Think about it, have you ever really been honored to your full potential in any group? Have you ever soared to your greatest heights? Have the groups on earth honored all their members? Have they disparaged non-members? The only group that is going to honor all life is the one where all are included equally. That is the group of humanity, where all are important.

52. Releasing Self-Loathing

A client messaged me about her foster dog. It almost bit the vet. She had already had a different foster dog that bit others, so she was frustrated. The thought crossed her mind for an instant about putting him down. This horrified her. She was inquiring if a session would help the situation. Was she attracting defensive dogs?

I had a sense of what the issue was. I asked her if she had had any plastic surgery. She said yes. She had implants. The two issues were related, so I agreed to do a session with her. When someone has elective surgery, the body sometimes feels defensive. Here it is doing everything to be the best body, yet it is not good enough. The defensive dog was a reflection of her issues. The connections may seem subtle at first, but the clues were there.

In the session, there were deep issues about self-loathing. It was really surprising because this woman is so intelligent, accomplished, and aware. I asked her about the elective surgery. She said she had implants but wanted them removed. They looked good; they weren't uncomfortable, but they made her uneasy. It was not the implants that made her uneasy but the emotional issues that were stored at the site of the implants that was causing the discomfort.

We started to work on the issues of self-loathing and then all of the sudden she felt Jewish to me. It was very funny because she was not Jewish in the present life, and energetically she didn't feel like Jewish energy. The scenario opened up of why she had to excel. Her past life in a Nazi death camp opened up to me. Women had to slip out of their dresses to be examined by a doctor to see if they were healthy enough to live. The sick ones were put to death. In that life, she actually had to prove herself worthy to survive. It was what drove her to excel in this lifetime and caused her to be super self-critical.

She was the one who recognized that the past life in a death camp was why she was compelled to rescue dogs. She was, on some level, trying to save herself. When the dog was being examined by the vet, it triggered the trauma of her being scrutinized by the doctor as to whether she should live or die. The defensiveness she saw in the dogs was a reflection of her own issues that were too unbearable to access.

As we released some of the issues, we both felt the energy around her upper ribs relax. It also came to my attention that the implants surgeon had a certain responsibility not to put his issues into his patients. It is similar to how a cook needs to prepare food with love. She was carrying a bit of the surgeon's issues in her breast area. We released that as well.

Taps to release self-loathing:

[Say each statement slowly and consciously out loud. Articulate each word and make a point to pause after each phrase. Say each statement three times while tapping on your head. Then say it a fourth time while tapping on your chest. Take a deep breath after finishing the series.]

"I release hating myself; in all moments."

"I release hating those who love me; in all moments."

"I release finding fault with those who love me; in all moments."

"I release treating myself as the enemy; in all moments."

"I release being my own enemy; in all moments."

"I release defiling myself; in all moments."

"I release attacking myself; in all moments."

"I release hiring someone to attack me; in all moments."

"I release rejecting my body; in all moments."

"I release hating my implants; in all moments."

"I release storing self-loathing in my body; in all moments."

"I release rejecting a part of myself; in all moments."

"I release hating my own beauty; in all moments."

"I release criticizing myself; in all moments."

"I release using self-criticism to show superiority; in all moments'

"I recant all vows and agreements between myself and self-loathing; in all moments."

"I remove all curses I have put on myself; in all moments."

"I dissolve all karmic ties between myself and self-loathing; in all moments."

"I remove all the pain, burden, limitations, and engrams that self-loathing has put on me; in all moments."

"I take back all the Joy, Love, Abundance, Freedom, Health, Success, Security, Companionship, Peace, Life, Wholeness, Beauty, Enthusiasm, and Contentment that self-loathing has taken from me; in all moments."

"I transcend self-loathing; in all moments."

"I shift my paradigm from self-loathing to Unconditional Self-love; in all moments."

"I am centered and empowered in Divine Self-love; in all moments."

The dogs were such a gift. They were, in a way, helping her look at what was too unbearable to see. The difficulty they were giving her was actually a gift. So many of our issues are gifts. The more we can recognize them, the more freedom we will have.

53. Give a Gift to Humanity

The movie *The Ten Commandments* is on now. The Pharoah just cursed the slaves as they set out upon the desert. He cursed them to suffer with such vengeance as he mourned the death of his only son. A curse is an intention that is fueled with passion and sealed with a belief. He cursed them forever.

People have suffered all over the world in every age. Pettiness, selfishness, and helplessness have forced the masses to suffer and to give up their power age upon age. It is disturbing that the Jewish people in the Ukraine have recently been ordered to register with the government. It does not matter that maybe it was a prank; the horrific history that this event elicits can not be revisited. The simple thought of the suffering that happened to the Jewish people brings physical pain to my body, and I am certain to many other sensitives. Maybe many others do not feel the intensity of the situation as physical pain the way some do, but the pain is still pressing upon us all.

Some may try to deny what happens in the world as a coping mechanism. It is understandable. It is actually better to withdraw all one's energy from a situation rather than fuel the flame. But people can withdraw themselves completely and consciously rather than unconsciously. By reclaiming their personal power, the grip that power has on all of humanity loosens. These taps are my humble attempt to do something proactive to assist the advancement of love in the world and to relinquish the heavy hand of control that has habitually gripped the world.

It is irrelevant which group is being persecuted, judged, slaughtered, or even eliminated. It is a crime against us all. The more we can release compartmentalizing people as "them or us," the more we can advance the cause of enlightenment on the planet. We are not helpless. It is a blessing that so many of us now realize that we are sacred vessels to advance Divine Love into the world. May these taps help.

The Jewish holiday of Passover, which celebrates the Exodus from Egypt depicted in the movie, falls around the same time as the Christian holiday of Easter. It is a special time for many. Please take a few minutes to do these taps. May it bring a little more reverence into your day and strengthen us all a little bit more in Divine Love.

Taps to release crimes against humanity:

[Say each statement slowly and consciously out loud. Articulate each word and make a point to pause after each phrase. Say each statement three times while tapping on your head. Then say it a fourth time while tapping on your chest. Take a deep breath after finishing the series.]

"I declare myself a surrogate for humanity; in all moments."

"I recant all vows and agreements between myself and all crimes against humanity; in all moments."

"I release all the trauma of all crimes against humanity; in all moments."

"I release being indifferent to crimes against humanity; in all moments."

"I release condoning any crimes against humanity; in all moments."

"I remove all curses between myself and all crimes against humanity; in all moments."

"I dissolve all karmic ties between myself and all crimes against humanity; in all moments."

"I withdraw all my energy from all crimes against humanity; in all moments."

"I remove all the pain, burden and limitations that all crimes against humanity have put on myself and all humanity; in all moments."

"I take back for myself and all humanity, all the Joy, Love, Abundance, Freedom, Health, Success, Security, Companionship, Creativity, Peace, Life, Wholeness, Beauty, Enthusiasm, and Contentment that all crimes against humanity have taken from myself and humanity; in all moments."

"I release resonating with crimes against humanity; in all moments."

"I release emanating with crimes against humanity; in all moments."

"I remove all crimes against humanity from my sound frequency; in all moments."

"I remove all crimes against humanity from my light body; in all moments."

"I shift my and humanity's paradigm from crimes against humanity to Joy, Love, Abundance, Freedom, Health, Success, Security, Companionship, Creativity, Peace, Life, Wholeness, Beauty, Enthusiasm, and Contentment; in all moments."

"I and humanity are centered and empowered in Joy, Love, Abundance, Freedom, Health, Success, Security, Companionship, Creativity, Peace, Life, Wholeness, Beauty, Enthusiasm and Contentment; in all moments."

"I make space in this world for Joy, Love, Abundance, Freedom, Health, Success, Security, Companion, Creativity, Peace, Life, Wholeness, Beauty, Enthusiasm and Contentment, for all humanity; in all moments."

"I remove all blockage to myself and humanity having more Joy, Love, Abundance, Freedom, Health, Success, Security,

Companionship, Creativity, Peace, Life, Wholeness, Beauty, Enthusiasm, and Contentment in this world; in all moments."

"I stretch my and humanity's capacity to accept more Joy, Love, Abundance, Freedom, Health, Success, Security, Companionship, Creativity, Peace, Life, Wholeness, Beauty, Enthusiasm, and Contentment in this world; in all moments."

54. Perfect the Dance

I spent time with my cousin who is a competitive break-dancer. He was telling me about a move that he is trying to perfect but was having difficulty with. I know nothing about break dancing. But as he was sharing his passion with me, I was inspired to assist him in quickly overcoming the plateau that he was on.

I told him that the difficulty was between the transitions from one move to another. This made sense to him because that was the word for the shift that he was having difficulty with (I did not know that). I told him that he could do the moves forever, but when he changed to the next one, he tripped himself up. His dance was an analogy for his journey.

In life, we gain momentum and are really caught up in what we are experiencing. We are sometimes resentful when we leave a good life. This resentment shows up in our present lives as not finishing projects. The ingrained memory of prematurely dying makes us say on some level, "why bother?" My cousin had died in his prime in many lives, and that subtle frustration was holding him back from being totally fluid in his movements in his dance.

My cousin needed to become more fluid. I led him through a bunch of taps to assist. I saw that he was storing certain issues in the transitions between the moves he had to make. He was also storing the same issues in his joints. As we did the taps, he felt energized, inspired, and wanted to get to the dance. As we released one issue, another issue would come to the surface and reveal itself as holding him back. He was also allowing issues of others he cared about to get in the way of being totally present in his dance.

Taps to improve one's fluidity:

[Say each statement slowly and consciously out loud. Articulate each word and make a point to pause after each phrase. Say each statement three times while tapping on your head. Then say it a

fourth time while tapping on your chest. Take a deep breath after finishing the series.]

"I release storing the frustration of dying into my transitions; in all moments."

"I release storing the frustration of dying into my joints; in all moments."

"I release storing limitations into my transitions; in all moments."

"I release storing limitations into my joints; in all moments."

"I release storing anger into my transitions; in all moments."

"I release storing anger into my joints; in all moments."

"I release storing unworthiness into my transitions; in all moments."

"I release storing unworthiness into my joints; in all moments."

"I release storing expectations into my transitions; in all moments."

"I release storing expectations into my joints; in all moments."

"I release storing genetic programming into my transitions; in all moments."

"I release storing genetic programming into my joints; in all moments."

"I release storing fear in my transitions; in all moments."

"I release storing fear into my joints; in all moments."

"I release storing failure in my transitions; in all moments."

"I release storing failure into my joints; in all moments."

"I release storing bullshit into my transitions; in all moments."

"I release storing bullshit into my joints; in all moments."

"I release storing other people's issues into my transitions; in all moments."

"I release storing other people's issues into my joints; in all moments."

"I infuse omniscience, omnipresence, and omnipotence into my transitions; in all moments."

"I infuse omniscience, omnipresence, and omnipotence into my joints; in all moments."

These taps will be helpful for any dancer, athlete, person with joint issues, those who don't finish projects, those who don't use their gifts, and everyone else.

55. Understanding Food and Weight Issues

There is a huge difference between having issues with food and being obese. They are two different emotional issues. Many people can have both, but it is good to get an understanding of the difference.

One of the most primal needs is to eat. Many lifetimes were spent foraging for food. As difficult as those experiences were, they were less complicated. People who binge eat are reverting to a less complicated experience.

When many people eat, they revert to a lifetime when they were starving. They are trying to feed an experience of the past with present life food. That is why fullness never registers. That is why mindful eating is effective; it keeps them in the present moment.

Many people have been part of a mass starvation, so when they eat, they are trying to feed a whole village through their meal. That is another experience people have that explains why someone can eat and eat and never get full. The void is too great.

Many people feel vulnerable being too thin. In past experiences, being thin was associated with poverty and sickness. People who have experienced horrific, emaciated bodies will have an aversion to being thin because it triggers lifetimes of disease and depravity. This is subconscious, and they live in incredible guilt because of this lack of understanding of the correlation.

People sometimes feel safer in a big body because they have been diminished and want to create the illusion of strength in themselves. They manifest a girth in their own frame out of fear of being weak.

Many have been abused because of their beauty. They have been sacrificed, raped, imprisoned, and been the victims of horrific attention because they stood out as the most beautiful. In past lives, the person in power could pluck anyone out of their lives and use them as a plaything and defile them. People who have been singled out in a bad way for their attractiveness will attempt to hide it in layers of obesity. It is a survival mechanism.

Each one of these issues has its own protocol of taps. Here are some to address each issue. When doing the taps, pay attention to the ones that cause the most reaction. It will be a clue to your own issues.

Taps to differentiate between food issues and weight issues:

[Say each statement slowly and consciously out loud. Articulate each word and make a point to pause after each phrase. Say each statement three times while tapping on your head. Then say it a fourth time while tapping on your chest. Take a deep breath after finishing the series.]

"I release the primal need to forage for food; in all moments."

"I release using foraging for food as a distraction from stress; in all moments."

"I release mourning my own innocence; in all moments."

"I release mourning a more innocent time; in all moments."

"I release the trauma of starving to death; in all moments."

"I release confusing hunger with starving to death; in all moments."

"I release the guilt of eating; in all moments."

"I release trying to feed the whole group through my body; in all moments."

"I dry up the void of depravity within; in all moments."

"I dry up the inner hunger; in all moments."

"I release defining being thin as unhealthy; in all moments."

"I release associating being thin with disease and poverty; in all moments."

"I release the trauma of being poor and diseased; in all moments."

"I release associating being thin as being invisible; in all moments."

"I release confusing being thin with being weak; in all moments."

"I release the fear of being weak; in all moments."

"I release protecting myself in a big body; in all moments."

"I release using weight to compensate for feeling weak; in all moments."

"I release confusing carrying extra weight with being strong and safe; in all moments."

"I release the fear of being attractive; in all moments."

"I release hiding my beauty; in all moments."

"I release using weight to hide; in all moments."

"I embrace my own beauty; in all moments."

These are a jumping off point in figuring out your own core beliefs about yourself, food, and weight. Use your findings to release punishing or imprisoning yourself.

56. Concentrated Love

If we get the mind out of the way, we can be more detached about what we are. We are a combination of a frequency of sound and an emanation of light. We have worked with our issues till we are blue in the face, and yet the mind acts as a monitoring system to prevent us from changing. A key to doing this is to perceive ourselves less as a solid ball of mass and more as a fluid emanation of love.

Since we are not solid, everyone else that we perceive is not solid either. We are not so contained. We spill into, overflow, and intermix with everyone. Maybe we have been diluting each other's effectiveness for too long. Maybe the ones who can adapt to the concept of being fluid have an advantage in changing the dynamics for all. We are all interconnected and the more we all give our all, the more we add something better to the mix.

One can be diluted by the light and sound of others, or one can decide to be concentrated love and affect others positively. Concentrated love, when mixed in the group, would add its loving properties to the group. It may sound silly to believe in a loving world for all. But it may be even sillier to be complacent and not utilize every loving intention to uplift all of humanity.

The Christian Bible quotes Jesus as saying "Lest we become like little children...." This technique is what a child would do. They would take what adults see as an impossible notion, pour all their enthusiasm into it, wear the resistance down, and manifest their goal. We have seen this when super-empowered children create multimillion dollar industries. We can do the same to make a better world.

This exercise is indulging the child in all of us that want a better life. Maybe it is silly to think it is possible. You don't have to believe for it to work. If you feel silly, do it as an homage to the victims of Sandy Hook. Or, do it so other children don't get nerve-bombed by their own government. Do this exercise so that all the children who took a trek of a lifetime and are sent away for their efforts can feel some intangible love. Do it so that all the children at this moment in a broken, war-torn city can feel an intangible sense that someone, anyone, cares and is doing something, although radical and unbelievable, to ease their suffering.

Taps to bring concentrated love into this world:

[Say each statement slowly and consciously out loud. Articulate each word and make a point to pause after each phrase. Say each statement three times while tapping on your head. Then say it a fourth time while tapping on your chest. Take a deep breath after finishing the series.]

"I declare myself concentrated fluid emanation of love; in all moments."

"I am a perpetual fluid emanation of concentrated love into the world; in all moments."

"I pour all my concentrated love into the world and uplift the universal 'We'; in all moments."

"I declare myself a surrogate for the universal 'We'; in all moments."

"I extract all pain from our sound frequency; in all moments."

"I extract all pain from our light body; in all moments."

"I infuse concentrated joy into our sound frequency; in all moments."

"I imbue concentrated joy into our light body; in all moments."

"I extract all hatred from our sound frequency; in all moments."

"I extract all hatred from our light body; in all moments."

"I infuse concentrated love into our sound frequency; in all moments."

"I imbue concentrated love into our light body; in all moments."

"I extract all poverty from our sound frequency; in all moments."

"I extract all poverty from our light body; in all moments."

"I infuse concentrated abundance into our sound frequency; in all moments."

"I imbue concentrated abundance into our light body; in all moments."

"I extract all slavery from our sound frequency; in all moments."

"I extract all slavery from our light body; in all moments."

"I infuse freedom and joy into our sound frequency; in all moments."

"I imbue freedom and joy into our light body; in all moments."

"I extract all disease from our sound frequency; in all moments."

"I extract all disease from our light body; in all moments."

"I infuse concentrated health into our sound frequency; in all moments."

"I imbue concentrated health into our light body; in all moments."

"I extract all failure from our sound frequency; in all moments."

"I extract all failure from our light body; in all moments."

"I infuse concentrated success into our sound frequency; in all moments."

"I imbue concentrated success into our light body; in all moments."

"I extract all fear from our sound frequency; in all moments."

"I extract all fear from our light body; in all moments."

"I infuse concentrated security into our sound frequency; in all moments."

"I imbue concentrated security into our light body; in all moments."

"I extract all isolation from our sound frequency; in all moments."

"I extract all isolation from our light body; in all moments."

"I infuse companionship into our sound frequency; in all moments."

"I imbue companionship into our light body; in all moments."

"I extract all programming from our sound frequency; in all moments."

"I extract all programming from our light body; in all moments."

"I infuse concentrated creativity into our sound frequency; in all moments."

"I imbue concentrated creativity into our light body; in all moments."

"I extract all war from our sound frequency; in all moments."

"I extract all war from our light body; in all moments."

"I infuse everlasting peace into our sound frequency; in all moments."

"I imbue everlasting peace into our light body; in all moments."

"I extract all death from our sound frequency; in all moments."

"I extract all death from our light body; in all moments."

"I infuse life into our sound frequency; in all moments."

"I imbue life into our light body; in all moments."

"I extract all devastation from our sound frequency; in all moments."

"I extract all devastation from our light body; in all moments."

"I infuse concentrated wholeness into our sound frequency; in all moments."

"I imbue concentrated wholeness into our light body; in all moments."

"I extract all ugliness from our sound frequency; in all moments."

"I extract all ugliness from our light body; in all moments."

"I infuse concentrated beauty into our sound frequency; in all moments."

"I imbue concentrated beauty into our light body; in all moments."

"I extract all complacency from our sound frequency; in all moments."

"I extract all complacency from our light body; in all moments."

"I infuse concentrated enthusiasm into our sound frequency; in all moments."

"I imbue concentrated enthusiasm into our light body; in all moments."

"I extract all darkness from our sound frequency; in all moments."

"I extract all darkness from our light body; in all moments."

"I infuse concentrated light into our sound frequency; in all moments."

"I imbue concentrated light into our light body; in all moments."

"I extract all discord from our sound frequency; in all moments."

"I extract all discord from our light body; in all moments."

"I infuse concentrated harmony into our sound frequency; in all moments."

"I imbue concentrated harmony into our light body; in all moments."

Doing this technique, sharing this technique, and holding an intention and a place for a beautiful shift in the world is an incredible gift to all. I see miracles every day. I create them sometimes with my loving intention combined with my gifts. Here is to you seeing an amazing miracle that you had a hand in.

57. Reconnecting to One's Divinity

I don't think people realize what the devastating ramifications that the concept of God has done to the psyche of the world. In the present day even, most of the hatred, wars, and fighting are motivated by not seeing God in the same light as the other side. This is not a new phenomenon. The holy wars lasted thousands of years, and many genocides were committed in the name of God. The Bible says that man was made in God's image but man switched it around. God was made in man's image, petty and possessive.

When I see atheists, I respect their journey. Seeing the akashic records of people, I see the torment that was caused in so many because they were not in step with the concept of God at the time. So many, if not all of us, were tortured, ostracized, humiliated, enslaved, and made to fight for the concept of God at the time. Some of us can look at those today who are killing in the name of their true God and see only a couple of degrees of separation between current events and their own personal journey towards enlightenment.

The concept of God being love works for me. If anything is not kind, diminishes another person or group, inflicts pain or suffering of any kind on anyone or anything, it is not loving; therefore, it is not God. With this definition, so many atheists I know are closer to God than those who try to micromanage the lives and behavior of others. If anyone tries to argue with me about my belief in this, it is evidence that they do not understand the qualities of God that I speak of, and so I do not engage them. Nor do I try to convince atheists that they are wrong in there NOT being a God. They have come by their vantage point as honestly as I have come by mine.

In the akashic records of so many are the records of the horrendous devastation that has occurred because of God. What is important to realize is that it was NEVER because of God but of man's interpretation of God. All the practices of abasement, sacrificing, fighting, and killing in the name of God were really done for the insecurities of man. The God of Love's hands are clean. Man's are not.

Man has mutilated the psyche of itself and others by interpreting God for others. Our relationship with the Divine is so personal and sacred that to listen to another person's understanding of It, is to deviate from our own truth. That is what has happened through our existence on earth; man has skewed the divine for others. It is only now that we are coming to the awareness of our own ability to decipher our own relationship with God. It is time to clean the slate of past misunderstandings and stand on the precipice of our own truth. Taps to reconnect to one's divinity:

[Say each statement slowly and consciously out loud. Articulate each word and make a point to pause after each phrase. Say each statement three times while tapping on your head. Then say it a fourth time while tapping on your chest. Take a deep breath after finishing the series.]

Here are the taps to reconnect with one's own divinity.

"I release personifying God; in all moments."

"I release diminishing God to attributes of man; in all moments."

"I release the belief that I disappointed God; in all moments."

"I release being abandoned by God; in all moments."

"I release the belief that I have failed God; in all moments."

"I release being rejected by God; in all moments."

"I release being afraid of God; in all moments."

"I release the belief that God is anything but love and loving; in all moments."

"I release diminishing myself for God; in all moments."

"I release harming others in the name of God; in all moments."

"I release using God as an excuse; in all moments."

"I release using God as a crutch; in all moments."

"I release the belief that God hates me; in all moments."

"I release associating God with self-shame; in all moments."

"I release being persecuted for my beliefs; in all moments."

"I release the pain and trauma of being ostracized; in all moments."

"I release being disillusioned by God; in all moments."

"I release being pitted against others for the sake of God; in all moments."

"I release the belief that God wants me to feel unworthy; in all moments."

"I remove the false sense of humility; in all moments."

"I release cowering to God; in all moments."

"I release all outmoded concepts and beliefs about God; in all moments."

"I release enslaving others to my concept of God; in all moments."

"I release interfering with others' relationship with God; in all moments."

"I release using God to feel superior to others; in all moments."

"I release using God to abuse power; in all moments."

"I release being subjected to force in the name of God; in all moments."

"I release the trauma of being sacrificed to God; in all moments."

"I release hating God; in all moments."

"I release the belief that I am separate from God; in all moments."

"I release the need to prove myself to God; in all moments."

"I release defining God as slavery; in all moments."

"I release diminishing others to please God; in all moments."

"I release allowing concepts of God to interfere with my relationship to God; in all moments."

"I recant all vows and agreements between myself and God; in all moments."

"I remove all curses between myself and God; in all moments."

"I dissolve all karmic ties between myself and God; in all moments."

"I remove all the pain, burden, limitations, and engrams that God has put on me; in all moments."

"I take back all the Joy, Love, Abundance, Freedom, Health, Life, and Wholeness that God has taken from me; in all moments."

"I remove all limiting concepts of God from my sound frequency; in all moments."

"I remove all limiting concepts of God from my light body; in all moments."

"I transcend all limiting concepts of God; in all moments."

"I redefine God as divine love; in all moments."

"I am centered and empowered in divine love; in all moments."

By releasing all these limiting concepts of God that we had in the past, we allow the true essence of God to imbue our energy. So the Zen of it is, by releasing God, we can actually be closer to God.

I would love to encourage anyone on the fence about God to do these taps to see if they feel a shift.

58. Uplifting Humanity

I was honored to facilitate a private remote session with Skye Daniels. She is such an AMAZING soul that the session ended up being about uplifting humanity. There are some selfless souls that reflect the issues of humanity in their own lives. Maybe we all do to an extent. Some of us live as surrogates for Goddess, or Humanity, or Love. If this is you, you may enjoy doing these taps to raise the bar.

As we were working on these universal releases, it felt like we were making history. That we were removing universal blocks that were preventing all from moving forward as a group in more Joy, Love, Abundance, and Freedom.

Taps to uplift humanity:

[Say each statement slowly and consciously out loud. Articulate each word and make a point to pause after each phrase. Say each statement three times while tapping on your head. Then say it a fourth time while tapping on your chest. Take a deep breath after finishing the series.]

"I release endorsing poverty; in all moments."

"I withdraw all my energy from poverty; in all moments."

"I release endorsing false humility; in all moments."

"I withdraw all my energy from false humility; in all moments."

"I release endorsing male domination; in all moments."

"I withdraw all my energy from male domination; in all moments."

"I release endorsing abuse of power; in all moments."

"I withdraw all my energy from the abuse of power; in all moments."

"I release endorsing slavery and sexual perversion; in all moments."

"I withdraw all my energy from slavery and sexual perversion; in all moments."

"I release endorsing need, want, and lack; in all moments."

"I withdraw all my energy from need, want, and lack; in all moments."

"I recant all vows and agreement between Humanity and money; in all moments."

I remove all curses between Humanity and money; in all moments."

"I dissolve all karmic ties between Humanity and money; in all moments."

"I remove all the shackles, pain, fear, burden, limitations, and engrams that money has put on Humanity; in all moments."

"I take back all the Joy, Love Abundance, Freedom, Health, Success, Security, Companionship, Creativity, Peace, Life, Wholeness, Beauty, Enthusiasm, Contentment, Confidence, Spirituality, and Enlightenment that money has taken from Humanity; in all moments."

"I neutralize the charge of money; in all moments."

"I shatter the glass ceiling of unworthiness that society has put on Humanity; in all moments."

"I shift the world's paradigm from the rigid structures of society to the loving flexibility of Humanity; in all moments."

"I infuse Humanity's sound frequency with Joy, Love Abundance, Freedom, Health, Success, Security, Companionship, Creativity, Peace, Life, Wholeness, Beauty, Enthusiasm, Contentment, Confidence, Spirituality and Enlightenment; in all moments."

"I imbue Humanity's light body with Joy, Love, Abundance, Freedom, Health, Success, Security, Companionship, Creativity, Peace, Life, Wholeness, Beauty, Enthusiasm, Contentment, Confidence, Spirituality and Enlightenment; in all moments."

"ALL OF HUMANITY resonates and emanates with Joy, Love, Abundance, Freedom, Health, Success, Security, Companionship, Creativity, Peace, Life, Wholeness, Beauty, Enthusiasm, Contentment, Confidence, Spirituality, and Enlightenment; in all moments."

"All of society surrenders to the empowerment and sanctity of Divine Love; in all moments."

"Humanity is centered, imbued, and empowered in Divine Love; in all moments."

As a confirmation from the Universe that we are truly making a difference, the phone call disconnected itself exactly at 11:11 a.m.

59. Releasing Torture

I was in the shower with the water running all over my face, and it occurred to me in that moment to send healing love to all the people who have ever been water-boarded. It had nothing to do with politics or being in agreement with anything on the surface. It had to do with helping them to maintain their connection with humanity.

That is why torture is so egregious. It separates an individual from humanity and creates an engram on their causal body that may take many lifetimes to undo.

Think of yourself as a 3-D old vinyl record. The grooves that are in it are all memories from all the experiences in all your lives. The ones that are less deep are the pleasant experiences. The ones that make the record skip (repeat experiences) are painful experiences and are deeply ingrained physically, emotionally, and mentally. These deepest grooves are the ones I read in private sessions and the ones I help to rub out or fill in so that the clients can return to their Joy. The reason torture is so horrendous is that it carves deep grooves in all components of the human experience by combining physical, emotional, and mental pain.

What the torturers don't realize is that they are obligated to assist that person in undoing what they have done to them. As a group, the same rule applies. Ignorance of the understanding of cause and affect does not excuse one from violating others. Denial will run out of steam as well. I have experienced torture in this lifetime, and I see it in the memory banks of my clients. Doing the following taps may assist lightening the burden that such acts have put on humanity. May all humanity feel lightness by you doing them.

Taps to release torture:

[Say each statement slowly and consciously out loud. Articulate each word and make a point to pause after each phrase. Say each

statement three times while tapping on your head. Then say it a fourth time while tapping on your chest. Take a deep breath after finishing the series.]

"I release the trauma of being tortured; in all moments."

"I release the guilt and trauma of torturing others; in all moments."

"I release condoning torture; in all moments."

"I release relinquishing my power to torture; in all moments."

"I recant all vows and agreements between myself and torture; in all moments."

"I release quantifying torture; in all moments."

"I dissolve the karmic pull of torture; in all moments."

"I remove all the pain, burden, and limitations that torture has put on me; in all moments."

"I remove all the pain, burden, and limitations I have put on all others through torture; in all moments."

"I take back all the Joy, Love, Abundance, Freedom, Health, Life, and Wholeness that being tortured has taken from me; in all moments."

"I withdraw all my energy from, and support of, torture; in all moments."

"I give back all that I have taken from others through means of torture; in all moments."

There are varying degrees of torture. Mental anguish and emotional upheaval in this life may be a playing out of past life torture. When souls are at the end of a leash outside, and all those they love are in the house, it is indeed torture to them. Who is to justify it? Who is to say that their suffering is any less valid than that of a human?

60. Repair Damage of Drug Use

I work with some amazing young adults who are really dynamic and very spiritually acute. It saddens me when I see these profound dynamos get trapped in the diminishing belief that drugs are harmless to the psyche. They have told me that this upcoming generation associates drugs with spirituality. (Haven't they heard of the sixties?) That is hypocrisy. It is the lie that they tell themselves. It saddens me to watch the potential of genius drop into complacency.

When I try to explain to them the difference between drugs and spirituality, I get that polite listening but closing down their receptivity. I understand the thinking that the people who don't do drugs don't know what they're talking about. But that place where they try to have drugs take them is where I go totally in control and with free will. Those who equivocate drugs with spirituality are as silly as those doing a healthy juice fast but using fruit punch instead of organic juice. The youth don't respect their parents' point of view because their parents are coming at it out of fear. I am explaining from experience. The place that drugs take one is not spiritual but a skewed illusion. It may seem so at first, like the mind enhances the experience of drugs, but the individual is being led around in a maze that leads nowhere.

My client confided in me that she felt pot was okay, but the other drugs were messed up. Many people believe this. Pot expands your energy field in a pretty even way. It leaves one feeling whole but with "spaces" between each atom. Though people feel the same, energetic influences are able to seep in. It is like unwittingly giving up one's free will because it feels natural.

Here is an analogy. Your energy field is your home. Doing pot is like opening windows and doors and trusting that no one will come in. Maybe some harmless energies come in to stay like house guests. Maybe they are coaxing you into opening your inner rooms.

Since there is no seemingly long term consequences, you agree. You open those inner chambers by using harsher drugs.

There are some savvy energies that are out there just waiting to take up residency in unsuspecting people. They are like seasoned criminals. When one mixes drugs with spirituality, there is no way to know what is real and what is illusion. These people have given up their home to these savvy energies. All their memories and experiences are recorded in pictures called akashic records. Think of this as the library of your house. When people do drugs and open up to influences, they are susceptible to having all their pictures stolen or altered. They can be energetically raped of all that they are. This is why people who do drugs look so empty. It is because they are.

I have had clients who have done mushrooms. This seems to have warped their energy field. The ones with issues have seen a dark presence out of the corner of their eye. One client was constantly internally berated about how evil she is. One client was just very paranoid. With all of them, I have assisted by reforming the walls of their energy field. I perceived them as wax with ridges in them. I rebuilt their walls for them. Whatever I did, the influences dried up and they got relief.

For anyone who has done mushrooms and suffers with this issue, I would suggest that they try the visualization that I just mentioned. Visualize your energy field as a wax cocoon that has an opening in it. Slightly melt the sides with your intention until you are all firmly encased once again. Then solidify the wax with your intention. Then visualize a burst of incredible Light and Love from within the size of a mushroom cloud and burn out any residual foreign matter.

If you have done pot and lost your focus, these taps to seal up your energy field may help you. It is not a quick fix. It is using your spiritual abilities while you still have the ability to close the doors.

Taps to repair energetic damage of drug use:

[Say each statement slowly and consciously out loud. Articulate each word and make a point to pause after each phrase. Say each statement three times while tapping on your head. Then say it a fourth time while tapping on your chest. Take a deep breath after finishing the series.]

"I repair and fortify my Wei Chi; in all moments."

"I disarm all foreign influences; in all moments."

"I blast out and dissolve all foreign energies with the intensity and purity of Divine Love; in all moments."

"I am centered and empowered in Divine Love; in all moments."

There is such empowerment knowing that whatever comes one's way can be handled with confidence. This is that invincibility that young people experience. When people can maintain that confidence throughout their life, they exude such attractiveness and success. This is my intention for the current young generation, and all the rest to come.

61. Releasing Subtle Forms of Masochism

I just finished a session with a very spiritual woman who sabotages herself. As I am facilitating the session, I am also receiving a download of information from my Spirit Guides on the pandemic of masochism that plagues the world.

Here is the definition of masochism: The condition in which gratification depends on one's suffering physical pain or humiliation.

At first, I was shown addictions as a form of masochism. How when you "use" you are shamed even as you do it but continue to do it. But then I was shown all these different addictions, preferences, and scenarios that seemed masochistic in nature:

- Choosing a 9 to 5 job over a life's passion
- All through history, woman being submissive to men
- Declaring ourselves unworthy in the eyes of our God
- Sending our heartiest people to war and deeming it noble
- Poisoning our own bodies with sugar and toxins
- Allowing our children to be killed in their schools and accepting it as the norm
- Decorating and even mutilating the body to meet an unreachable standard of beauty
- Poisoning our own environment and choosing ill health over addressing the issue
- Giving our power over to governing factions that insult our intelligence
- Allowing ourselves to be manipulated by companies so we can be mildly entertained
- Worshiping manufactured celebrities that make us feel inferior in comparison

If these issues aren't masochistic, they hedge eerily close to it.

Taps to release subtle forms of masochism:

[Say each statement slowly and consciously out loud. Articulate each word and make a point to pause after each phrase. Say each statement three times while tapping on your head. Then say it a fourth time while tapping on your chest. Take a deep breath after finishing the series.]

"I declare myself a surrogate for society in doing these taps" (optional)

"I release distracting myself with masochism; in all moments."

"I release society being distracted by masochism; in all moments."

"I release sabotaging myself with masochism; in all moments."

"I release society being sabotaged by masochism; in all moments."

"I strip off all the illusion and intrigue of mass masochism; in all moments."

"I release being enslaved to masochism; in all moments."

"I release society being enslaved to masochism; in all moments."

"I recant all vows and agreements between myself and masochism; in all moments."

"I recant all vows and agreements between society and masochism; in all moments."

"I remove all curses between myself and masochism; in all moments."

"I remove all curses between society and masochism; in all moments."

"I sever all ties cords between myself and masochism; in all moments."

"I sever all ties and cords between masochism and society; in all moments."

"I dissolve all karmic ties between myself and masochism; in all moments."

"I dissolve all karmic ties between society and masochism; in all moments."

"I shatter all mystique of masochism; in all moments."

"I remove all the pain, burden, limitations, and engrams that masochism has put on me; in all moments."

"I remove all the pain, burden, limitations, and engrams that masochism has put on society; in all moments."

"I take back all the Joy, Love, Abundance, Freedom, Health, Success, Security, Companionship, Creativity, Peace, Life, Wholeness, Beauty, Enthusiasm, Contentment, Spirituality, Empowerment, Enlightenment, Dance, and Ingenuity that masochism has taken from me; in all moments."

"I retrieve for society all the Joy, Love, Abundance, Freedom, Health, Success, Security, Companionship, Creativity, Peace, Life, Wholeness, Beauty, Enthusiasm, Contentment, Spirituality, Empowerment, Enlightenment, Dance, and Ingenuity that masochism has taken from it; in all moments."

"I release resonating with masochism; in all moments."

"I release society resonating with masochism; in all moments."

"I release emanating with masochism; in all moments."

"I release society emanating with masochism; in all moments."

"I remove all masochism from my sound frequency; in all moments."

"I remove all masochism from society's sound frequency; in all moments."

"I remove all masochism from my light body; in all moments."

"I remove all masochism from society's light body; in all moments."

"I shift my paradigm from masochism to Joy, Love, Abundance, Freedom, Health, Success, Security, Companionship, Creativity, Peace, Life, Wholeness, Beauty, Enthusiasm, Contentment, Spirituality, Empowerment, Enlightenment, Dance and Ingenuity; in all moments."

"I shift society's paradigm from masochism to Joy, Love, Abundance, Freedom, Health, Success, Security, Companionship, Creativity, Peace, Life, Wholeness, Beauty, Enthusiasm, Contentment, Spirituality, Empowerment, Enlightenment, Dance and Ingenuity; in all moments."

"I am centered and empowered in Divine Love; in all moments."

"Society is centered and imbued in Divine Love; in all moments."

"I shift the world's paradigm from society to Humanity; in all moments."

I was trying to make this a shorter set of taps to accommodate some people's preference. But when I was writing these, I heard a huge crack in my home as if the building was settling. I opted to listen and typed out the long version. It is too important of an issue to glaze over. It has been glazed over for too long.

62. Primed for Enlightenment

There have always been spiritual factions assisting the inhabitants of the world in reaching enlightenment. Enlightenment is a physiological process of stripping away the ego from the true self. It is what St. Paul described as getting knocked down by the Light of God on the road to Damascus. When it happens, the person is left with a purity of truth and serves others from a sacred place. There are many misconceptions about enlightenment. After the process, the ego is reintegrated into the psyche, but it is with a heightened awareness of the difference between ego and one's true self that the individual continues.

Reaching enlightenment is becoming more possible with our interconnectedness. When it happened for me, I was locked up by others, and I cannot help feeling that this was orchestrated. As I assist others in reaching enlightenment, I can't help but think that this is in divine accordance with my purpose. When I came back from imprisonment, I was never angry; maybe this is why. Maybe I realized on some level that I would make good use of the experience.

No true spiritual path is gratuitous. Every single grain of truth that was folded over into a religion was a seed to lead individuals to the heart of God. The road map is not reaching providence. Complacency is offensive to the spiritual greats who have dedicated their existence to bringing others to truth. They have not done this so that one individual can feel warm and fuzzy. They have not done this, so one group or individual feels superior to another. They have not done this so that someone has a leg up on another. They have done this to uplift all.

Maybe it is a huge experiment to see if humans can pull themselves up by the bootstraps and embrace the spiritual nature that is in their grasp. Maybe then the desire to serve others is as compulsive as a salmon swimming upstream. Maybe all the war, strife, and injustice that this world has seen is the perfect breeding ground for enlightened souls. Once enough people transform through the process of enlightenment, we will reach a tipping point and all of humanity will follow suit. This is my intention for sharing all these techniques.

Recently, some of my clients have been getting a sense of being ready for enlightenment. It is almost like they found me to help them prepare. One client who did experience the process believes that she would not have been ready without our work. Another client realized that she still has an ingrained fear of being an individual. It is an astute awareness. Here are the taps to assist with that subtle issue.

Taps to be a pipeline of divine love into this world:

[Say each statement slowly and consciously out loud. Articulate each word and make a point to pause after each phrase. Say each statement three times while tapping on your head. Then say it a fourth time while tapping on your chest. Take a deep breath after finishing the series.]

"I release the fear of being separated from the ego; in all moments."

"I release the fear of losing my mind; in all moments."

"I release the fear of the responsibility of enlightenment; in all moments."

"I release the fear of something better; in all moments."

"I release the fear of the unknown; in all moments."

"I release being programmed for the mundane; in all moments."

"I release the fear of being separated from the herd; in all moments."

"I release the fear of my own greatness; in all moments."

"I release the fear of my own insignificance; in all moments."

"I make space in this world for my own enlightenment; in all moments."

"I remove all obstacles to my own enlightenment; in all moments."

"I stretch my capacity for my own enlightenment; in all moments."

"I release the fear of losing it all; in all moments."

"I connect to my own vortex; in all moments."

"I remove all limitations; in all moments."

"I open up the heavens and walk into my own stillness; in all moments."

"I release the fear of losing myself; in all moments."

"I release the fear of the realization of not knowing who I am; in all moments."

"I release micromanaging the universe; in all moments."

"I cut all strings and cords between myself and the ego; in all moments."

"I release the belief that my greatness is contingent on another; in all moments."

"I recant my vow to not transcend until every sentient being has transcended; in all moments."

"I release waiting for someone to save me; in all moments."

"I release waiting to be discovered; in all moments."

"I release the fear of facing myself; in all moments."

"I make space in this world to transcend the mind; in all moments."

"I remove all blockages to transcending the mind; in all moments."

"I stretch my capacity to transcend the mind; in all moments."

"I release reacting to outer stimuli; in all moments."

"I release an aversion to my own stillness; in all moments."

"I release feeling and believing that I am unworthy to serve; in all moments."

"I am centered and empowered in my own enlightenment; in all moments."

These taps may create a powerful shift in the individual. May the experiences they bring be life-changing. Also please realize that feeling alone and being alone are two different things. There are always spiritual guides to assist even if one does not recognize or acknowledge their presence.

63. Removing Fat Cells

Yet more taps on the physicality.

Taps to remove fat cells:

[Say each statement slowly and consciously out loud. Articulate each word and make a point to pause after each phrase. Say each statement three times while tapping on your head. Then say it a fourth time while tapping on your chest. Take a deep breath after finishing the series.]

"I release all the issues stored in all fat cells; in all moments."

"I release holding on to fat cells; in all moments."

"I release identifying with fat cells; in all moments."

"I release personifying a fat cell; in all moments."

"I release using fat cells to protect myself; in all moments."

"I release the genetic propensity to rely on fat cells; in all moments."

"I release using fat cells as a buffer; in all moments."

"I release being at the mercy of fat cells; in all moments."

"I release using fat cells for solace; in all moments."

"I release using fat cells to define myself; in all moments."

"I recant all vows and agreements between myself and all fat cells; in all moments."

"I collapse all fat cells; in all moments."

"I remove all curses between myself and all fat cells; in all moments."

"I dissolve all karmic ties between myself and all fat cells; in all moments."

"I cut all the cords and ties to all fat cells; in all moments."

"I remove all the pain, burden, limitations, and engrams that all fat cells have put on me; in all moments."

"I take back all the Joy, Love, Abundance, Freedom, Health, Success, Security, Companionship, Creativity, Peace, Life, Wholeness, Beauty, Enthusiasm, and Adventure that all fat cells have taken from me; in all moments."

"I withdraw all my energy from all fat cells; in all moments."

"I dissolve all fat cells into divine love; in all moments."

"I release harboring fat cells; in all moments."

"I release resonating with fat cells; in all moments."

"I release emanating with fat cells; in all moments."

"I remove all fat cells from my sound frequency; in all moments."

"I remove all fat cells from my light body; in all moments."

"I shift my paradigm from all fat cells to Joy, Love, Abundance, Freedom, Health, Success, Security, Companionship, Creativity, Peace, Life, Wholeness, Beauty, Enthusiasm, and Adventure; in all moments."

"I transcend all fat cells; in all moments."

"I am centered and empowered in Joy, Love, Abundance, Freedom, Health, Success, Security, Companionship, Creativity, Peace, Life, Wholeness, Beauty, Enthusiasm, and Adventure; in all moments."

64. Make Everything New Again

Did you ever get excited about doing a project but then start thinking about what it entails? You run through all the steps that you need to do to get started and all the equipment you need to collect. You run through the scenario in your head and then lose your enthusiasm. Have you ever done this?

The thing is, the scenario in your head doesn't know all the little surprises that will happen or the wonderful encounters that we will have. The scenario is the dead skin of a collection of old images. That is why children have so much enthusiasm; everything is being processed through a new brain.

Taps to regain your sense of wonder:

[Say each statement slowly and consciously out loud. Articulate each word and make a point to pause after each phrase. Say each statement three times while tapping on your head. Then say it a fourth time while tapping on your chest. Take a deep breath after finishing the series.]

"I release squelching my own Joy; in all moments."

"I release diminishing my own enthusiasm; in all moments."

"I release being immersed in complacency; in all moments."

"I release being seeped in indifference; in all moments."

"I release being limited by fear; in all moments."

"I remove all the pain, burden, and limitations that fear, indifference, and complacency have put on me; in all moments."

"I remove all the pain, burden, and limitations that I have put on all others due to fear, indifference, and complacency; in all moments."

"I remove all limiting thoughts and feelings that separate me from Joy, Love, Abundance, Freedom, Health, and Wholeness; in all moments."

"I break through and dissipate all resistance to being in complete Joy, Love, Abundance, Freedom, Health and Wholeness; in all moments."

"I make space in this world to live in complete Joy, Love, Abundance, Freedom, Health and Wholeness; in all moments."

"I remove all blockages to living in complete Joy, Love, Abundance, Freedom, Health and Wholeness; in all moments."

"I stretch my capacity to live in complete Joy, Love, Abundance, Freedom, Health, and Wholeness; in all moments."

"I declare myself a beacon of Joy, Love, Abundance, Freedom, Health, and Wholeness in the world; in all moments."

Maybe it's time to get empowered by getting your joy and enthusiasm back!

65. Healing in All Dimensions

I facilitated a private remote session with one who amazingly shares her gifts. She has experienced physical issues even with all her talents to heal. We delve deeply in her sessions. In a past life, I saw her with metal braces. She had polio. The braces seemed to be a trigger that brought in issues for her from another dimension. In another dimension, she was harvested for parts and experienced being turned into a cyborg.

She experienced such suffering in that dimension that not only did she want to help everyone in this life, but she also felt an obligation to ease their suffering in another dimension. It was the reason that she was not getting total relief in this life. It was like she was holding her foot open to the other dimension so she could help them too.

Taps to heal in all dimensions:

[Say each statement slowly and consciously out loud. Articulate each word and make a point to pause after each phrase. Say each statement three times while tapping on your head. Then say it a fourth time while tapping on your chest. Take a deep breath after finishing the series.]

> **"I recant all vows and agreements between myself and everyone and everything; in all moments and in all dimensions"**

> **"I remove all curses between myself and everyone and everything; in all moments and in all dimensions"**

> **"I dissolve all karmic ties between myself and everyone and everything; in all moments and in all dimensions"**

"I remove all the pain, burden, limitations, and engrams that everyone and everything have put on me; in all moments and in all dimensions"

"I remove all the pain, burden, limitations, and engrams that I have put on everyone and everything; in all moments and in all dimensions"

"I take back all the Joy, Love, Abundance, Freedom, Health, Success, Security, Companionship, Creativity, Peace, Life, Wholeness, Beauty, Enthusiasm, Contentment, Spirituality, Enlightenment and Confidence that everyone and everything have taken from me; in all moments and in all dimensions"

"I give back all the Joy, Love, Abundance, Freedom, Health, Success, Security, Companionship, Creativity, Peace, Life, Wholeness, Beauty, Enthusiasm, Contentment, Spirituality, Enlightenment and Confidence that I have taken from everyone and everything; in all moments and in all dimensions"

"I release resonating with everyone and everything; in all moments and in all dimensions"

"I release emanating with everyone and everything; in all moments and in all dimensions"

"I remove everyone and everything from my sound frequency; in all moments and in all dimensions"

"I remove everyone and everything from my light body; in all moments and in all dimensions"

"I shift my paradigm from everyone and everything to Joy, Love, Abundance, Freedom, Health, Success, Security, Companionship, Creativity, Peace, Life, Wholeness, Beauty, Enthusiasm, Contentment, Spirituality, Enlightenment and Confidence; in all moments and in all dimensions"

"I transcend everyone and everything; in all moments and in all dimensions"

"I repair and fortify the Wei Chi of all of my bodies; in all moments and in all dimensions"

"I repair and fortify the Wei Chi of all those I have damaged; in all moments and in all dimensions"

"I align all my bodies; in all moments and in all dimensions"

"I am centered and empowered in divine love; in all moments and in all dimensions"

66. Story of Saving a Spouse

I really don't know how to explain these taps. They came through when I worked with a client who holds the highest intention for humanity. She is so open-minded, but her husband was less so. It felt like on some abstract level, in the imagination, that he was trapped in this prism of power. Those are the words that came through that resonated with my client. Before the session, she was feeling that we would need to do some taps to help him. But it is impossible for me to interfere in someone's psychic space.

When two people are energetically joined as in marriage or being intimate, they share space. It felt like her husband being trapped in a prism of power was her business. Because they share space, she is able to do taps to help free him of the prism of power. These taps seemed very powerful to her. The visuals that I saw were souls being trapped in something that looked like the death star from the *Star Wars* saga.

As she was performing these taps to save her husband, it felt like she was literally pulling him out of this dark orb. What was interesting is the image I had of him. In this life he is a fireman. He saves people from dark burning buildings. It felt like, on some abstract level, he chose this profession to work out a deep unconscious need to save himself and others from this prism of power. I also wonder if people who have been to war would benefit from these taps as well.

Taps to assist a loved one:

[Say each statement slowly and consciously out loud. Articulate each word and make a point to pause after each phrase. Say each statement three times while tapping on your head. Then say it a fourth time while tapping on your chest. Take a deep breath after finishing the series.]

"We release being trapped in all prisms of power; in all lifetimes, realities, and dimensions"

"We release being diminished by all prisms of power; in all lifetimes, realities, and dimensions"

"We release being rendered helpless by all prisms of power; in all lifetimes, realities, and dimensions"

"We release being enslaved by all prisms of power; in all lifetimes, realities, and dimensions"

"We release being manipulated by all prisms of power; in all lifetimes, realities, and dimensions"

"We recant all vows and agreements between ourselves and all prisms of power; in all lifetimes, realities, and dimensions"

"We remove all curses between ourselves and all prisms of power; in all lifetimes, realities, and dimensions"

"We dissolve all karmic ties between ourselves and all prisms of power; in all lifetimes, realities and dimensions"

"We sever all cords and connections between ourselves and all prisms of power; in all lifetimes, realities, and dimensions"

"We withdraw all our energy from all prisms of power; in all lifetimes, realities, and dimensions"

"We shatter all prisms of power; in all lifetimes, realities, and dimensions"

"We free all souls that we have trapped in all prisms of power; in all lifetimes, realities, and dimensions"

"We remove all the fear, pain, burden, limitations, engrams, cords and ties, and control devises that all prisms of power have put on us; in all lifetimes, realities, and dimensions"

"We remove all the fear, pain, burden, limitations, engrams, cords and ties, and control devises that we have put on all others for all prisms of power; in all lifetimes, realities, and dimensions"

"We take back all the Joy, Love, Abundance, Freedom, Health, Success, Security, Companionship, Creativity, Peace, Life, Wholeness, Beauty, Enthusiasm, Contentment, Confidence, Light, Music, Spirituality and Enlightenment that all prisms of power have taken from us; in all lifetimes, realities and dimensions"

"We give back all the Joy, Love, Abundance, Freedom, Health, Success, Security, Companionship, Creativity, Peace, Life, Wholeness, Beauty, Enthusiasm, Contentment, Confidence, Light, Music, Spirituality and Enlightenment that we have taken from all others for all prisms of power; in all lifetimes, realities, and dimensions"

"We release resonating with all prisms of power; in all lifetimes, realities, and dimensions"

"We release emanating with all prisms of power; in all lifetimes, realities, and dimensions"

"We remove all prisms of power from our sound frequency; in all lifetimes, realities, and dimensions"

"We remove all prisms of power from our light body; in all lifetimes, realities, and dimensions"

"We shift our paradigm from all prisms of power to Joy, Love, Abundance, Freedom, Health, Success, Security, Companionship, Creativity, Peace, Life, Wholeness, Beauty, Enthusiasm, Contentment, Confidence, Light, Music, Spirituality, and Enlightenment; in all lifetimes, realities, and dimensions"

"We transcend all prisms of power; in all lifetimes, realities, and dimensions"

"We repair and fortify our Wei Chi; in all lifetimes, realities, and dimensions"

"We are centered imbued and empowered in Divine Light, Love and Music; in all lifetimes, realities and dimensions"

67. Removing All Genetic Dis-eases

There is a belief that genetic diseases are caused by one of our relatives who came before us and had difficult issues. They stored the issues in their DNA and passed them down to many who came afterwards. That makes sense because some genetic diseases haven't always been part of our lineage. They are a newer phenomenon.

In a BodyTalk session, I was told that one of my issues was passed down by my father's grandmother who was very unhappy. In my sessions, its effects were released from me. But what about my siblings who could be affected by this relative? What if I released the pain and anguish of this relative as a means to release it from all who came after her? What if all genetic diseases could be released by healing or disconnecting from all the relatives who came before us? Why not try? What if it isn't just diseases but genetic propensity to have undesirable traits that we can release? Maybe our lives and the lives of many others can be made better by sending our ancestors love and easing their pain. What a concept! Maybe it has never been tried on a mass scale. Let's try something outside the box.

Here are the taps to assist in disconnecting from all our past relatives. May it relieve many people.

[Say each statement slowly and consciously out loud. Articulate each word and make a point to pause after each phrase. Say each statement three times while tapping on your head. Then say it a fourth time while tapping on your chest. Take a deep breath after finishing the series.]

"I release carrying the pain and dis-ease of all my ancestors; in all moments."

"I release identifying with the angst of all my ancestors; in all moments."

"I release being enslaved to the angst of all my ancestors; in all moments."

"I release the genetic propensity for pain and dis-ease; in all moments."

"I release storing pain and angst in my DNA; in all moments."

"I release being a victim of my ancestor's angst; in all moments."

"I recant all vows and agreements between myself and all my ancestors; in all moments."

"I remove all curses between myself and all my ancestors; in all moments."

"I dissolve all karmic ties between myself and all my ancestors; in all moments."

"I remove all the pain, burden, limitations, and engrams that all my ancestors have put on me; in all moments."

"I remove all the pain, burden, limitations, and engrams that I have put on all my ancestors; in all moments."

"I give back all the Joy, Love, Abundance, Freedom, Health, Success, Security, Companionship, Creativity, Peace, Life, and Wholeness that I have taken from all my ancestors; in all moments."

"I take back all the Joy, Love, Abundance, Freedom, Health, Success, Security, Companionship, Creativity, Peace, Life and Wholeness that all my ancestors have taken from me; in all moments."

"I withdraw all my energy from all my ancestors; in all moments."

"I release resonating with all my ancestors; in all moments."

"I release emanating with all my ancestors; in all moments."

"I remove all my ancestors from my sound frequency; in all moments."

"I remove all my ancestors from my light body; in all moments."

"I shift my paradigm from any or all of my ancestors to the purity and stillness of now; in all moments."

"I am centered and empowered in Joy, Love, Abundance, Freedom, Health, Success, Security, Companionship, Creativity, Peace, Life, and Wholeness; in all moments."

Science has discovered that DNA can be changed. This is an organic tool with a focused intention to shift one back into health.

68. Uplifting Humanity by Releasing the Vanities

It is fortunate that I am able to see the akashic records of clients and know what their issues are so that I can address them. A recent client had been an abuser of power on a grand scale. It is a very important lesson to knowing compassion. In the present life, I could get a sense of her records and how she has made life difficult for others in her stubbornness.

In her first session, she really compartmentalized my work, and it was a bit off-putting. She seemed to value only the components of it to which she had a strong reaction. The other parts we seemed to dismiss. In her session, the images that I was seeing were all of Nazi Germany during World War II. They were more than an abuse of power; they were a disregard for human life. I perceived her as a high ranking official in the Nazi regime. Her whole session was addressing this issue. When her session was over, the exchange was as cold and thankless as if I had handed her dry cleaning. But I was comforted by knowing that this session benefited humanity in some way. Releasing her dynamics with the world, released the world from whatever she had unleashed on them. This is how I approach every single session, as if it unties some of the karmic strings on some people and loosens the ones on all others as a by-product.

I was surprised when she contacted me for another session. I refused to give it to her before we talked about the first session. I was surprised that she actually knew she had benefited greatly from the session because of her lack of gratitude. I explained how she left me feeling, and she seemed genuinely surprised. She thought I was hard on her in the first session. She had no idea what was to come in the second session.

Because I am releasing issues that people would otherwise have to experience, the client still needs to absorb the lesson that they would have been learning on their own. With this woman, I had to be very direct to help compensate for her denial. In other clients, it can be a process that happens within them and is none of my business after the session. I will support them, but I don't even remember sessions or many of the clients after a session.

There is a subversive exchange that happens between people on an energetic level. To understand this, think of talking to teenagers and having them say what you want them to say, but you know they are holding contempt for you. Since I perceive mostly in energy, this is the dynamic I address in people. They seem confused at first, but I let them know what they really are doing. To be called on it is confusing yet refreshing to them.

On the surface, she was very polite, but energetically she was seething with contempt. Those layers that were being released did not want to go. It was them that I was addressing with my strong tone. It was the thick layers of facade that I was addressing and stripping off. Clients know this somewhat because I will toggle between very harsh tones and my usual kindness. Also, what clients may not realize is that while I am addressing them, I am also moving energy with an energetic intention.

At the beginning of her second session, I was surprised by this woman's voice. She was warm and kind. I was very pleased about the change from the first session. Still, I honestly explained to her how she was the only person I ever left a session feeling so unappreciated that it felt like an abyss. I also explained that after her session, I checked out her Facebook page to see if I could tell which member of the Nazi party she reminded me of. I told her how when I saw this one photo of her, that it left me cold. I asked her if she were Hitler. This seems silly to say out loud, but I wanted her to get a sense of the magnitude of the abuse of power that I was tuning into.

From the beginning of the session to the end, she convulsed in huge sobs. I gave her no sympathy. The image of the plights of the world that were devastated by power left me unwavering in compassion. Energetically, she needed to experience the lack of compassion to which her power plays had subjected the world. If someone did not know the inner dynamic that was playing out, they would have thought I was ruthless. But it was what was necessary for this session.

I was actually very pleased with her that she was so receptive in the session. But I did not allow her to know that. When bringing up the photo, she admitted (with a hint of pride that she was not aware of) that she had an evil streak in her. That needed to be stripped from her. The fact that the session was so difficult for her was evidence of just how deep the session was.

She wanted to address her judgments and jealousies. When I facilitate a session, I am conscious of how the victims of my clients are going to benefit from my clients energetically giving back all they have taken from the victims. I am also aware of the benefit all their victims receive by them erasing all their transgressions. I performed this particular session from the point of view of what people who were affected by the abuse of power would want it to look like. They would want her to feel a hint of what they had experienced. They would not have been disappointed. This was an incredibly intense session, and I am so proud of her for allowing me to share this with everyone.

Here are some of the taps I shared with her. There are some that brought her into convulsive laughter. You may recognize which ones. I handed out the taps as if Hitler himself was doing the session. That is very harsh, but it describes the level of responsibility I take in doing these sessions. It is incredibly effective. That analogy gives a good perspective to anyone doing the taps. Do them from the vantage point of abusing power and be a surrogate to release deep injustices in the world and regain balance. The taps begin with releasing the vanities. These are anger, greed, lust, attachment and vanity.

[Say each statement slowly and consciously out loud. Articulate each word and make a point to pause after each phrase. Say each statement three times while tapping on your head. Then say it a fourth time while tapping on your chest. Take a deep breath after finishing the series.]

"I release abusing power; in all moments."

"I release giving my free will over to the vanities; in all moments."

"I release succumbing to the vanities; in all moments."

"I release worshiping the vanities; in all moments."

"I release being enslaved to the vanities; in all moments."

"I release wielding power for the vanities; in all moments."

"I release craving world domination; in all moments."

"I release perpetuating the vanities; in all moments."

"I release choosing the vanities over love; in all moments."

"I release the relentless pursuit for the vanities; in all moments."

"I release an allegiance with evil; in all moments."

"I release endorsing evil; in all moments."

"I release being the personification of evil; in all moments."

"I withdraw all my energy from evil; in all moments."

"I recant all vows and agreements between myself and the vanities; in all moments."

"I remove all curses between myself and the vanities; in all moments."

"I dissolve all karmic ties between myself and the vanities; in all moments."

"I remove all the pain, burden, limitations, and engrams that the vanities have put on me; in all moments."

"I remove all the pain, burden, limitations, and engrams that I have put on the world due to the vanities; in all moments."

"I release endorsing Putin; in all moments."

"I release providing a blueprint for war; in all moments."

"I release creating war in the world; in all moments."

"I release being responsible for the conflict between Palestine and Israel; in all moments."

"I withdraw all my energy from the vanities; in all moments."

"I withdraw all my energy from war; in all moments."

"I take back all the Joy, Love, Abundance, Freedom, Life, and Wholeness; in all moments."

"I give back all the Joy, Love, Abundance, Freedom, Life, and Wholeness that I have taken from the world due to the vanities; in all moments."

"I release resonating with the vanities; in all moments."

"I release emanating with the vanities; in all moments."

"I remove all of the vanities from my sound frequency; in all moments."

"I remove all the vanities from my light body; in all moments."

"I shift my paradigm from the vanities to Joy, Love, Abundance, Freedom, Life, and Wholeness; in all moments."

"I transcend the vanities; in all moments."

"I remove all masks, walls, and armor; in all moments."

"I repair and fortify the Wei Chi of all my bodies; in all moments."

"I am centered and imbued in Divine Love; in all moments."

"I emanate and resonate Divine Love to every corner of the world; in all moments."

"I dissolve everything that is not motivated by Divine Love; in all moments."

This exercise is an incredible gift that my client allowed me to share with everyone. The taps may seem really harsh. But on some level, if we are not doing everything in our own lives to overcome the vanities and abusing power, we are adding to the conflict in the world. This life is the tipping point, and what we do here—although no one will pat us on the back for it—is our part in uplifting the quality of life for everyone on the planet. We are not bystanders in life. The more people who do these taps, the easier it will be for others to recognize their importance. I encourage everyone to do them and to share.

69. Embracing One's Higher Purpose

I facilitated a private remote session with someone who was experiencing writer's block. She was more than halfway through her project, but she was getting in her own way. As she was feeling empowered by writing, she was coming up against a past life trauma that made her feel guilty. The closer she came to manifesting her truth, the closer she brushed up against the trauma that prevented her from sharing her truth in a past life. The manifestation was depression and compulsive eating.

What came through was a past life in Cathars. Cathars is the site of the twelfth century genocide that took place in southern France. It was a whole village of peaceful monks who practiced the alchemy of turning their physical state into the golden state of higher consciousness. They lived as the personification of the Holy Grail.

The monks were given a choice. They were either to renounce their beliefs or walk into a huge fire to their death. Most walked in. The monks who went last would pull the first monks out of their bodies so that they would feel no pain. I was the last monk to go into the fire. No one was left to free me. I was left with the pain and burden of the circumstance. That is why I am so familiar with the incident.

My client was a monk there as well. But she renounced her faith to live. She was starved and tortured, but she lived. The guilt from renouncing her vocation singed deep within her. Whenever she felt close to doing something uplifting, she was pulled back into the guilt and anguish of that time. She was unable to connect with her Spirit Guides or her own intuitive side because it brought her own betrayal to the surface. Her compulsive eating was a means of telling her conscious mind that she was NOT being starved and tortured. It was a way of separating herself from the pain.

It did her good to hear that her Spirit Guides were not mad at her. She would not have been able to do anything. All the guilt and shame were getting in the way. When we finished the taps, I energetically tuned into her writing and told her where it was tangled. She could see it after I showed her, and she was now equipped to finish her project and share her gifts.

Taps to reconnect with one's highest purpose:

[Say each statement slowly and consciously out loud. Articulate each word and make a point to pause after each phrase. Say each statement three times while tapping on your head. Then say it a fourth time while tapping on your chest. Take a deep breath after finishing the series.]

"I recant renouncing my higher purpose; in all moments."

"I release the pain and trauma of being tortured; in all moments."

"I release the belief that my Spirit Guides hate me; in all moments."

"I release betraying my higher purpose; in all moments."

"I release the fear of being tortured; in all moments."

"I release confusing my higher purpose with death; in all moments."

"I release confusing my higher purpose with torture; in all moments."

"I release playing it safe; in all moments."

"I recant all vows and agreements between myself and torture; in all moments."

"I remove all curses between myself and torture; in all moments."

"I dissolve all karmic ties between myself and torture; in all moments."

"I remove all the pain, burden, limitations, and engrams that torture has put on me; in all moments."

"I withdraw all my energy from torture; in all moments."

"I take back all the Joy, Love, Abundance, Freedom, Health, Life and Wholeness that torture has taken from me; in all moments."

"I make space in this world to manifest my higher purpose; in all moments."

"I remove all blockages to living my higher purpose; in all moments."

"I stretch my capacity to live my higher purpose; in all moments."

"I accept and embrace my Spirit Guides; in all moments."

"I am centered and empowered in Divine Love; in all moments."

70. Releasing the Addiction to Television

Sometimes there is nothing on television, but some people find a need to have it on anyway. Some families use television as a means to connect without really connecting. Some were plopped down in front of the TV when they were young to distract them from being upset or to entertain them.

From our pet's point of view, they don't know we are looking at something when we sit in front of the TV. They think that we are just sitting in one spot looking at a wall all day. At least they look out a window at real things. Who is better off?

Television, while entertaining, is also a huge energy drain, a source of manipulation, and over-watching it is a form of complacency. In some cases, it is more addictive than sugar. In fact, some addictions go hand in hand. There is a huge correlation, I am sure, with watching television and over-indulging in junk food. That is the whole purpose of television as a business: to sell everyone things they would not otherwise think they needed.

Taps to release the addiction to television:

[Say each statement slowly and consciously out loud. Articulate each word and make a point to pause after each phrase. Say each statement three times while tapping on your head. Then say it a fourth time while tapping on your chest. Take a deep breath after finishing the series.]

"I release being addicted to television; in all moments."

"I release confusing television for family; in all moments."

"I release confusing television for friendship; in all moments."

"I shatter the illusion of television; in all lifetimes"

"I release using television as a crutch; in all moments."

"I release replacing my joy with television; in all moments."

"I release replacing love with television; in all moments."

"I release inhibiting my own creativity by watching television; in all moments."

"I release trading in my abundance to watch television; in all moments."

"I release choosing television over freedom; in all moments."

"I release confusing television for reality; in all moments."

"I release choosing television over reality; in all moments."

"I release using television as a security blanket; in all moments."

"I release allowing television to dumb down my consciousness; in all moments."

"I release choosing television over adventure; in all moments."

"I release choosing television over life; in all moments."

"I release lowering my vibration to the level of television; in all moments."

"I release being manipulated by television; in all moments."

"I shift my paradigm from television to Joy, Love, Abundance, Freedom, Health, Success, Security, Companionship, Peace, Life, and Wholeness; in all moments."

71. Healing One's Own Fibonacci Sequence

The Fibonacci Sequence was discovered by a medieval mathematician. It is a sacred geometry equation that is present in every structure of nature, including man. As a mathematic equation, it looks like this:

1+1=2, 1+2=3, 2+3=5, and so on.

Every spiral, every leaf, every seashell is evidence of this simple equation.

Each step is important as a foundation for the next step. It is an exacting science. If one step is left out, there is no structure to support the structure that ensues. This may explain the reason why so many people who win the lottery quickly lose the money. They had left out a series of steps in learning how to invest money.

So many people want to skip a process in life. I have clients who want to make drastic changes in their living conditions. When I suggest that they make small moves, they reject the idea. There is a fear that if they make a small move, they will be as entrenched in the next step as where they are now. They are afraid of risking a change that will not be good.

They prefer to wait until a sure thing presents itself. They want a safety net on life. But by not changing and adapting, they create a prison for themselves. They have to walk through the equation of one plus one so they can get to two. But they want to start at one and get to a hundred and skip all the steps in between in the Fibonacci sequence.

[Say each statement slowly and consciously out loud. Articulate each word and make a point to pause after each phrase. Say each statement three times while tapping on your head. Then say it a

fourth time while tapping on your chest. Take a deep breath after finishing the series.]

"I release the pain and trauma of being uprooted; in all moments."

"I release holding on to the devastation of war; in all moments."

"I release the fear of being uprooted; in all moments."

"I release the fear of change; in all moments."

"I release defining change as devastation; in all moments."

"I release the fear of crossing over; in all moments."

"I release confusing change with crossing over; in all moments."

"I release wanting a safety net; in all moments."

"I release choosing security over freedom; in all moments."

"I release being enslaved to security; in all moments."

"I release creating my own imprisonment; in all moments."

"I release avoiding change; in all moments."

"I release the fear of being stuck in purgatory; in all moments."

"I release the fear of getting stuck in the next step of my Fibonacci Sequence; in all moments."

"I release being stuck in a stagnant state; in all moments."

"I make space in this world for the manifestation of my highest Joy, Love, Abundance, Freedom, Health, Success, Confidence, Enthusiasm, Life, and Wholeness; in all moments."

"I remove all blockages between myself and the manifestation of my highest Joy, Love, Abundance, Freedom, Health, Success, Confidence, Enthusiasm, Life and Wholeness; in all moments."

"I stretch my capacity to accept the manifestation of my highest Joy, Love, Abundance, Freedom, Health, Success, Confidence, Enthusiasm, Life, and Wholeness; in all moments."

"I fortify every step in my own Fibonacci Sequence with the manifestation of my highest Joy, Love, Abundance, Freedom, Health, Success, Confidence, Enthusiasm, Life and Wholeness; in all moments."

"I collapse all time and space and secure the highest manifestation of my Joy, Love, Abundance, Freedom, Health, Success, Confidence, Enthusiasm, Life and Wholeness; in all moments."

"I shift my paradigm from complacency to the highest manifestation of my Joy, Love, Abundance, Freedom, Health, Success, Confidence, Enthusiasm, Life and Wholeness; in all moments."

"I am centered and empowered in the highest manifestation of my Joy, Love, Abundance, Freedom, Health, Success, Confidence, Enthusiasm, Life and Wholeness; in all moments."

72. Even More Taps on Food Issues

Taps to release food issues:

[Say each statement slowly and consciously out loud. Articulate each word and make a point to pause after each phrase. Say each statement three times while tapping on your head. Then say it a fourth time while tapping on your chest. Take a deep breath after finishing the series.]

"I release eating out of boredom; in all moments."

"I release eating as a coping mechanism; in all moments."

"I release eating because I am sad; in all moments."

"I release eating to fill a void; in all moments."

"I release eating to feel loved; in all moments."

"I release eating to feel comfort; in all moments."

"I release eating to feel safe; in all moments."

"I release eating to kill time; in all moments."

"I release eating to feel busy; in all moments."

"I release eating as a form of distraction; in all moments."

"I release eating for entertainment; in all moments."

"I release eating to be social; in all moments."

"I release eating to celebrate; in all moments."

"I release thinking of food as a friend; in all moments."

"I release the fear of being hungry; in all moments."

"I release eating to nurture myself; in all moments."

"I release being obsessed with food; in all moments."

"I release using food as a hobby; in all moments."

"I am centered and satiated in Joy, Love, Abundance, Freedom, Health, Life, and Wholeness; in all moments."

73. Release Being Conditioned

We are conditioned by advertisers to be taken from. That is why we are hesitant to be giving. There has always been someone that is there to take. Advertisers have become savvy in using what is sacred to us to open up our receptiveness, and then they harvest from our essence.

This is the manipulative nature of advertising. We have been so conditioned by this process in the last 60 years that it is difficult to trust a sincere sentiment. Whatever life event brings us joy, there is a commercial about it to take something from us. They are not just taking our money; they are taking our trust and our free will. We are being robbed and programmed.

Christmas morning--Maxwell house, child returning home--Folgers, Mother's Day--Hallmark, first day of school--Staples. Everyone reading this is pulling up the images of the commercials that I just mentioned. This is programming. We happily pull them up because they are so ingrained.

Even the upliftment of humanity was sponsored by Coca Cola in the 70s. No wonder everyone got disillusioned at wanting to teach the world to sing; instead, they just drank a Coke and called it a day!

[Say each statement slowly and consciously out loud. Articulate each word and make a point to pause after each phrase. Say each statement three times while tapping on your head. Then say it a fourth time while tapping on your chest. Take a deep breath after finishing the series.]

"I release being programed; in all moments."

"I release trading programmed images for truth; in all moments."

"I remove all the images that were programmed into me; in all moments."

"I release being a pawn for advertisers; in all moments."

"I release giving away my free will; in all moments."

"I release trading my Joy, Love, Abundance, Freedom and Wholeness for security; in all moments."

"I release being part of the herd mentality; in all moments."

"I release being a money distributor; in all moments."

"I strip the illusion off those who lie to me; in all moments."

"I see truth beyond the lie; in all moments."

"I release being used; in all moments."

"I transcend being used; in all moments."

"I strip all the illusion off the users; in all moments."

"I shift my paradigm from being used to Joy, Love, Abundance, Freedom, Health, Life, and Wholeness; in all moments."

"I am centered and empowered in Divine Love; in all moments."

74. Embracing Your Ultimate Truth

Sometimes, we feel burdened because we try to come to terms with our internal truth without abandoning external truth. It can leave us feeling lost, dejected, or confused.

Taps to embrace your ultimate truth:

[Say each statement slowly and consciously out loud. Articulate each word and make a point to pause after each phrase. Say each statement three times while tapping on your head. Then say it a fourth time while tapping on your chest. Take a deep breath after finishing the series.]

"I release being enslaved to external truth; in all moments."

"I release trading my ultimate truth for external truth; in all moments."

"I release trading my ultimate truth with someone else's truth; in all moments."

"I release betraying my ultimate truth; in all moments."

"I release squelching my ultimate truth; in all moments."

"I release giving my allegiance to external truth: in all moments."

"I release being fragmented by external truth: in all moments."

"I release allowing external truth to shake my confidence in my ultimate truth; in all moments."

"I withdraw all my energy from external truth; in all moments."

"I recant all vows and agreements between myself and external truth; in all moments."

"I remove all curses between myself and external truth; in all moments."

"I dissolve all karmic ties between myself and external truth; in all moments."

"I remove all the pain, burden, limitations, and engrams that external truth has put on me, in all moments."

"I take back all the Joy, Love, Abundance, Freedom, Health, Success, Security, Companionship, Peace, Life, and Wholeness that external truth has taken from me; in all moments."

"I release resonating with external truth; in all moments."

"I release emanating with external truth; in all moments."

"I remove all external truth from my sound frequency; in all moments."

"I remove all external truth from my light body; in all moments."

"I transcend external truth; in all moments."

"I shift my paradigm from external truth to my ultimate truth; in all moments."

"I am centered and empowered in Divine Love; in all moments."

75. Happy Birthday!

A birthday is a great time to take inventory. It is a special day of acknowledgement. Some birthdays are disappointing because we have expectations of others making the day special. Here is to taking your power back by giving yourself a gift of freedom. Happy birthday to everyone! Celebrate you!

Taps to release on your birthday:

[Say each statement slowly and consciously out loud. Articulate each word and make a point to pause after each phrase. Say each statement three times while tapping on your head. Then say it a fourth time while tapping on your chest. Take a deep breath after finishing the series.]

"I release the fear and hesitation of returning to earth; in all moments."

"I release being homesick for heaven; in all moments."

"I release the trauma of being born; in all moments."

"I release being disappointed in my parents; in all moments."

"I release being a disappointment in my situation; in all moments."

"I release the trauma of being a mistake; in all moments."

"I release feeling unwanted; in all moments."

"I release being rejected by my mother; in all moments."

"I release being abandoned by my father; in all moments."

"I release being the enemy of my siblings; in all moments."

"I release being ignored; in all moments."

"I release being invalidated; in all moments."

"I release feeling unsafe; in all moments."

"I release having to be the adult; in all moments."

"I release losing my childhood; in all moments."

"I release being an inconvenience; in all moments."

"I release the belief that I am in the wrong place; in all moments."

"I release being numb and despondent; in all moments."

"I release being bound to any vivaxis; in all moments."

"I release being confined to any astrological vivaxis; in all moments."

"I release being limited by my astrological sign; in all moments."

"I free myself to be all I am capable to be; in all moments."

"I release the belief I don't have a choice; in all moments."

"I release feeling the need to be anywhere other than where I AM; in all moments."

"I remove myself from autopilot; in all moments."

"I take back my empowerment; in all moments."

"I am centered and imbued in Divine Love; in all moments."

"I celebrate me; in all moments."

*a vivaxis is an energetic link to the place of birth or a negative energy merely because it was imprinted on you.

76. Father's Day Taps

Fathers have been given an impossible role in this society. They are flawed people who are supposed to perpetuate the facade that men are superior and play that part every day. It is no wonder that so many of them desert their post. In stereotypes, we accept mothers for being flawed because they nurture, and we have dads there to make us feel safe. But that is not really the scenario that plays out for so many.

Taps to change relationship with father:

[Say each statement slowly and consciously out loud. Articulate each word and make a point to pause after each phrase. Say each statement three times while tapping on your head. Then say it a fourth time while tapping on your chest. Take a deep breath after finishing the series.]

"I release hating dad; in all moments."

"I release disappointing dad; in all moments."

"I release being disappointed in my dad; in all moments."

"I release letting my dad down; in all moments."

"I release the belief that dad hates me; in all moments."

"I release worshiping my dad; in all moments."

"I release the pain in realizing that dad is flawed; in all moments."

"I release defining flawed as broken; in all moments."

"I release the fear of becoming my dad; in all moments."

"I release being beat up by my dad; in all moments."

"I release being abandoned by my dad; in all moments."

"I release being my dad's scapegoat; in all moments."

"I release being my dad's target; in all moments."

"I release being raped by my dad; in all moments."

"I release being betrayed by my dad; in all moments."

"I release defining my relationship with my dad as me being unworthy; in all moments."

"I release the pain and trauma of being punished; in all moments."

"I release the belief that God is punishing me; in all moments."

"I release the pain and trauma of being invisible to my dad; in all moments."

"I release being afraid of my dad; in all moments."

"I release using my dad to formulate my relationship with God; in all moments."

"I recant all vows and agreements between myself and dad; in all moments."

"I remove all curses between myself and dad; in all moments."

"I dissolve all karmic ties between myself and dad; in all moments."

"I remove all the fear, shame, pain, burden, limitations, and engrams that my dad has put on me; in all moments."

"I take back all the Joy, Love, Abundance, Freedom, Health, Success, Security, Companionship, Creativity, Peace, Life, Wholeness, Beauty, Enthusiasm, Contentment, Creativity, Confidence, and Enlightenment that my dad has taken from me; in all moments."

"I am centered and empowered in divine love; in all moments."

These taps will help take the pressure of your dynamics with your dad. Maybe it can alleviate a lot of angst or pain that the societal role of fathers has put on everyone. Say all the statements above. One never knows which one is going to alleviate that internal pressure and bring more Joy, Love, Abundance, Freedom and Wholeness.

May all the grown children who need these taps get validation and completion in doing these.

77. The Underbelly of Mother's Day

I facilitated a long distance session with a woman who was having a strong reaction to her mother moving close. We all know the politically correct thing to say, "Suck it up! She gave birth to you!" But this mentality does such a disservice to many. It is a very invalidating point of view.

Immediately, when I tuned into the woman, I saw her as a sweet little girl in a pretty little dress. Her mother was lighting matches and handing them to her over and over again so she would burn herself. Then she would just start dropping them on her and burning her as they fell on her. The child, in her innocence, kept reaching for them and engaging the adult. The adult turned into a dark form and was coaxing the child to play games and then hurt her.

The next scene was of the little girl hiding in the dark and being coaxed out by a convincing voice that made promises to her. She was drawn out of hiding and murdered after being tortured by the woman who was her mother in this lifetime. Her brothers in the present life were also victims in this past life.

The scene after that was her being subjected to a horrific surgery that removed parts of her spine. This was a routine procedure performed in a certain period so that slaves could not run away. Her mother in this life is the one who sentenced her to that fate. Her mother still treated her as property and prey. Those lifetimes were bleeding through to the present.

It was obvious from the scenarios that this person was stalking her in her lifetimes, which was really confusing because she was born to the woman. The woman moving close to her was a hint that this woman was following her from lifetime to lifetime. She could either "suck it up" for a few more lifetimes and respect the concept of mother, or she could do the work that we were doing together and sever all connections to this woman. Can anyone possibly judge her for severing all ties?

This woman was sabotaging her own happiness because of these deep-seated experiences. She was hesitant to have a wonderful wedding that she deserved because she did not want this person near anything sacred to her. To do so felt like being that little child that was trusting one more time and getting killed for it. She couldn't enjoy the thought of having children with the man she adored because part of her was terrified that they would become prey to the mother.

Taps to release connection to one's mother:

[Say each statement slowly and consciously out loud. Articulate each word and make a point to pause after each phrase. Say each statement three times while tapping on your head. Then say it a fourth time while tapping on your chest. Take a deep breath after finishing the series.]

"I release hating _____; in all moments." (We used her given name not the title of mother so as not to be connected anymore.)

"I release the trauma of being born to _____ ; in all moments."

"I release the trauma of living with a predator; in all moments."

"I release the trauma of having a masochist for a mother; in all moments."

"I release the trauma of having a sadist for a mother; in all moments."

"I release the trauma of being stalked by _____; in all moments."

"I release being imprisoned by _____ ; in all moments."

Enlightenment Unveiled

"I release the trauma of being murdered by _____; in all moments."

"I release defining motherhood as tolerating the enemy; in all moments."

"I recant all vows and agreements between myself and _____; in all moments."

"I remove all curses and spells between myself and _____; in all moments."

"I remove all the pain, burden, limitations, and engrams that _____ has put on me; in all moments."

"I take back all the Joy, Love, Abundance, Freedom, Health, Success, Security, Companionship, Peace, Life, Wholeness, Beauty, Enthusiasm, and Contentment that _____ has taken from me; in all moments."

"I transcend having a relationship with _____; in all moments."

"I make myself and my family invisible to _____; in all moments."

"I engulf myself and my family in a protective globe of light; in all moments."

What came through in the session validated all her angst at such a deep level.

I did do something else that may be viewed as unconventional. I gave this woman permission to move away from her mother and to never look back. It is what she so desperately wants to do. I just validated her by agreeing with her truth.

These taps work with anyone in your life that you get an uncomfortable feeling about. I encourage you to do them and feel validated by doing so. And give yourselves permission to disconnect.

78. Reclaiming Truth

There is an innate truth that exists. It is a higher essence of morality and integrity that exists beyond where and when those concepts were tainted. Beyond is even the wrong word. They exist within. Truth is our true nature. In human form, we thought it was lost. But no. It is our own essence. It is time to reclaim it. Time to stop believing the "lie."

We are all tired of the lie. The one that says we are not good enough. The one that says we need to fight and kill to be whole. The lie that makes us focus so much of our energy on outer appearances rather than in nurturing each other in so many intangible ways. The lie proclaims only humans are important, and there is a whole hierarchy within that. The lie makes us concede that rich white men are revered, so the rest of us concede to their whims in all matters. They change laws and manipulate facts to stroke their petty sense of morality. Facts are not truth. They are a justification of a stance. Facts are part of the lie. So many of us are tired of living and watching the lie.

[Say each statement slowly and consciously out loud. Articulate each word and make a point to pause after each phrase. Say each statement three times while tapping on your head. Then say it a fourth time while tapping on your chest. Take a deep breath after finishing the series.]

"I release believing the lies; in all moments."

"I release being vested in lies; in all moments."

"I release being comforted by the lies; in all moments."

"I strip off the illusion of all lies; in all moments."

"I release being swayed by lies; in all moments."

"I release circumnavigating truth around lies; in all moments."

"I release conceding to the lies; in all moments."

"I release switching out truth for the lies; in all moments."

"I release perpetuating the lies; in all moments."

"I release living a lie; in all moments."

"I recant all vows and agreements between myself and all lies; in all moments."

"I remove all curses between myself and all lies; in all moments."

"I dissolve all karmic agreements between myself and all lies; in all moments."

"I remove all the pain, burden, limitations, and engrams that all lies have put on me; in all moments."

"I take back all the Joy, Love, Abundance, Freedom, Health, Life, and Wholeness that all lies have taken from me; in all moments."

"I release resonating with lies; in all moments."

"I release emanating with lies; in all moments."

"I remove all lies from my sound frequency; in all moments."

"I remove all lies from my light body; in all moments."

"I shift my paradigm from all lies to Joy, Love, Abundance, Freedom, Health, Life, and Wholeness; in all moments."

"I am centered and empowered in the sanctity of absolute truth; in all moments."

If nothing else, these taps will help individuals feel like they are taking a personal stance. They don't have to rally for a cause; they don't have to hop on a moral high horse. They are just a way of drawing a line in the sand that holds a place for a higher truth in this world. It is a silent, reverent calling to arms.

79. Redefining Motherhood

I facilitated a session with a young woman contemplating motherhood. She had many reservations, but they manifested as one mass of confusion. The first thing that she would not admit to herself was that although she loved her husband, it was not a storybook romance. Their relationship didn't reach the depth of fairytale romances. She was concerned about being connected for life to her husband as the father of her baby.

When I tuned in, I knew that she was harboring all the feelings about motherhood. But the baby that she was carrying was a true fairytale love. Her husband was the perfect father that would give this baby what he needed. This perspective reassured her.

The next issue was all these dynamics with her mother. She did not want to be annoyed with the baby like she was annoyed with her mother her whole life. She also didn't want to be like her mother. She identified negative traits with motherhood. I led her through a series of taps that brought some relief. But then more disturbing layers were revealed.

She described the feeling of being led through her life and losing control. The imagery of a past life emerged. She was being led to slaughter. Slowly and methodically she was moving closer and closer to her horrific death. There was no compassion, there was no kindness, just a methodical bludgeoning. This is the feeling that was being subliminally evoked every time she had a major milestone in her life. She was correlating each event as a step closer to a horrific outcome. Motherhood was just another one of those steps.

When I helped her release this correlation, I inadvertently coughed. She told me that when I coughed, she had a strange tingling on the roof of her mouth. She was getting a sense of the imagery that I saw when I coughed. She was a newborn. She was unwanted, maybe because she was born a girl. She was put in a burlap bag at birth and taken out to the pond and drowned. It made her confuse birth with death and death with love. When she learned about this lifetime, it made her realize why she got freaked out when she thought about the amniotic sac. In her baby body, she confused the burlap sack with the amniotic sac.

As she was releasing these old engrams, images of many Mother's Day cards with wonderful sayings were running through my perception. It was if a higher definition of motherhood was being downloaded into her. She felt much lighter. It was like untangling confusion and peeling off layers of trauma at the same time. The baby will now open her up to a love she has not experienced in so many of her lifetimes. It will almost be a means to actualize all the work we have done together and for her to truly and deeply experience an incredible ethereal love.

Taps to redefine motherhood:

[Say each statement slowly and consciously out loud. Articulate each word and make a point to pause after each phrase. Say each statement three times while tapping on your head. Then say it a fourth time while tapping on your chest. Take a deep breath after finishing the series.]

"I release defining motherhood as controlling; in all moments."

"I release defining motherhood as needy; in all moments."

"I release defining motherhood as negative; in all moments."

"I release defining motherhood as being the enemy; in all moments."

"I release the fear of becoming my mother: in all moments."

"I release the fear of being hated; in all moments."

"I release the fear of losing my freedom; in all moments."

"I release the fear of letting my baby down; in all moments."

"I release defining motherhood as imprisonment; in all moments."

"I release correlating motherhood with looming death; in all moments."

"I release the fear of being trapped by motherhood; in all moments."

"I recant all vows and agreements between myself and motherhood; in all moments."

"I remove all curses between myself and motherhood; in all moments."

"I dissolve all karmic ties between myself and motherhood; in all moments."

"I remove all the pain, burden, limitations, and engrams that motherhood has put on me; in all moments."

"I take back all the Joy, Love, Abundance, Freedom, Health, Life, and Wholeness that motherhood has taken from me; in all moments."

"I redefine Motherhood as Joy, Love, Abundance, Freedom, Health, Life, and Wholeness; in all moments."

80. Cleansing Ourselves of Energetic Parasites

When I was a little girl, we would go out at night and get night crawlers to use as bait. The best time to find them was in a torrential downpour. The reason being that worms can drown underground. So they have to come to the surface when it is raining to breathe.

I have noticed the phenomenon that when there are happy events, some people are the most miserable. It is like all these triggers come to the surface to annoy them. Think of the holidays, retreats, or spiritual events where there is joy everywhere, and some people get agitated even more.

It is like the joy and happiness drowns the energetic parasites that stay hidden otherwise. They may hide and seek out an existence through attaching to us, and we co-exist without much awareness of them. Sure they may create annoyances, cravings, fears, and angers in us, but we just accept them as part of our own make up.

When these agitations come up, we can use them as an opportunity to identify these annoyances and address them. As soon as we feel an annoyance of any kind, we can use the technique of zapping them with divine love and dissipating them on contact. Thinking of ourselves as a human parasite zapper can be a great shift in our perspective. It is a refreshing shift to welcome the opportunities to be agitated, so we can release them and feel more spacious in our energy field.

Taps to zap out foreign energies:

[Say each statement slowly and consciously out loud. Articulate each word and make a point to pause after each phrase. Say each statement three times while tapping on your head. Then say it a fourth time while tapping on your chest. Take a deep breath after finishing the series.]

"I zap out all lies pretending to be truth; in all moments."

"I zap out all stealing presenting itself as borrowing; in all moments."

"I zap out all nightmares masquerading as reality; in all moments."

"I zap out all prisons that are presenting themselves as happy-ever-after; in all moments."

"I zap out all hells that are camouflaged as heaven; in all moments."

"I zap out all desecration that is pretending to be sacred; in all moments."

"I zap out all demons pretending to be God; in all moments."

"I zap out all poison that disguises itself as fruit; in all moments."

"I zap out all mutilation that is thought to be healing; in all moments."

"I zap out all power posing as love; in all moments."

"I zap out all evil that pretends to be innocence; in all moments."

"I zap out all ignorance that passes itself off as enlightenment; in all moments."

81. Release Being Indoctrinated

I facilitated a private remote session for a new client. At first, clients think they are going to tell me all their issues. I refuse to let them. It is more authentic if I tell them what I am perceiving.

As soon as I tuned in, I sensed an energetic ganglion a little bit below the heart chakra. It was a storage place for all this woman's issues. She was very positive and likable. She was dumping all her issues in this one main spot that would be out of the way. As I was explaining this, she couldn't resist telling me she had a hiatal hernia.

I started to perceive a long tentacle of this ganglion branching out in her back and wrapping around her left shoulder. She confirmed that she had pain in that shoulder. I also perceived a tentacle branching down her right leg. I sensed it causing painful veins in that leg. She confirmed. She also told me it was affecting her bladder.

I saw only one past life for her and it was the cause of many of these issues. I saw her as a soldier in a large militia for a Russian dictator. She was in a heavy uniform and standing at attention. She had her left arm out and was standing very rigid. To move was to be deemed weak or useless. She had to override all her natural body functions to conform and survive. It was affecting her in the present life. She also confirmed another thing that I suspected—that she disliked the cold.

It is always exciting when new clients can feel the shifts in their body as we do the releasing. She felt that pain in her left shoulder release, and she felt tingling in her body, which signifies the energy flowing. She did feel some warmth as well. As I emoted into the congestion in the energy ganglion, she perceived a change and sensed it crumble.

Taps to release being indoctrinated:

[Say each statement slowly and consciously out loud. Articulate each word and make a point to pause after each phrase. Say each statement three times while tapping on your head. Then say it a fourth time while tapping on your chest. Take a deep breath after finishing the series.]

"I release the trauma of being indoctrinated; in all moments."

"I release relinquishing my power to indoctrination; in all moments."

"I recant all vows and agreements between myself and all indoctrination; in all moments."

"I remove all curses between myself and all indoctrination; in all moments."

"I dissolve all karmic ties between myself and all indoctrination; in all moments."

"I remove all the pain, burden, limitations and engrams that all indoctrination has put on me; in all moments."

"I take back all the Joy, Love, Abundance, Freedom, Health, Success, Security, Companionship, Peace, Life and Wholeness that all indoctrination has taken from me; in all moments."

"I release resonating with all indoctrination; in all moments."

"I release emanating with all indoctrination; in all moments."

"I remove all indoctrination from my sound frequency; in all moments."

"I remove all indoctrination from my light body; in all moments."

"I transcend all indoctrination; in all moments."

"I shift my paradigm from all indoctrination to Joy, Love, Abundance, Freedom, Health, Success, Security, Companionship, Peace, Life and Wholeness; in all moments."

"I repair and fortify my Wei Chi; in all moments."

"I am centered and empowered in Divine Love; in all moments."

It doesn't matter how one registers the shifts. The important thing is that there is a change.

82. Change Allegiance

I have been facilitating remote sessions with clients who have been loyal to the Third Reich. It shows up in this lifetime as thick walls of being stubborn and believing one is right at all costs.

I feel very fortunate to be able to go back to that time with people and try to show them what they are missing in life. It seems to swing between either having a lack of remorse or having a lack of gratitude. When I asked one client why she did not feel broken about what she partook in, she quantified it with, "We have all abused power in the past." This is true. But her rationale was depicted as spiritual superiority that was parallel to the physical superiority into which she was indoctrinated in that past life.

This is the reason why I am happy to see a client break down. When one is devastated, it means the walls and facade of denial are tumbling down. It is cracking the shell. When the shell is cracked, it allows people to get back into touch with humanity. Nobody wants to feel awful. But what if feeling awful was equivocated with waking up? What if it meant the currents of power that are still lingering today could lose the wind that fills their sails?

Would you do it? Would you break down the walls of facade in yourself and risk feeling awful for a bit if it helped power lose its grip in the world?

Taps to release the grip of power:

[Say each statement slowly and consciously out loud. Articulate each word and make a point to pause after each phrase. Say each statement three times while tapping on your head. Then say it a fourth time while tapping on your chest. Take a deep breath after finishing the series.]

"I release being removed from humanity; in all moments."

"I release being a pawn for power; in all moments."

"I release using superiority as a form of denial; in all moments."

"I release condoning power and oppression; in all moments."

"I withdraw all my energy and support from power; in all moments."

"I release worshiping power; in all moments."

"I release choosing power over Love; in all moments."

"I release all indifference to the casualties of power; in all moments."

"I shift my paradigm from power to Love; in all moments."

83. Releasing Pain Marathon

I facilitated a remote session on a wonderful healer. She has been working on herself for many years. She has been dealing with pain and thought she had done all she could to address the issues. After her session, she was surprised at the oversight. There was much revealed.

When I tuned in for her session, I saw her in a past life groveling on her knees in excruciating pain to God. There was a flood of memories of times when she was subservient to God. She said she had done extensive work in releasing these issues. But they were showing up in her session.

We went through the whole protocol on her relationship with God. We then went through the whole protocol with her relationship with all of God's minions. It brought great relief. Under that layer there were some interesting findings. One was that she had done a lot of work on her issues with God, but her God issues were hiding in her body under the auspices of pain. She had converted her God issues to physical pain. She was thinking of pain in God terms as if it were omniscient and omnipotent.

Here are some of the taps that we did and that I have done with others, specifically around pain.

Taps to release pain:

[Say each statement slowly and consciously out loud. Articulate each word and make a point to pause after each phrase. Say each statement three times while tapping on your head. Then say it a fourth time while tapping on your chest. Take a deep breath after finishing the series.]

"I release being at the mercy of pain; in all moments."

"I release giving pain my power; in all moments."

"I release using pain to validate myself; in all moments."

"I release using pain as a crutch; in all moments."

"I release being enslaved to pain; in all moments."

"I release using pain as an excuse; in all moments."

"I release using pain to feel important; in all moments."

"I release using pain to punish myself; in all moments."

"I release using pain to declare myself unworthy; in all moments."

"I release the belief that pain is omniscient; in all moments."

"I release the belief that pain is omnipresent; in all moments."

"I release the belief that pain is omnipotent; in all moments."

"I release worshiping pain; in all moments."

"I release being trapped in hell; in all moments."

"I release converting hell into pain; in all moments."

"I release using pain to express being in hell; in all moments."

"I release making a God out of Pain; in all moments."

"I release storing hell in my nerve endings; in all moments."

"I recant all vows and agreements between myself and pain; in all moments."

"I remove all curses between myself and pain; in all moments."

"I sever all strings and cords between myself and all pain; in all moments."

"I dissolve all karmic ties between myself and pain; in all moments."

"I sever all strings and cords between myself and my pain body; in all moments."

"I step out of my pain body and disintegrate it; in all moments."

"I remove all the pain, burden, limitations, and engrams that pain has put on me; in all moments."

"I take back all the Joy, Love, Abundance, Freedom, Health, Success, Security, Companionship, Creativity, Peace, Life, Wholeness, Beauty, Enthusiasm, Contentment, Spirituality, Enlightenment and Confidence that pain has taken from me; in all moments."

"I release being permeated in pain; in all moments."

"I withdraw all my energy from pain; in all moments."

"I annihilate all concepts of pain; in all moments."

"I annihilate all memories of pain; in all moments."

"I annihilate all feelings of pain; in all moments."

"I annihilate all physical components of pain; in all moments."

"I convert all pain to a joyous expression of gratitude; in all moments."

"I release resonating with pain; in all moments."

"I release emanating with pain; in all moments."

"I remove all pain from my sound frequency; in all moments."

"I remove all pain from my light body; in all moments."

"I shift my paradigm from pain to Joy, Love, Abundance, Freedom, Health, Success, Security, Companionship, Creativity, Peace, Life, Wholeness, Beauty, Enthusiasm, Contentment, Spirituality, Enlightenment and Confidence; in all moments."

"I transcend pain; in all moments."

"I am centered and empowered in Divine Love; in all moments."

"I resonate and emanate Divine Love; in all moments."

84. Release the Drama from Friendships

I facilitated a private remote session with a lovely client who felt picked on in work situations. It was obvious that she was a very kind person and prided herself on being nice. But there were a few times with her interactions in job situations that she felt victimized. The scenarios always started the same. She was nice to everyone, but the people who started out being her friends became her ruthless enemies. She felt she was the victim. Also, she kept telling me about incredible pain in her left shoulder.

I saw the core issue being played out in one of her past lives. It was a scene of an arena with a lion's den. She and people that were her friends and family, her closest allies, were forced to fight to the death for the amusement of others. This scenario played out in her present life between her and particular coworkers who were most likely the same people from that past life. Except in this lifetime, they were creating drama. They were mimicking the entertainment in the present through the drama they were giving to onlookers in the past.

I made her look at the fact that the people she had problems with were not bad people. Both she and they were unconsciously acting out behavior from the past. They were not the bad ones, and she was not an innocent. It was a dance that they had done many lifetimes ago, and it was playing out in the present lifetime.

The issue of the arm was the pain of holding a heavy shield to defend her life in that past situation. The trauma was so devastating that the emotional and physical pain was bleeding through to the present. By being aware of the connection, it unhooked the unconscious defense that my client was reenacting in this life.

Taps to release the drama from friendships:

[Say each statement slowly and consciously out loud. Articulate each word and make a point to pause after each phrase. Say each

statement three times while tapping on your head. Then say it a fourth time while tapping on your chest. Take a deep breath after finishing the series.]

"I release the belief that I am a victim; in all moments."

"I release the pain and trauma of being a victim; in all moments."

"I release being a victim; in all moments."

"I release creating or being pulled into drama; in all moments."

"I release making enemies out of friends; in all moments."

"I release the trauma of being pitted against my friends and peers; in all moments."

"I release the trauma of being sent to the lion's den; in all moments."

"I release the trauma of being eaten alive; in all moments."

"I release playing out conflict for the amusement of others; in all moments."

"I release turning friendship into conflict; in all moments."

"I release seeing enemies in friends; in all moments."

"I release being defensive; in all moments."

"I release being in attack mode; in all moments."

"I lay down my sword and shield; in all moments."

"I shift my paradigm from victim to Joy, Love, Abundance, Freedom, Life and Wholeness; in all moments

"I am centered and empowered in Divine Love; in all moments."

85. Success Marathon

There are so many people that are talented and passionate about creating their own business, but get sabotaged along the way somehow. There is much that goes into birthing a new creative venture. Everything must align just right. Just as a human baby starts out as two single cells, a new venture is a concept that perpetuates itself until it is self-sustaining.

We get so filled up with the energy of a new idea at its point of conception; however, it takes a while to gestate. It has to be treated with a healthy dose of protection, respect, and reverence. Self-doubt and past failures get in the way. Also, what will success entail?

The following is a set of taps for anyone wanting to manifest anything. It could be a new business, a project, a change in their life, or a new direction.

Taps for success:

[Say each statement slowly and consciously out loud. Articulate each word and make a point to pause after each phrase. Say each statement three times while tapping on your head. Then say it a fourth time while tapping on your chest. Take a deep breath after finishing the series.]

"I release doubting myself; in all moments."

"I release dissipating my own effectiveness; in all moments."

"I release giving my power away; in all moments."

"I release comparing my success with past failures; in all moments."

"I release expecting success to look a certain way; in all moments."

"I release micromanaging the course of success; in all moments."

"I release putting fears into my success; in all moments."

"I release overlaying failure onto my success; in all moments."

"I release the need to convince others of my success; in all moments."

"I release allowing others to sabotage my success; in all moments."

"I release allowing others to interfere with my success; in all moments."

"I release the fear of success; in all moments."

"I release confusing success for death; in all moments."

"I release the interruption of my success through death; in all moments."

"I release the trauma of success bleeding away from me; in all moments."

"I release the fear of abusing power; in all moments."

"I release defining success as a form of enslavement; in all moments."

"I shatter all preconceived concepts of success; in all moments."

"I release defining success as an abuse of power; in all moments."

"I release all false humility; in all moments."

"I release cursing my success; in all moments."

"I release the aversion to my own success; in all moments."

"I release confusing success with arrogance; in all moments."

"I release dissipating the energy of my success through talking; in all moments."

"I recant all vows and agreements between myself and all failures; in all moments."

"I remove all curses between myself and all failures; in all moments."

"I dissolve all karmic ties between myself and all failures; in all moments."

"I sever all cords and strings between myself and all failures; in all moments."

"I remove all the pain, burden, limitations, and engrams that all failures have put on me; in all moments."

"I take back all the joy, love, abundance, freedom, confidence, success, and wholeness that all failures have taken from me; in all moments."

"I withdraw all my energy from failure; in all moments."

"I release resonating with failure; in all moments."

"I release emanating with failure; in all moments."

"I remove all failure from my sound frequency; in all moments."

"I remove all failure from my light body; in all moments."

"I shift my paradigm from failure to success; in all moments."

"I transcend failure; in all moments."

"I infuse success into my sound frequency; in all moments."

"I infuse success into my light body; in all moments."

"I resonate with success; in all moments."

"I emanate with success; in all moments."

"I make space in this world to manifest my greatest success; in all moments."

"I remove all blockages to manifesting my greatest success; in all moments."

"I stretch my capacity to manifest my greatest success; in all moments."

"I am centered and empowered in my greatest success; in all moments."

86. An Aversion to Eating

Some people have an aversion to eating. I have uncovered a few of the reasons in my private remote sessions. One of my clients was a food tester for royalty and was poisoned to death. One client's spouse put rat poison in the food and the client died miserably. One client had to eat rotten food in squalor to survive. Another client starved to death with a whole group of people, so she felt guilty about eating anything at all.

Our body image is so skewed because we are more than a physical body. We have an astral body that is very similar to the physical. Some people can get a sense of it when they look at themselves. You know how there are times when you look in the mirror and you just look so beautiful? This is you seeing the energetic light and love just pouring through yourself. When you look in the mirror and you look distorted or big, you are looking at your astral body and believing it is your physical body. You can do this because you are looking at yourself through your astral eyes.

I know someone who felt so vulnerable in group settings that she made herself really huge as a little girl just so she could be seen. She ended up manifesting a huge physical body for herself. It was not quite the affect that she hoped for since the huge presence made her even more invisible to attention.

The body is fluid like a river in the sense that it changes continuously depending on the thoughts and feelings fed to it. If one could realize that they do more good in the world and for themselves by simply changing their thoughts, we would truly have a grass roots revolution.

Taps to release an aversion to eating:

[Say each statement slowly and consciously out loud. Articulate each word and make a point to pause after each phrase. Say each statement three times while tapping on your head. Then say it a

fourth time while tapping on your chest. Take a deep breath after finishing the series.]

"I release the fear and trauma of being poisoned; in all moments."

"I release the pain and anguish of being poisoned to death; in all moments."

"I release the trauma of having to survive on squalor; in all moments."

"I release the disgust of eating rotting garbage; in all moments."

"I release the guilt of eating when so many have gone hungry; in all moments."

"I release trying to starve myself out; in all moments."

"I release hating food; in all moments."

"I release hating myself; in all moments."

"I release punishing myself; in all moments."

"I release wanting to disappear; in all moments."

"I release trying to punish others by starving; in all moments."

"I release using starving myself to communicate my pain; in all moments."

"I release feeling out of control; in all moments."

"I release being starved for attention; in all moments."

"I release being starved to be heard; in all moments."

"I recant my vow of martyrdom; in all moments."

"I release being a martyr; in all moments."

"I release mourning a past life; in all moments."

"I release feeling trapped in an experience; in all moments."

"I release using physical and emotional drama to stand out; in all moments."

"I release starving to be validated; in all moments."

There are so many varying factors to why we do what we do. These taps may give you a clue as to what motivates you on a subliminal level.

87. Autoimmune Disease

I connected with someone who had an autoimmune issue. Autoimmune is an issue where the body attacks itself. Many times the body is in conflict with itself in the course of life. There are many devastating examples.

Many people have an aversion to killing, yet they are forced to defend their land in war. That sets up a dichotomy in them which is worse if they don't believe the cause for war is a noble one. Many times through history people have been used as pawns for those hungry for power.

We love our children so much. But there have been times in many of our pasts where we were raped and impregnated by men who have been our enemy. The love of our child is mixed with hatred for their other parent. This creates a dichotomy as well. Interestingly, it can create a conflict in the child as well.

Many times we have loved and been scorned, been humiliated when we tried and failed putting our lifeblood into a cause. Other times we died defeated or in anguish, abandonment, or despair. These register strongly on the future "us" we embody.

Autoimmune may be these conflicts being played out at a cellular level. Maybe this is the psyche's way to bury the turmoil, so we don't have to feel anything emotional. Maybe it is a form of self-punishment for past transgressions. If so, here are some taps to bring a reality check to the physical body and to clear cellular conflict. It is worth a try.

Taps for autoimmune disease:

[Say each statement slowly and consciously out loud. Articulate each word and make a point to pause after each phrase. Say each statement three times while tapping on your head. Then say it a

fourth time while tapping on your chest. Take a deep breath after finishing the series.]

"I release all self-loathing; in all moments."

"I release all inner conflict; in all moments."

"I release punishing myself; in all moments."

"I release attacking myself; in all moments."

"I release all cellular confusion; in all moments."

"I release being my own worst enemy; in all moments."

"I release the pain and trauma of living with the enemy; in all moments."

"I disarm the struggle between love and hate within myself; in all moments."

"I release the pain and trauma of being forced to kill; in all moments."

"I release willingly killing; in all moments."

"I release being entrenched in guilt, pain, and trauma; in all moments."

"I release being paralyzed in dis-ease; in all moments."

"I release the genetic propensity for self-defeat; in all moments."

"I release carrying the burden of disappointment of all my ancestors; in all moments."

"I recant all vows and agreements I have made with myself; in all moments."

"I remove all curses I have made with myself; in all moments."

"I dissolve all karmic ties I have tangled myself in; in all moments."

"I remove all the guilt, pain, fear, limitations, engrams and self-destructive mechanisms that I have put on myself; in all moments."

"I take back all the Joy, Love, Abundance, Freedom, Health, Success, Security, Companionship, Creativity, Peace, Life, Wholeness, Enthusiasm, Contentment and Enlightenment that I have kept from myself; in all moments."

"I release pushing away all the Joy, Love, Abundance, Freedom, Health, Success, Security, Companionship, Creativity, Peace, Life, Wholeness, Enthusiasm, Contentment and Enlightenment; in all moments."

"I shift my paradigm from dis-ease to self-love; in all moments."

"I release resonating with dis-ease; in all moments."

"I release emanating with dis-ease; in all moments."

"I remove all dis-ease from my sound frequency; in all moments."

"I remove all dis-ease from my light body; in all moments."

"I transcend all dis-ease; in all moments."

"I am centered and empowered in Joy, Love, Abundance, Freedom, Health, Success, Security, Companionship, Creativity, Peace, Life, Wholeness, Enthusiasm, Contentment and Enlightenment; in all moments."

If you have a loved one that is incapacitated, you can do these taps for them by using the word "we" instead of "I." Some will argue with this saying that you will be taking on their karma by doing this, but I disagree. If you love someone who is incapacitated, you are already in it with them. Also, there's a spiritual law that trumps all other spiritual laws. It is the law of love.

Love is a karma-less act. If you don't agree, just don't do the taps. But any personal aspersions to me for sharing will just be chalked up as a lack of compassion and understanding of the spiritual law of love.

We are here to love. That is the one abiding law of the land. I am centered and empowered in knowing that love is a karma-less act.

88. Attracting Money

Most people think that they would welcome a windfall if it landed in their lap, but what they don't realize is their own dynamics with money have already been set up by them. If they are not attracting something in their life, they are the ones repelling it from themselves.

In private sessions, such things as believing money is the root of all evil, or that only selfish, powerful people have money have kept many people from attracting it. There was one client who, in a past life, was so disgusted by the behavior of the rich that he vowed never to have money because he didn't want to abuse power. These latent dynamics prevent monetary abundance from flowing in this life.

In sessions, we untangle the dynamics with money on all levels. Afterwards, often the client will get evidence that the session was effective immediately. They will get a tax refund they weren't expecting, a client will pay them unexpectedly, or they will get an opportunity to earn more. The important thing to realize is to NOT set your expectations by your standards or by what society agrees to accept. Be the exception to every rule in excellence.

Taps to Attract Money:

[Say each statement slowly and consciously out loud. Articulate each word and make a point to pause after each phrase. Say each statement three times while tapping on your head. Then say it a fourth time while tapping on your chest. Take a deep breath after finishing the series.]

"I release hating money; in all moments."

"I release the belief that money is evil; in all moments."

"I release defining money as an abuse of power; in all moments."

"I remove all curses between myself and money; in all moments."

(a curse is any negative statement charged with emotion)

"I release feeling shame around having money; in all moments."

"I release repelling money; in all moments."

"I release the belief that I am unworthy of money; in all moments."

"I release the fear of having money; in all moments."

"I release the belief that I am unworthy to have money; in all moments."

"I make space in this world to have an abundance of money; in all moments."

"I remove all blockages to having money; in all moments."

"I stretch my capacity to have an abundance of money; in all moments."

Abundance, just like love, is a birthright. If everyone else agrees on some level to push love and abundance away, you do not have to agree. This is the personal component of being your own person.

89. The Need to Join

Needing to be a part of a group is a primal urge of survival. It is how a school of fish tricks a big predator into thinking it is one big fish. A gazelle will survive a predator's attack by staying deep within the herd. Those on the outskirts are targeted. It is the same with people. Those who were more powerful or vocal in a group were the ones that were targeted by the powers that be. They were pulled out of the group and destroyed.

When we join a group, we pool all our energy into it. We agree to becoming the energetic average of the greatest and least of all the members. It is great for survival but not so great for culminating our individuality. Everyone is pooling their resources and receiving an allotment of the average. One cannot receive more than what is there for any group member unless they are in charge of the group allotment.

The leaders get to decide where the energy goes. This is fine for those who have put less energy in, but for those who have put more in, and are not the leaders, it is a way of squelching their greatness. They may want to look at that primal need to be a part of the group and why it is so terrifying not to be included.

Some are going to be afraid to do this technique. I suggest they challenge that fear. Think of these taps as wiping the slates clean to eliminate any unconscious control that they have been under. They can make fresh alliances with any group that they still choose to be a part of, but with more discernment. Let's stop giving our power to unworthy causes: those who are abusing our goodwill for the gain of those in a position. Let's redefine the lines of what we will allow. We don't have to do anything outwardly. We can just peacefully inwardly withdraw ourselves, and no one will be the wiser but us.

Taps to remove one's self from the herd:

[Say each statement three times while tapping on your head. Then say it a fourth time while tapping on your chest. Take a deep breath after finishing the series.]

"I release the fear and trauma of being separated from the herd; in all moments."

"I release the need to be accepted; in all moments."

"I release the pain and trauma of being abandoned; in all moments."

"I release the need to belong; in all moments."

"I release equivocating individuality with being preyed upon; in all moments."

"I recant all vows and agreements to all groups; in all moments."

"I withdraw all my support for all groups; in all moments."

"I remove all curses between myself and all groups; in all moments."

"I release being controlled by the group; in all moments."

"I release being manipulated by the group; in all moments."

"I release being duped by the group; in all moments."

"I dissolve all karmic ties between myself and all groups; in all moments."

"I withdraw all my energy from all groups; in all moments."

"I remove all the pain, burden, limitations, and engrams that all groups have put on me; in all moments."

"I take back all the Joy, Love, Abundance, Freedom, Health, Success, Security, Companionship, Peace, Life, Wholeness, Beauty, Enthusiasm, and Contentment that all groups have taken from me; in all moments."

I withdraw all my energy from all groups; in all moments."

I transcend all groups; in all moments."

"I shift my paradigm from group dynamics to individual empowerment; in all moments."

"I shift my paradigm from all groups to Joy, Love, Abundance, Freedom, Health, Success, Security, Companionship, Peace, Life, Wholeness, Beauty, Enthusiasm and Contentment that all groups have taken from me; in all moments."

If you need an argument for regaining your power from all groups, realize that this is how society has been running the show for so long. Withdrawing your energy means not condoning such power plays that have been whittling the rights of the individual for so long. This is your way to be empowered without joining an outward revolution (which is another group).

90. Being in Perpetual Success

I facilitated a remote session with a successful realtor. She was getting exasperated with the cycle that appeared in her earnings. She would work so hard for a sale and put all her energy into it. Funds would get very low and then a sale would come through, and she was living in abundance again. It was interesting to get an image of why this was happening to her.

I was shown the past life cycle of "the kill." The whole tribe would rally around the process of taking down a big animal. They would then go from starving to feasting. It was the process of going from famine to feast. Her sales cycle was mimicking the cycle of hunting. She wasn't getting more than one big sale at a time because in hunting there was only one kill taken down at a time. Otherwise, it would spoil. Only one kill was needed at a time.

It occurred to me that many people who are living paycheck to paycheck have synchronized their financial life with the cycle of hunting. Just getting by is a primal memory that they unconsciously draw upon. Here are some taps to break the cycle:

[Say each statement three times while tapping continuously on your head. Then say it a fourth time while tapping on your chest.]

"I release synchronizing my life with primal survival; in all moments."

"I release mimicking primal survival cycles; in all moments."

"I release being limited by primal cycles of survival; in all moments."

"I release being trapped in survival mode; in all moments."

"I release the trauma of dying in survival mode; in all moments."

"I recant all vows and agreements between myself and survival mode; in all moments."

"I remove all curses and engrams between myself and survival mode; in all moments."

"I dissolve all karmic ties between myself and survival mode; in all moments."

"I remove all the pain, burden, limitations, and programming that survival mode has put on me; in all moments."

"I take back all the Joy, Love, Abundance, Freedom, Health, Success, Security, Companionship, Creativity, Peace, Life, and Wholeness that survival mode has taken from me; in all moments."

"I release resonating with survival mode; in all moments."

"I release emanating with survival mode; in all moments."

"I remove all of survival mode from my sound frequency; in all moments."

"I remove all of survival mode from my light body; in all moments."

"I transcend being in survival mode; in all moments."

"I shift my paradigm from primal mode to Joy, Love, Abundance, Freedom, Health, Success, Security, Companionship, Creativity, Peace, Life, and Wholeness; in all moments."

"I make space in this world for perpetual success and multiple abundance; in all moments."

"I remove all blockages to being in perpetual success and multiple abundance; in all moments."

"I stretch my capacity to accept perpetual success and multiple abundance; in all moments."

I am centered and empowered in perpetual success and multiple abundance; in all moments."

The more we move out of unconscious, habitual existence, the more we can manifest all that brings us Joy, Love and Abundance. There is nothing more liberating that realizing our own potential.

91. An Energetic Vitamin

Do you know why affirmations don't always work? Because as one says them, for some people, the mind is going a mile a minute and reminds them of all the instances of the opposite. For example, if you use the affirmation, "I am abundant," the mind will remind you of all the bills and problems to refute the affirmation.

A way to bypass the mind's discernment is to not deal with the issues as if you are dealing with the physical body. The mind only controls what it understands. In metaphysical terms, we are not a solid form. We are a frequency of sound and an emanation of light. The mind does not know how to refute when we work in light and sound. It is above its pay scale.

These taps are meant to add to the quality of your essence without the mind knowing how to negate it. Enjoy these. These are like taking a positive vitamin and gushing it right into your energy field. You can do these taps daily.

Taps to bypass the mind:

[Say each statement slowly and consciously out loud. Articulate each word and make a point to pause after each phrase. Say each statement three times while tapping on your head. Then say it a fourth time while tapping on your chest. Take a deep breath after finishing the series.]

> **"I resonate with Joy, Love, Abundance, Freedom, Health, Success, Security, Companionship, Creativity, Peace, Life, Wholeness, Beauty, Enthusiasm, Contentment, and Confidence; in all moments."**

> **"I emanate with Joy, Love, Abundance, Freedom, Health, Success, Security, Companionship, Creativity, Peace, Life, Wholeness, Beauty, Enthusiasm, Contentment, and Confidence; in all moments."**

"I infuse Joy, Love, Abundance, Freedom, Health, Success, Security, Companionship, Creativity, Peace, Life, Wholeness, Beauty, Enthusiasm, Contentment, and Confidence into my sound frequency; in all moments."

"I imbue Joy, Love, Abundance, Freedom, Health, Success, Security, Companionship, Creativity, Peace, Life, Wholeness, Beauty, Enthusiasm, Contentment, and Confidence into my light body; in all moments."

Print these out. Keep them in your wallet. Post them on your wall. Start your day with them. Do these taps before you go to a meeting. Do them before you go to a family occasion. Make them a daily routine. Do them as a sacred prayer to honor yourself. Because you are worthy and you deserve to realize that you are already all of these.

92. Vibrate with Love

Your thoughts and words can either be glass ceilings or a springboard into the heavens. You are the navigator. That is how you are empowered. Before you speak, or before you even think, ask yourself if what you are about to manifest is something that will elevate yourself and others, or is it something that will sink all of you. Get a sense of what the words you say feel like.

I see it when I post something. I try to extend the highest loving intention to the farthest reaches possible. Then someone will say something that will pull people back to a heavy place. Notice it for yourselves. Which pages do you like to go to? How high can you hold a vibration? You are empowered to manifest and hold a place for extreme awesomeness!

Taps to raise one's vibrations:

[Say each statement slowly and consciously out loud. Articulate each word and make a point to pause after each phrase. Say each statement three times while tapping on your head. Then say it a fourth time while tapping on your chest. Take a deep breath after finishing the series.]

"I release dumbing myself and others down; in all moments."

"I transcend the mundane human thought process; in all moments."

"I release being trapped in habitual mind loops; in all moments."

"I release ruling out possibilities; in all moments."

"I release shutting doorways with 'no'; in all moments."

"I release putting limitations on my capabilities; in all moments."

"I release shutting down viable components of my brain; in all moments."

"I shift my paradigm from thinking to knowing; in all moments."

"I awaken direct knowing within myself; in all moments."

"I activate the dormant parts of my brain; in all moments."

"I release being trapped in a time/space continuum; in all moments."

"I consciously access my own vortex; in all moments."

"I shift my paradigm from human consciousness to God consciousness; in all moments."

"I consciously choose to resonate as an advanced being through choosing uplifting words and thoughts; in all moments."

"I hold space in this world for a higher vibrational frequency; in all moments."

"I remove all blockages to being a higher vibrational frequency; in all moments."

"I stretch my capacity to be a higher vibrational frequency; in all moments."

"I strengthen my endurance to be a higher vibrational frequency; in all moments."

"I connect with higher frequency beings in a reverent state of Divinity; in all moments."

"I am centered and empowered in Divine Love; in all moments."

"I vibrate and resonate with Divine Love and emanate it to all; in all moments."

The more expansive we can think of ourselves, the greater we can make a difference in our lives and all those we care about. We can leave a golden footprint in the world.

93. Creating Better "Vision"

These taps came through while facilitating a powerful private remote session with a regular client. When people are open to my work, we can go deep to core issues and harvest the tools for everyone to benefit. My client said that she was nearsighted, and while I took her through these particular taps, her vision cleared up. She is not certain it is 20/20, but she felt a huge shift.

Taps to create better "vision":

[Say each statement three times while tapping on your head. Then say it a fourth time while tapping on your chest. Take a deep breath after finishing the series.]

"I convert all my need into being; in all moments."

"I convert all my hope into knowing; in all moments."

"I convert all my dreams into experiencing; in all moments."

"I convert all my wants into having; in all moments."

"I convert all my wishes into expressions; in all moments."

"I convert all my desires into contentment; in all moments."

"I convert all my conflicts into peace; in all moments."

"I convert all my lamenting into joyful expression; in all moments."

"I convert all my self-doubt into the manifestation of my truth; in all moments."

"I convert all my procrastination into living my purpose; in all moments."

94. Be a Pipeline of Divine Light, Love, and Song into This World

So many people feel helpless at the current state of the world, yet they don't realize what a powerful conduit they are to pour Divine Love into the world. If everyone who is feeling helpless, would forgo all worry, opinions, and fears and just start pouring their love into the world, it would make the profound difference they are waiting to see. The world is a big pool, but look what has been achieved through history with a Nelson Mandela or a Mother Theresa perpetually pouring their love in to fill it. Imagine if we all poured our love into the world while going about our day.

It is a trapping of the ego to feel small and insignificant. Having a little opinion of yourself is having a big ego. Having a sense of your dynamic ability to uplift all those in your awareness is more in balance. We have all been inspired about the child that decides to make a difference in the world and does. We have all secretly wanted to be that child and are.

So much of what we view on television is a stagnant pool of negative energy. People tap into it and open a door to it by choosing to watch the shows that they do. People who do this consistently can't discern the negativity of watching television with the reality of life. In fact, they become so conditioned by stagnant energy that they become a conduit of negativity by professing gloom and perpetuating the views that they have adopted by immersing themselves in the negativity of television. They have to somehow be weaned off the negativity that they have become accustomed to. It is a challenge because it has created such a comfort level within them.

Here are some taps to do to keep your pipeline of Divine Love pumping and flowing out into the world no matter what you are doing. There are side benefits, of course. Maybe one will feel more confident and less insignificant. For those who do feel small, may I suggest when you declare yourself a perpetual pipeline that you visualize being a HUGE hose and not some itty bitty garden hose. There is an infinite amount of Divine Love. The flow can never dry up. People cut themselves off from the flow.

Taps to be a pipeline of divine love into this world:

[Say each statement slowly and consciously out loud. Articulate each word and make a point to pause after each phrase. Say each statement three times while tapping on your head. Then say it a fourth time while tapping on your chest. Take a deep breath after finishing the series.]

> **"I declare myself a perpetual pipeline for Divine Light, Love, and Song to pour into this world; in all moments."**

> **"I remove all blockages to perpetually pouring Divine Light, Love, and Song into this world; in all moments."**

> **"I stretch my capacity to perpetually pour Divine Light, Love, and Song into the world; in all moments."**

> **"I am a perpetual pipeline of Divine Light, Love, Song, Health, Joy, Beauty, Abundance, and Healing into this world; in all moments."**

> **"I am uplifted by the process of Divine Light, Love, Song, Health, Joy, Beauty, Abundance, and Healing perpetually flowing through me; in all moments."**

These are great taps to do every day. You may even want to start a journal to write down the shifts that you notice by doing these taps. Please share, and please give them to those who are feeling overwhelmed or hopeless. It is through sharing the love that we heal ourselves. Once more people understand this, we will see dynamic shifts happen in the world.

95. Manifesting Universal Joy

There is a restless state that happens when people realize that they have no desires. When they realize that they need for nothing, crave nothing, and really want nothing, they will fall back on habitual thinking and create something negative about this state. They will interpret the lack of want and need as a negative, and it becomes a means to rev up the habitual thinking. They will call it apathy or depression. No. It is not. There is a different caliber to it.

This is where self-discipline comes in. When the lack of craving and desire first appears, it is so foreign that we sometimes manufacture something to want and need. It will force us to obsess over something. This is fine for a while, but there will be no lasting satisfaction in that. Our new higher state is more at peace with just enough. It prefers it.

So instead of trying to kick back into primal mode of gathering and collecting, try something new. If there is nothing to do, do nothing. If there is nowhere to go, go nowhere. There are so many tools to expand the Joy, Love, Abundance and Freedom of each moment until time itself falls away. It is the beauty of the new paradigm.

Enhance the experience of each moment by pouring attention into it. Give attention to all the things in your home. Feed the birds (and squirrels), nurture a garden, connect to a tree, play an instrument, write a song, pull out the craft from long ago. These are all arsenal in bringing peace to this world. The more we expound upon peace in our own lives, the more we create space for it in this world.

Taps to manifest universal joy:

[Say each statement slowly and consciously out loud. Articulate each word and make a point to pause after each phrase. Say each statement three times while tapping on your head. Then say it a fourth time while tapping on your chest. Take a deep breath after finishing the series.]

"I release denying the moment, in all moments."

"I release denying myself peace; in all moments."

"I release the fear of facing myself; in all moments."

"I release being a stranger to myself; in all moments."

"I release being my own enemy; in all moments."

"I release creating conflict out of habit: in all moments."

"I forgive myself; in all moments."

"I grant myself peace; in all moments."

"I recant all vows and agreements that I have made with myself; in all moments."

"I remove all curses I have put on myself; in all moments."

"I dissolve all karmic ties I have meshed myself in; in all moments."

"I sever all strings and cords that I have tangled myself in; in all moments."

"I remove all the pain, burden, limitations, and engrams I have put on myself; in all moments."

"I take back all the Joy, Love, Abundance, Freedom, Health, Success, Security, Companionship, Creativity, Peace, Life, Wholeness, Beauty, Enthusiasm, Confidence and Enlightenment that I have kept from myself; in all moments."

"I infuse Joy, Love, Abundance, Freedom, Peace, and Wholeness into my sound frequency; in all moments."

"I imbue Joy, Love, Abundance, Freedom, Peace, and Wholeness into my light body; in all moments."

"I resonate and emanate with Joy, Love, Abundance, Freedom, Peace, and Wholeness; in all moments."

"I am centered and empowered in Joy, Love, Abundance, Freedom, Peace, and Wholeness; in all moments."

"I make space in this world for Universal Joy, Love, Abundance, Freedom, Peace, and Wholeness; in all moments."

"I remove all blockages to Universal Joy, Love, Abundance, Freedom, Peace, and Wholeness in this world; in all moments."

"I stretch my capacity to manifest Universal Joy, Love, Abundance, Freedom, Peace and Wholeness in this world; in all moments."

"I am centered and empowered in Universal Joy, Love, Abundance, Freedom, Peace and Wholeness; in all moments."

Testimonials About Jen's Work

I have found your divinely guided taps that you have lovingly shared profoundly effective and efficient. So wonderful you will be sharing this wisdom in a book. I will definitely buy it. Love and gratitude.

M. B., UK

≈

I was a skeptic! I've been in such intense pain for so long. I had nothing to lose and everything to gain. But I must let you know that my pain level is so much better today! I'm reminding my body to just relax and be and enjoy some pain free time! Thank you, thank you for sharing! It has been amazing!

M. B., Texas

≈

Jen is a generous and gifted healer. I suffered from a lot of anxiety and Jen cleared a lot of that up for me, helping me let go of anxious patterns.

The taps have changed me over time in a very subtle but powerful way. Since doing them for about nine months now, I no longer fear people reading my writing. I've gotten stronger and don't care so much what others think. I no longer have to get angry at others to protect my space. This was important for someone with so little self-esteem. I trust my instincts more too. Jen has helped me to clear out the noise and chatter in my mind and emotions and tune into truth.

When I say Jen is generous, she is one of these rare people who has integrity. She really puts it back on you—she wants you to take responsibility to create a world that you love. She clears the emotions or thoughts that may be in the way, but expects you to practice living a life where you are not a victim. She acts like she wants you to operate without her—instead of what some healers want which for you to become dependent on them. I recommend you do Jen's deep taps and work with her!

T. K., Professor and Writer

≈

Before meeting Jen, I had never experienced taps. I had no idea what they were, how they were done, or their potential benefits. The first time I did them I was little embarrassed and taken aback. I couldn't understand what was happening during the taps, but they are powerful. Jen's words are powerful.

Her taps guide you through hard truths and realizations in a safe and controlled way. In our busy lives we tend to over analyze things and harp on negativity. Taps allow you to pinpoint those areas while realizing their existence and releasing them from yourself rather than keeping them in. Sometimes, you can feel the release during the taps through a feeling of weightlessness, or changes in your breathing, brief discomfort, or sometimes even crying. These help assist in your release and can help you feel even better after completing the taps.

The gift of Jen is her ability to come up with the taps and figure out what truths and realizations need to be brought to the surface. It's something that makes her a wonderful and valuable healer. I can't imagine my life without taps or Jen. If you are scared or nervous, open your heart. You will be amazed at the love and wholeness you are capable of when you learn a healthy way to deal with and release the negativity and hardships of life.

C.H., Veterinarian

≈

Jen, the taps you post have helped me so much more than any other methods I have tried. They make me laugh, cry, and give me chills.

Some remind me of past lives and help me remember things I have experienced. They energize me and release stagnant energy and give me hope to go on when I think I can't.

N.C.F., Chiropractor

≈

Just wanted to let you know I'm new to tapping. When I do your taps regardless of what they are meant for; I always come away better for it. I feel a lightness, happiness and just overall positive. Of course I don't understand why it works, but I can gleefully attest that it does. You make my heart smile with much gratitude.

C.G., Office Manager

≈

I had never heard of tapping until a friend added me to Jen Ward's Facebook page. I've battled depression for decades. Prescriptions masked the symptoms without healing the problem and caused unpleasant side effects. Counseling made me feel worse. After being introduced to Jen's taps, I decided it couldn't hurt to try. The relief I felt after my first set was profound. I've done her taps for six months, and I'm free of both the hopelessness and the fear of it returning. It's a simple, harmless technique that removes the burdens of existence and clears the pathways to allow for peace and love.

A. S., Stay-at-Home Mom

≈

Jen, I've been carrying some of your writings around with me in my purse for emergencies. Well, I met a man who really needed help, I gave him all of the papers I had. He came back and told me it changed his life. He cried all night and made copies and shared with five people who also needed help. And the love keeps flowing....

I printed out your post called, "Be Worthy" for a friend who is very evolved and knowledgeable. He was impressed. I'm seeing people's pain in their eyes lessen just from reading your writings.

Robin, Real Estate, Seeker

≈

Another session with incredible, selfless, loving healer Jen Ward! Words cannot articulate what past life incarnation's wounds and samskaras are being released in our sessions as a result of Jen Ward. Jen IS an Intuitive, Clairvoyant, Empathic, Reiki Master, Energy Healer.

J.J.H.

≈

Another session with Jen Ward today. REALLY!! I am indebted to such a selfless, incredible healer who has the ability to see anything one is holding onto that impedes one from moving forward. The best investment you can make is in yourself, in your healing, to propel you forward to get back to your pure nature and experience joy, abundance, freedom and love in every moment of every day.

≈

Let me say that after my time with Jen in a session, I am transformed. I'm like a dry plant that's been watered. It might not be noticeable because some of the changes take time to develop. When you just water a dry plant, it still looks dry until its roots can absorb the water. Then a while later, you look again and the plant has come back to LIFE.

I am so grateful that God has sent a messenger to help me. Not to help me think better, or feel better, but to BE better. Thank you, Jen, for the mission you are on has watered me like a plant.

≈

Jen has helped me so much. I will for the rest of my life hold her high in esteem to all my friends! She helped me--although she is hesitant to take credit, saying it was ALL in me--to 1. Recover a long lost friendship with my best friend, 2. Give up horrible feelings of insecurity, 3. Come to newfound understandings as to my mighty place in the Universe, where before I was a beggar and a disheartened slave, 4. Gave me renewed hope, 5. Gave me a vision as to what I, myself, can do to continue to reap the rewards of my newfound Self, and 6. Taught me to LOVE all over again. She did MORE than all that! She built me up when I was struggling and very, very down. She did all this, never once embarrassed me or hurt my feelings, or was inquisitive or nosey. She charges so little for the renewed life she gives. On my list of Time Magazine's top ten people, she's number 1 or 2!

≈

The only way I could describe Jen's work is by saying she is an intuitive shamanic EFT and sound healer. Let me explain. Her work is to facilitate the release of past lives traumas, fears, and beliefs. Usually, these come from extremely traumatic experiences of being hurt or hurting other people and I have to stress both. It is as traumatic having been a victim as having been a perpetrator.

She is not here to hear you whine or explain. She is here to blast you with her sword of truth. For this reason, I wouldn't be surprised if she worked within the energy of Archangel Michael. At the end of the session, I felt really shaken but so much lighter, like a weight had been shifted off my shoulders. There were some very painful moments, but there is nothing like releasing old energies that keep you trapped.

I am impressed by the purity of her work. Jen is truly a genuine healer.

≈

I had a session with Jen Ward today. At first, it was strange. Then as the time went on, it was like I lost tons, and I mean tons. Do you know what it is like when you let go of years and lifetimes of baggage? Well that is how you lose tons. It only took about an hour with Jen. It was such a great feeling to find yourself letting go of the hurt you do to yourself or allowed others to do. To start the process of self-love to be the person God expects me to be to have the abundance. The abundance of all.

If you want to feel self-love and feel the abundance of all, to lose tons—I am not talking about body weight I am talking about inner weight the kind that weighs us all down—I am so thankful to Jen for the help.

In love and light may we all prosper in abundance through the love of God.

≈

My life has themes and patterns. Well, I had gotten myself into a pattern that was no longer useful to me. That is where Jen comes in. She has a natural gift of "unsticking" us from our patterns and ourselves. To do that, she has to get creative and uses methods that might seem unconventional, but they work. My session with Jen is unique to me, but what I can tell you is that she listens to her inner voice and does what she needs to do, so you can start to manifest the light that is within for all to see. Blessings to Jen for her bravery and fortitude when helping others.

A.P.

≈

Jen Ward's healing energy work is changing my life profoundly, and bringing her to your attention is a great pleasure and honor. I was one who thought that "answers" to my personal quandaries were received by diligent searching and disciplined spiritual attention...MY work to believe in and discover. Well then there are nudges to follow...and I followed Jen's blog and thought a personal session with her might be a good thing? To express my gratitude and convey the miraculous benefits is a great challenge because real healing involves more than meets the eye, and there's no "therapy" I've encountered that means as much as our "releasing energy" sessions. To feature Jen and her loving work around your uplifting formats would be a blessing to mankind, sincerely. Thank you for this venue to express my gratitude to Jen!

≈

Rarely in life does one meet a person like Jen Ward The impact she has had on countless lives is remarkable and immeasurable and cannot be denied. I cannot say that I know a more passionate person than Jen, and her message is one of healing and love. She has a unique perspective and is very enlightening.

Tina
New York

≈

I find myself both humbled and grateful to be able to share with Jen Ward. Being able to diligently process and take account of both our subjective and objective experience in a search for the Truth is an all too rare commodity to find nowadays. The human psyche, and how it plays into our existential reality, is a complex subject which is not to say that it is complicated, just that there is so much of it to navigate, that without a truthful heart for something beyond ourselves, we are merely at the behest of those forces within life that are so compelling as to create an illusion of separation.

Jen sees beyond this to a Truth where she realizes that the only thing that stands in the way of our relationship with the Divine, each other, and the natural world around us is the thing we get out of bed every morning and believe we are that thing that makes us believe we are different to everyone else…ourselves. Blessings always.

≈

I have been a student of ESP, the occult, and parapsychology since my first ESP experience at the age of ten. I am a spiritual writer and reader. I must tell you that I have NEVER met a more spiritual person than Jen Ward. If you are truly interested in exposing people to real spirituality, love, and knowledge of themselves and their relationship to God, there is no one I could recommend more highly than Jenuine Ward.

Michael
Florida

≈

Jen Ward is amazing. She handles everything with grace, loving kindness, and gentleness. Her wisdom and insight are some things that can be experienced by reading her work. She is inspirational. She is also loving, kind, graceful and so giving to others.

≈

Jen Ward has helped make me a better mother, wife, friend, and human being. She is the real deal. She has also helped my children and husband. Just when you think something can't be solved Jen will be there to breakthrough whatever it is that prevents your evolution. She is AMAZING! Try a session and you will understand. The world is a better place because of Jen Ward."

J.B.H.
Baltimore

≈

I have read many of Jen's posts, and she has kept me going day to day. I see small things that she has said that have made a great impact; she has made me think at times, and I have become stronger. A huge difference, I keep reading, and finding more each day as she posts.

≈

This year Jen Ward helped me...I was stiff with osteoarthritis of the knees, and all the exercise I did was of little help. Jen worked on the phone with me. The first time I was feeling better but had no idea to connect the dots until a few months and two more sessions with Jen went by (as well as my 65th birthday). Now I am very flexible in mind and body.

≈

I must tell you, Jen Ward changed my life forever! This woman, Jen Ward, is the most enlightened person I've ever had the privilege of meeting. She seems to have what the old sages called illumined mind. She makes Edgar Cayce's work look like child's play. She doesn't share knowledge, she shares understanding. She uncovered stuck points in my past that had prevented me from creating a successful life for myself. Now, that's all changed. Everyone likes me more, the people at work, my cats even come sit on my lap more, I have true ease, I have a pleasant personality for once. It might sound exaggerated, but she knows how to uncover parts of you that are old and helps you become an ever greater whole. Get a session with Jen Ward! It'll be your gift to yourself for the year, and it'll be the best gift you could get! Hands down.

≈

A dear friend of mine referred me to Jen Ward. We have had two sessions thus far, and each time felt what I believe to be stagnant energy exit directly through my chest and limbs. Her gifts go beyond spiritual healing, she cleanses your karma. She is powerful in a way that I never knew existed and, incredibly, with no pomp or ego.

≈

I attribute much of my success to coaches. These have included sports, career, sales, executive, and even resume coaches. However, the most powerful coach I have ever had has been Jen Ward of jenuinehealing.com. I have called her my energy coach for over three years. I'm not sure how she does it, but she can make me feel like a million bucks!

C.D.
Baltimore

≈

I believe in Jen Ward and her extremely high level of consciousness. Her love is bigger than global.... Her story is one worth knowing. Jen gives to humanity a gift that is beyond compare.

Rochester, NY

≈

I went to Jen for neck trouble. I was scared because the pain was so intense at night I had trouble sleeping. I felt like my head wasn't sitting properly on my spine. I had spent years in and out of chiropractors' offices, but I wasn't in a position where I lived to see one, nor did I feel on an intuitive level that they could solve the problem at this point in my life. So I had a session with Jen, and it has been almost a week now, and I am free of the severe neck and back pain with only a memory of soreness. I'm grateful for Jen's work and these simple but profound taps.

≈

Last night, in my evening contemplation, I had a possible solution to a situation I was working on in my own life, and I thought that I could message this possible fix to Jen Ward and see what she thought about it. But by then it was late, and I was tired so I didn't send the Facebook message. I just thought about it instead.

Well, all throughout the night, I came to realize that I was receiving inner instructions from none other than Jen Ward, and when I woke up, I woke up refreshed, and with a great solution for my situation!

I also woke up an hour earlier than usual, full of energy, enthusiasm, and new hope! This is amazing! Who do you know who can also do this? Isn't this usually reserved for the leaders who truly help restore the freedom of Soul? I believe it is. Thank you, Jen!

≈

I followed my spirit, which handed me a gift. My discussion with Jen evolved into some healing and clearing opportunities. In the middle of this, she suddenly said she was getting some sound waves and asked if I had sung as a kid, "We are marching to Pretoria," and I don't know why, but YES, we sang that as kids!!! I haven't thought of that song in forever! And so I did taps on being a soldier. They were so helpful.

Working through stuff takes bravery for me. I am grateful for renewed self-trust and for Jen's in-the-moment immediacy of how she works. Thank you.

K.B.
New York

≈

Jen is a friend, as well as a faithful healer, conduit, prolific writer, energy-sensor. I have worked with many folks in the healing profession—personally as well as professionally—and I have never encountered anyone who works with such immediacy of understanding and truth. It is fascinating to watch her work. Her deep understanding of the energetic nature of the universe lends itself to profound written and verbal exclamations. Plus, Jen has a wonderfully witty and wry sense of humor. GET TO KNOW HER! Jen uplifts and helps a lot of people.

≈

Just had a really powerful healing session with Jen Ward. It reminded me who I am in the deepest way possible. Lifetimes and lifetimes were just illuminated and healed with the remembrance of that joyous, loving, light self, who can carry that into this world, not the other way around. That is my call to action and my call to just be. To emanate light and love for the entire universe. If you are feeling out of touch, in need of healing, or needing to release old ways of being, I highly recommend her.

M.D.F.

≈

I am an energy healer myself and have had MANY sessions with different healers. Today was one of the most powerful sessions I have ever experienced. Jen was able to take me deeper than others. Her ability to identify with me at such deep levels has already made such an intense difference. I just know that to be true. She is an amazing gift, and I truly honor her for the gift of healing she has achieved through her own work! If you are willing to go DEEP, please don't hesitate to connect with this Master Healer.

K.N.

≈

Jen has just given me some priceless help, got me to tap for some health issues that would appear to have roots in previous lives. Starting to feel better already, my vision has become clearer and everything is brighter; can't wait to see what more wonderful effects I will get. Bless you Jen.

M.H.

≈

And my journey continues with each session I have with Jen Ward. As well, the results keep growing just as the effects and realizations of meditation stays with you after you have meditated. One continues to awaken, open, more and more as with each passing moment. Every session is powerful with Jen, and each session feels more powerful than the previous and today it felt like once again another layer was peeled away. Actually many. Once again, I felt a HUGE breakthrough. My heart is opening, and as a result, so is my hand. I feel I can hold hands with abundance, hold hands with love, I feel free! Thank you Jen...love you so.

J.H.
Arizona

≈

As a spiritual truth seeker, the thing I know is that many of our problematic issues are connected to previous lives where the curtain has been drawn and we can't see the direct cause of fears and anxieties. This is not kooky hearsay but documented reality, if one really wants to know their personal truth of troubling matters. I've experienced the benefits of numerous therapy sessions, but there comes a time when you know to follow your gut and be open to other possibilities. In heeding my inner guidance, I found, on-line, jenuinehealing.com. Profoundly helpful to the extent that I can risk any and all judgments if just one individual is sparked and guided to consider Jen Ward's assistance. Suffering and living in the shadows of our best good can be dramatically eased and eliminated with understanding the puzzle pieces that created our present challenges, whatever they may be.

M.M., School Teacher

≈

Remember John of God? I just had a session with Jen Ward and I got more out of one session with her than of all the times that I visited JOG in person. I've been to Brazil and Omega many times to see him and gave up. I would suggest you investigate her and consider sharing her gift with the rest of the world.

C.W.

≈

First session with Jen this morning and I had no idea what to expect or how deep-seated the negative energy was held in my body until she began clearing the layers...Jen was able to get to the heart of the matter within the first 10-15 minutes! I've been through months of therapy that didn't come close to removing the blockages that Jen did in one hour, and she started the session knowing nothing about me! Amazing. Life-changing. Freeing. Jenuine. Above All, Love.

Thank You, Jen!

K.D.H.

≈

I recently came across a woman, Jen Ward, who has a remarkable gift for healing. Because of her, I am finally able to "re-frame" a lot of issues in my mind that were totally crippling my life. To say I was skeptical when my fiancee told me about her would be an understatement. I'm fairly open-minded, but it took me six months before I finally booked an appointment with a "sound healer"—but I was blown away at how much we were able to work through in less than two hours!

I've been to traditional counselors, Christian counselors, military counselors, psychics, energy healers, hypnotists, counselors of various other religions—you name it—I've tried it. They all helped to various degrees, but I was amazed at the progress and emotional release I experienced with one session with this lady. I have found someone to help me overcome the obstacles that I've constructed for myself over the years, and I am looking forward to finally living the life that was intended for me. I'm not sure I've ever been this excited about living!

(Jen, if you see this, your method still seems a bit crazy to me lol, but it DEFINITELY works! Thank you!)

J.B.
Veteran

≈

Last week my husband had a session with Jen on the phone. It wasn't two hours until he was telling me that he felt more "empowered" and had more energy. Today, he told me on my way home that he loved and missed me. When I did arrive home today he immediately wanted me to see that he had cleared off several large piles of papers from his desk. Those papers had been there in the same place for many years. That is a first I think. Thank you Jen Ward for all you do in the service of others.

A.Q.P.

≈

I was drawn to Jen, because I could tell she is a healer of action, one who can facilitate a real shifting and healing, and TEACH me something great, instead of just being all "let's talk it out" (I would have politely hung up the phone asap!). Jen, as I expected, was firm when needed to get through any resistance and to affect positive good shifts in my energy. The room became very warm, and I felt heat all through my body! I could sense good energy too and Jen's warm big heart!

Jen worked on all of the layers, bodies, and today I feel much more empowered and alive, and good! What is great about Jen is her ability to keep her client firmly rooted in the healing process, great results, and out of any fear-based stuff.

I am very grateful for Jen! I am also surprised and happy that Jen followed up with me the next day, to make sure I was alright! Jen is a light. Bless you and much peace!

≈

I'd say the Jen Ward is the best thing to happen to me since I met my better half, and got married. I HAVE NEVER promoted anyone's work, but this is life-changing for me.

With tears in my eyes I'm just now realizing the magnitude of what has happened to me. I will tell everyone for the rest of my life what massive help came through you, my humble friend. Bless you, and may God kiss your animals every day!

≈

In my lifetime, I have not met another person on the level as Jen. She does her work by telephone, and I was surprised to notice she was really tuned in to know what was going on with me. I wish everyone who wants growth would realize how worth it this is. I moved from thinking to being!

≈

I, for one, can certainly attest to the wonder of those private sessions! Those sessions are so valuable. I'm on a new road now after my session. So much so that I count that day as a starting point to a NEW ME! My experience was also that you are a person who carefully safeguards the feelings of everyone you talk to and even just communicating with you opens the heart. I can't say enough about the LOVE you have in your heart, so pure and so giving, and I was the recipient! I think wonderful good thoughts about you and your mission.

≈

Jen, the day of my session with you was like getting a new set of tires for my car. I still have to drive to my destination, but now I can get traction and no longer am prone to getting a flat as often. Thank you, dear Jen!

≈

I went back to work today, and my boss who is quite sensitive hugged on me lots! She said she could feel the love coming from me and good energy! So more confirmation that my energy shifted! I knew you were the person that would help me make a shift. Thank you!

I feel an inner peace that only comes from God the good. Thanks for everything.

≈

Jen discovered the root cause of my almost tape-recorded type responses to living situations and helped me erase the tape and replace it with a vital response to a heart-felt concern someone was voicing. I don't know how she learned this stuff, for it comes natural to her, but it's perhaps because she's an empath. Anyone who is wondering, let me tell you, you will be so glad you discovered this key to a life of vibrancy, a life of loving God, and your fellow human beings and pets.

≈

I had the most wonderful realization today. Because of Jen, one of my emotional sores was "not being wanted" or "being left out." I thought over the years I had healed that tenderness, but a series of recent events bought it back up, and I realized there was more to be done.

The exquisitely beautiful part of the event was the realization that the person who I felt was orchestrating the exclusion was really mirroring back to me an untruth I was holding in my consciousness. Jen, how beautiful is that! It felt like source love wanted me to see how I was wounding myself. I am so wrapped up in the wonder and love of it all that I could almost worship at the feet of the God child who mirrored this back to me.

≈

It matters not why I held or why others held me down so tightly at all. It matters not any of the whys or how comes. What has been released and transformed in divine love is the result and the only matter that matters! Wow! To be free is one thing, to know and feel it is another and an amazing gift to self! I am in a space of gratitude from this connection. I am bathing in awesome energy right now thanks to a wonderful, albeit at times very challenging, healing session with the very awesome Jen Ward. Her unique style is awesome, and I understood the reason for it. I must say, Jen does remind me of only one other unique expression of all that is, and I so welcomed her straightforward approach. Jen is an amazing, gifted healer within divine love.

T.P.C.

≈

I was wondering if you are part of my Soul group because it struck me so profoundly when I heard your voice on the phone how familiar you sounded and felt. I have been going internal for a few days, meditating. I woke up at 4 a.m. the night before last and realized how light my body felt and teared up because I didn't even realize, even with doing energy work, how very heavy I had felt before. Thank you so much! That person is being so friendly to me now I don't know how to react. It feels so...awkward. I feel so clear and centered in myself.

I feel balanced, grounded and patient in my own self. Things don't "eat" at me. I'm able to let them go. I'm understanding me better and feel like I have matured so beautifully. Frustrating things happen, but my approach is different. I'm above it. I reflect and can move on. I feel like I used to grab the pain and hurt and tuck it in my pocket before. It was clouding who I was and who I wanted to be. Thank you for everything! Our sessions are definitely not over. I just wish I could get my partner to see you! He could use it! Thank you again!

≈

I have been feeling full" and "bloated." Tried everything to relieve that! You showed me that it was the dichotomy I had between eating meat and the current loving philosophy I am trying to adopt. That was the problem. I immediately feel less restriction and bloating! This is a huge difference in how I'm feeling physically! I was uncomfortable sitting and bending forward with huge discomfort, a "big belly" feeling, gone! Can't wait for our one-on-one! Love you Jen! Thank you for loving me as I love you!

≈

Releasing Deeply Engrained Masochism

The operative word here for me is "deeply." Yes, Jen Ward released deeply engrained masochism in me this morning! WOW. I am free! Words can never suffice or adequately articulate my gratitude for such a boon. Deeply rooted samskaras, thought processes, behavior patterns all wiped out in one fell swoop by a session with Jen. Lifetimes of pain, and in this lifetime, the repeating of veiled notions, self-destructive behaviors all in which I gave away my power all too freely. With humility I give thanks, Jen.

≈

Hi Jen. I wanted to share with you and thank you for my freedom. I have been doing a lot of your taps that you share. I can't put into words how grateful I am. I have been afraid of the dark since I was a child because I have always felt a presence. It would physically disturb me in my sleep and I always felt watched. I was never sure what it was or care to know at this point, but I was never able to have good night's sleep unless my husband or my dog shared the bed with me. So when I would go out of town, I would get terrible sleep, next to none. I would dread the idea of even falling asleep by myself.

It was also embarrassing for me to admit as an adult that I was terrified of the dark and telling people why. I was afraid of sounding like a crazy person. Last week, I went out of town, and when it was time for me to go to bed, I wasn't afraid, and I slept the whole night without any disturbances. I never had a night's sleep like that away from home. It was amazing! I'm so grateful to have found you in my life. Thank you for sharing your gift; it is a rare and wonderful blessing!

Why I like working with Jen: I was in Scientology for a while and had a tremendous amount of wins, gains and freedom from it, but for me, I noticed I was giving up my freedom to them as I was advancing. The reason I like working with Jen so much is that she intuitively knows much of their "tech," and I receive gains without giving up my freedom. Thank you, Jen! You're spot on!

≈

Jen, I had a dream about you the other night. You did a session on the phone with me through my dream. You had a Belgian or Danish accent. Very interesting! You transmitted verbal recordings of what I went through with my miscarriage. It was healing and I thank you!

You are with me, healing in a transient way! You have the same strong love for all of humanity. And you give your whole heart to all of us, the same (strength) no matter who we are and how we react or how much we accept or don't accept that love. Thank you for all you do. Love you!

≈

Jen, I have been noticing some interesting things since my session with you and coming here and doing the taps. I could swear these taps were for me. After I did them, I remembered that yesterday I didn't write because I burned both hands.

Then I read another post you had written before taking a nap and it felt like you had done psychic surgery on me in my sleep. I could hear your voice explaining something to me in detail with many examples flashing through my mind, and I was blown away. I woke up from the shame of what you were talking about and great remorse or embarrassment, and I fell back asleep again, and you continued to work on me. It was incredible.

≈

Clear the Clouds of Self-Imposed Ceilings!

Unexpected, powerful, simply amazing! I was shocked at what Jen was telling me. I had no idea these things were actually holding me back! She gave me a new awareness and opportunity to embrace spiritual freedom like nothing else I have ever experienced. Thank you Jen, for your priceless gift of hope, and your uniquely unselfish spirit of genuine healing.

D.S.
Motivational Speaker

≈

I want to start off by saying what an amazing person Jen is. She has so much love, yet she does not sugar coat anything. That is what I love about her. She brings the truth, and it's like a much needed slap in the face. It was for me! She brought to my attention that I go about getting things the wrong way, like a spoiled brat, which is true. This is something I'm glad she brought up because I couldn't see it before.

As soon as I saw that truth, I instantly wanted to be a better person. She also went on to tell me about my son and me; we weren't connecting as mother and son, but I never knew why this was. For her to know exactly what my situation is, just amazes me. She just knows. She led me through some taps to help with this. They definitely helped. I feel so much closer to my son since the session. It's an awesome feeling, like a huge weight being lifted off. It's unexplainable.

≈

Sharing this intentionally with all my friends and associates that are interested in releasing what no longer serves their highest good and offering an introduction to a most wonderful healer who can help you replace worn-out concepts with ideas and belief systems that work. True, I am a Religious Science minister, and within the parameters of R.S. in the forefront is, "Change your Thinking, Change your Life." I introduce you now to Jen Ward. Friend her, visit her page. Many of her techniques are simply given, and she is available for private counseling as well. Give yourself a gift. Blessings all!

≈

Transformative healing session today with the amazing Jen Ward. She saw straight into me and gave me exactly what I needed. She also opened up a healing channel between me and this lovely animal that I never knew existed! If you're ready to cut through the fog, clear out what's holding you back at the root, and blast your heart wide open, sign up for a phone or in-person session at jenuinehealing.com. This is deep, powerful work and not for the faint of heart. Prepare yourself for an epic unfolding.

≈

I experienced profound emotional release and clearing during a long-distance phone session with Jen Ward. Within 10 seconds, her sounds cut through my pain body and expressed ancient grief. I wept, purified. She is firm, sharp, crystal clear. Her taps, healing. By the end, I was light, radiant, expansive. I highly suggest following her page, doing her taps and investing in a session, if you are called. Be prepared for shift beyond expectation. Thanks for being, Jen.

≈

I have been following Jen's tapping posts for a while now and recently had a strong sense that I wanted to work with her to help me free up some limiting patterns around creative passion. I am thrilled to share that yesterday's session has already reaped benefits. The best way I can think to describe it is that I have a renewed sense of inner expansion, inner space within which to create. It's like clearing out a densely cluttered garage housing all sorts of unused and outdated items such that it had been impossible to even walk around in it.

Now I feel freed up, I can see where to put my work table and materials, things of my choosing, rather than living with clutter someone else put there in another time. Perhaps it's coming Present to the here and now rather than living in a shadowy past that was crowding out my life force. I anticipate that this is just the beginning of an inner flowering as the work and processes deepen. Thank you, Jen, for sharing your healing insights and for being a playful channel for unconditional love.

≈

About the Author

Jen Ward is an Ascended Master. This entails being a Reiki Master, gifted healer, inspirational speaker, author of many books and an innovator of a healing modality for self-empowerment. She offers a simple but dynamic protocol to assist individuals in clearing up all their energy imbalances (karma) with every person, experience, belief system and the Universe. She enables all those struggling, to cross the bridge of self-discovery, with her encouragement and instruction. Her passion is to empower the world by encouraging all individuals in their own miraculous healing adventure.

Jen is considered a sangoma, a traditional African shaman who channels ancestors, and clears energy by emoting sounds and vocalizations. An interesting prerequisite to being a sangoma is to have survived being on the brink of death. When it was first revealed that Jen was a sangoma, she had not yet fulfilled the rigorous prerequisites necessary. However, in April 2008, through a series of traumas, she returned to civilization meeting all the requirements. She passed through the transforming process of enlightenment. She returned to the world of humanity a devout soul inspired to serve.

Jen currently works diligently in the physical world and in the worlds of energy to assist all souls to reach greater heights of awareness and empowerment. Those who believe they have "arrived," may be the most entrenched in the mental realms. They can painlessly free themselves without relinquishing the comfort of their current belief system. All that needs to be released will fall away naturally. Fear, in all its subtle forms of denial and judgment, will naturally fall away.

Many people report receiving healing assistance from Jen or protection in the dream state and even more subtle realms. Jen is passionate to shatter the mentality of sitting at the feet of another. She shares truth and wisdom graciously and abundantly. Jen makes the practice of doling out truth in increments to set up the dynamic of personality worship obsolete. Her passion is to assist the world over the brink of all perceived limitations, beyond the mind's scope, into the realms of enlightenment.

Other Books by Jen Ward

Grow Where You Are Planted: Quotes for an Enlightened "Jeneration." Inspirational quotes that are seeds to shift your consciousness into greater awareness.

Perpetual Calendar: A Daily Calendar of SFT Tapping Exercises to Maintain Joy, Love, Abundance, Health and Freedom. 369 days of powerful taps to use as a daily grounding practice for those who find meditation difficult.

Children of the Universe. Passionate prose to lead the reader lovingly into expanded consciousness.

Letters of Accord: Assigning Words to Unspoken Truth. Truths that the Ancient Ones want you to know to redirect your life and humanity back into empowerment.

The Do What You Love Diet: Finally, Finally, Finally, Feel Good in Your Own Skin. Revolutionary approach to regaining fitness by tackling primal imbalances in relationship to food.

Emerging from the Mist: Awakening the Balance of Female Empowerment in the World. Release all the issues that prevent someone from embracing their female empowerment.

Affinity for All Life: Valuing Your Relationship with All Species. This book is a means to strengthen and affirm your relationship with the animal kingdom.

The Wisdom of the Trees. If one is struggling for purpose, they can find love, and truth by tuning into the Wisdom of the Trees.

Chronicles of Truth. Truth has been buried away for way too long. Here is a means to discover the truth that lies dormant within yourself.

Healing Your Relationships. This book is a means to open up communications and responsiveness to others so that clarity and respect can flourish again in society.

How to Awaken Your Inner Dragon: Visualizations to Empower Yourself and the World. Tap into the best possible version of yourself and the world.

Collecting Everyday Miracles: Commit to Being Empowered. This book is a thought provoking means to recreate the moment of conception with everyday miracles. It is through gratitude and awareness. This is what this book fosters.

The SFT Lexicon: Spiritual Freedom Technique. Tap into the powerful ability of the mind to self heal.

Past Lives, Dreams and Inspiration. People are starving for truth. Unfortunately, they have been conditioned to dismiss their dreams and all remnants of past lives in discovering their own trajectory connection to truth. This book gives life to the expansiveness of self-discovery through one's past lives and dream experiences. There is no greater form of inspiration than discovering one's own depth.

All books are available on Jen's website www.JenuineHealing.com.

Made in the USA
Monee, IL
13 February 2021